What People Are Sayi... ks

"*Pets Welcome*™ *is the definitive guide to traveling with your pet—and the hotels, inns and resorts that welcome them."*
Pet Business News

"*More than just a travel guide . . . this book selects only those establishments that offer superior service and care for pet owners traveling with their pets."*
Pet Age

"*Discover the best places to lodge with Fido by referring to Pets Welcome*™"
Dog World

"*A perfect guidebook to hotels, inns and resorts."*
Los Angeles Times

DEDICATION

As "cover girl," officer manager of Bon Vivant Press
and owner of authors Kathleen and Robert Fish,
I would like to share the joys of our vacations and working
trips to produce our *Cooking Secrets* series.

Special thanks to my bon vivant canine pals,
Paige, Danny, Brian and Joey.

– Dreamer Dawg

NATIONAL EDITION

Pets Welcome

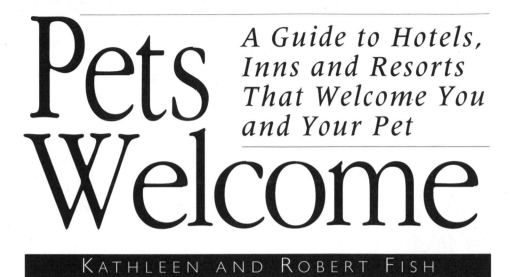

A Guide to Hotels, Inns and Resorts That Welcome You and Your Pet

KATHLEEN AND ROBERT FISH

BON VIVANT

Library of Congress Cataloging-in-Publication Data

Pets Welcome™ National Edition
A Guide to Hotels, Inns and Resorts That Welcome You and Your Pet

Fish, Kathleen DeVanna
Fish, Robert N.
CIP 98-071370
ISBN 1-883214-27-0
$19.95 softcover
Includes index

Copyright © 2000 by Kathleen DeVanna Fish and Robert N. Fish

Cover photography by Robert N. Fish
Editorial direction by Judie Marks
Associate editing by Nadine Guarrera
Cover design by Abalone Design Group
Illustrations by Robin Brickman, Illustrator; Gopa Design; and
    Gerrica Connolly, Design Studio
Type by Masterproof and Cimarron Design

Published by Bon Vivant Press
a division of The Millennium Publishing Group
P.O. Box 1994
Monterey, CA 93942

Printed in the United States of America
by Banta Book Group

Introduction

T raveling with those we love and whose company we enjoy can be one of life's great pleasures. Our pets can be counted among those who enrich our lives. How many vacations have been dampened or cut short over the years because you either couldn't find an appropriate sitter for your beloved pets or you simply couldn't bear to leave them behind?

Hundreds of resorts, hotels, inns, guest ranches and bed and breakfasts throughout the United States welcome pets with open arms. That's why Pets Welcome™ will be a handy resource for you — to help you discover and select some of the best places to stay when traveling with your four-legged companions.

Pets Welcome™ caters to all kinds of budgets by offering an array of lodging options, ranging from the luxurious and romantic to the quirky and rustic. We have researched and ranked a broad spectrum of places, from romantic hideaways to inns that have made a trademark name for themselves in the hospitality industry.

Each location, selected for its ambiance, guest amenities and pet friendliness, has been artfully described. In addition, original pen-and-ink artist's renderings share a glimpse of each place's waiting character and charm. We have bestowed each with our three-, four- or five-paw designation.

Whether you and your pet are seasoned traveling companions or venturing out for the first time, you will be well served by the Humane Society's traveling tips regarding transportation, security and pet care while "on the road." These helpful hints provide insight into traveling by car, plane, boat or train, offering specialized guidance on crating animals, documentation and basic care.

It is our hope that as you travel throughout the United States, you will return time and time again to this book as you would to your favorite inn—finding comfort in knowing that the places found within welcome both you and your pet, that details are both useful and intriguing and that it can open doors to new and exciting adventures. In fact, we hope you use it so much that it becomes, well, dog-eared.

Contents

Abbreviations Used in this Book

AAA   American Automobile Association

ABA   American Breeders Association

AKC   American Kennel Club

AARP   American Association of Retired Persons

Top Ten Travel Tips

1 Bring your pet's own food, dishes, litter and litter box, leash, collar with I.D. tags, a first-aid kit and a bottle of water from home. These will make your pet more comfortable, decrease the chances of an upset stomach from a strange brand of food and help prepare you for emergencies. Maintain the normal feeding and walking schedules as much as possible. Be sure to bring old bath towels or paper towels in case of an accident and plastic bags in which to dispose of your pet's waste. It is a good idea to bring a picture of your pet for identification purposes in case you and your pet become separated.

2 Bring your pet's vaccination records with you when traveling within the state, and a health certificate when traveling out of state. If you plan on boarding him at any time during your vacation, call the kennel to reserve his space, to see what they require you to bring and to find out if they require a health certificate.

3 Bring your pet's favorite toys, leash, grooming supplies, medications, bedding and waste removal supplies. It is a good idea to bring an old sheet or blanket from home to place over the hotel's bedding, just in case your pet gets on the bed. It also will come in handy to protect your car seats from pet hair and dirty paws.

4 Tape the address of where you are staying on the back of your pet's I.D. tag, or add a laminated card or new I.D. tag to your pet's collar, or add a second collar with a friend's or family member's phone number. It is always a good idea to have a second contact person on your pet's collar in case of a natural disaster so that someone out of your area can be contacted if you and your pet become separated.

5 Do not leave your pets unattended in the hotel room. The surroundings are new and unfamiliar to your pet, which may cause him to become upset and destroy property he normally would not, or to bark excessively and disturb your neighbors. You will also run the risk of his escaping. If a maid should open the door to clean your room, the pet may see that as a chance to escape to find you, or he may attack the maid out of fear.

6 Train your pet to accept being in a crate. This will come in handy if you ever need to travel by plane. Make sure the crate has enough room for your pet to stand up comfortably and to turn around inside. Be sure to trim your pet's nails so they don't get caught in the crate door or ventilation holes. Crates come in handy in hotel rooms, too. If your pet is already used to being in a crate, he will not object if you leave him in one long enough to go out to breakfast. Never take your pet with you if you will have to leave him in the car. If it is 85° F outside, within minutes the inside of the car can reach over 160° F, even with the windows cracked, causing heat stroke and possible death. According to The Humane Society of the United States, the signs of heat stress are: heavy panting, glazed eyes, a rapid pulse, unsteadiness, a staggering gait, vomiting or a deep red or purple tongue. If heat stoke does occur, the pet must be cooled by dousing him with water and applying ice packs to his head and neck. He should then be taken to a veterinarian immediately.

7 When your pet is confined to a crate, the best way to provide water is to freeze it in the cup that hooks onto the door of the crate. That way they will get needed moisture without the water splashing all over the crate. Freezing water in your pet's regular water bowl also works well for car trips.

8 Be sure to put your pet's favorite toys and bedding in the crate. Label the crate with "LIVE ANIMAL" and "THIS END UP," plus the address and phone number of your destination, as well as your home address and phone number and the number of someone to contact in case of an emergency.

9 When traveling by plane be sure to book the most direct flights possible. The less your pet has to be transferred from plane to plane, the less chance of you being separated. This is also very important when traveling in hot or cold weather. You don't want your pet to have to wait in the cargo hold of a plane or be exposed to bad weather any longer than necessary. Check with the airlines for the type of crate they require and any additional requirements. They are very strict about the size and type of crate you may carry on board.

10 Do not feed your pet before traveling. This reduces the risk of an upset stomach or an accident in his crate or your car. When traveling by car, remember that your pet needs rest stops as often as you do. It is a good idea for everyone to stretch their legs from time to time. If your pet is unfamiliar with car travel, then get him accustomed to the car gradually. Start a few weeks before your trip with short trips around town and extend the trips a little each time. Then he will become accustomed to the car before your trip and it will be more pleasant for all involved.

Traveling With Your Pet

Courtesy of The Humane Society of the United States (HSUS)
2100 L Street, N.W.
Washington, D.C. 20037

 f you are planning a trip and you share your life with a pet, you have a few decisions to make before you set off. The following are some tips to help you plan a safer and smoother trip for both you and your pet.

SHOULD YOU TRAVEL WITH YOUR PET?

Some pets are not suited for travel because of temperament, illness or physical impairment. If you have any doubts about whether it is appropriate for your pet to travel, talk to your veterinarian.

If you decide that your pet should not travel with you, consider the alternatives: have a responsible friend or relative look after your pet, board your pet at a kennel or hire a sitter to visit, feed and exercise your pet.

If a friend or relative is going to take care of your pet, ask if that person can take your pet into his or her home. Animals can get lonely when left at home alone. Be sure that your pet is comfortable with his or her temporary caretaker and any pets that person has.

If you choose to board your pet, get references and inspect the kennel. Your veterinarian or local shelter can help you select a facility. If you are hiring a sitter, interview the candidates and check their references. (A pet sitter may be preferable if your pet is timid or elderly and needs the comfort of familiar surroundings during your absence.)

Whatever option you choose, there are a few things to remember. Your pet should be up to date on all vaccinations and in sound health. Whoever is caring for your pet should know the telephone number at which you can be reached, the name and telephone number of your veterinarian, and your pet's medical or dietary needs. Be sure that your pet is comfortable with the person you have chosen to take care of him or her.

If You Plan to Travel With Your Pet

THE PRE-TRIP VETERINARY EXAMINATION

Before any trip, have your veterinarian examine your pet to ensure that he or she is in good health. A veterinary examination is a requisite for obtaining the legal documents required for many forms of travel.

In addition to the examination, your veterinarian should provide necessary vaccinations such as rabies, distemper, infectious hepatitis and leptospirosis. If your pet is already up to date on these, obtain written proof.

Your veterinarian may prescribe a tranquilizer for the pet who is a nervous traveler; however, such drugs should be considered only after discussion with your veterinarian. He or she may recommend a trial run in which your pet is given the prescribed dosage and you can observe the effects. Do not give your pet any drug not prescribed or given to you by your veterinarian.

LEGAL REQUIREMENTS

When traveling with your pet, it is always advisable to keep a health certificate (a document from your veterinarian certifying that your pet is in good health) and medical records close at hand. If you and your pet will be traveling across state lines, you must obtain from your veterinarian a certificate of rabies vaccination.

Although pets may travel freely throughout the United States as long as they have proper documentation, Hawaii requires a 120-day quarantine for all dogs and cats. Hawaii's quarantine regulations vary by species, so check prior to travel.

If you and your pet are traveling from the United States to Canada, you must carry a certificate issued by a veterinarian that clearly identifies the animal and certifies that the dog or cat has been vaccinated against rabies during the preceding thirty-six-month period. Different Canadian provinces may have different requirements. Be sure to contact the government of the province you plan to visit.

If you and your pet are traveling to Mexico, you must carry a health certificate prepared by your veterinarian within two weeks of the day you cross the border. The certificate must include a description of your pet, the lot number of the rabies vaccine used, indication of distemper vaccination and a veterinarian's statement that the animal is free from infectious or contagious disease. This certificate must be stamped by an office of the U.S. Department of Agriculture (USDA). The fee for the stamp is $4.

Get Ready to Hit the Road

TRAVEL CARRIERS

Travel carriers are useful when your pet is traveling by car; they are mandatory when your pet is traveling by air. Your pet's carrier should be durable and smooth-edged with opaque sides, a grille door, and several ventilation holes on each of the four sides. Choose a carrier with a secure door and door latch. If you are traveling by air, your carrier should have food and water dishes. Pet carriers may be purchased from pet-supply stores or bought directly from domestic airlines. Select a carrier that has enough room to permit your animal to sit and lie down, but is not large enough to allow your pet to be tossed about during travel. You can make the carrier more comfortable by lining the interior with shredded newspaper or a towel. (For air-travel requirements, see the "Traveling by Air" section.)

It is wise to acclimate your pet to the carrier in the months or weeks preceding your trip. Permit your pet to explore the carrier. Place your pet's food dish inside the carrier and confine him or her to the carrier for brief periods.

To introduce your pet to car travel in the carrier, confine him or her in the carrier and take short drives around the neighborhood. If properly introduced to car travel, most dogs and cats will quickly adjust to and even enjoy car trips.

CAREFUL PREPARATION IS KEY

When packing, don't forget your pet's food, food and water dishes, bedding, litter and litter box, leash, collar and tags, grooming supplies, a first-aid kit and any necessary medications. Always have a container of drinking water with you.

Your pet should wear a sturdy collar with I.D. tags throughout the trip. The tags should have both your permanent address and telephone number and an address and telephone number where you or a contact can be reached during your travels.

Traveling can be upsetting to your pet's stomach. Take along ice cubes, which are easier on your pet than large amounts of water. You should keep feeding to a minimum during travel. (Provide a light meal for your pet two or three hours before you leave, if you are traveling by car, or four to six hours before departure, if you are traveling by airplane.) Allow small amounts of water periodically in the hours before the trip.

On Your Way

TRAVELING BY CAR

Dogs who enjoy car travel need not be confined to a carrier if your car has a restraining harness (available at pet-supply stores) or if you are accompanied by a passenger who can restrain the dog. Because most cats are not as comfortable traveling in cars, for their own safety as well as yours, it is best to keep them in a carrier.

Dogs and cats should always be kept safely inside the car. Pets who are allowed to stick their heads out the window can be injured by particles of debris or become ill from having cold air forced into their lungs. Never transport a pet in the back of an open pickup truck.

Stop frequently to allow your pet to exercise and eliminate. Never permit your pet to leave the car without a collar, I.D. tag and leash.

Never leave your pet unattended in a parked car. On warm days, the temperature in your car can rise to 160°F in a matter of minutes, even with the windows opened slightly. Furthermore, an animal left alone in a car is an open invitation to pet thieves.

TRAVELING BY AIR

Although thousands of pets fly without experiencing problems every year, there are still risks involved. The HSUS recommends that you do not transport your pet by air unless absolutely necessary.

If you must transport your companion animal by air, call the airline to check health and immunization requirements for your pet.

If your pet is a cat or a small dog, take him or her on board with you. Be sure to contact airlines to find out the specific requirements for this option. If you pursue this option, you have two choices: airlines will accept either hard-sided carriers or soft-sided carriers, which may be more comfortable for your pet. Only certain brands of soft-sided carriers are acceptable to certain airlines, so call your airline to find out what carrier to use.

If your pet must travel in the cargo hold, you can increase the chances of a safe flight for your pet by following these tips:

- Use direct flights. You will avoid the mistakes that occur during airline transfers and possible delays in getting your pet off the plane.

- Always travel on the same flight as your pet. Ask the airline if you can watch your pet being loaded into and unloaded from the cargo hold.

- When you board the plane, notify the captain and at least one flight attendant that your pet is traveling in the cargo hold. If the captain knows that pets are on board, he or she may take special precautions.

- Do not ship pug-nosed dogs and cats (such as Pekingese, Chow Chows and Persians) in the cargo hold. These breeds have short nasal passages that leave them vulnerable to oxygen deprivation and heat stroke in cargo holds.

- If traveling during the summer or winter months, choose flights that will accommodate the temperature extremes: early morning or late evening flights are better in the summer; afternoon flights are better in the winter.
- Fit your pet with two pieces of identification — a permanent I.D. tag with your name, home address and telephone number, and a temporary travel I.D. with the address and telephone number where you or a contact person can be reached.
- Affix a travel label to the carrier, stating your name, permanent address and telephone number, and final destination. The label should clearly state where you or a contact person can be reached as soon as the flight arrives.
- Make sure that your pet's nails have been clipped to protect against their hooking in the carrier's door, holes and other crevices.
- Give your pet at least a month before your flight to become familiar with the travel carrier. This will minimize his or her stress during travel.
- Your pet should not be given tranquilizers unless they are prescribed by your veterinarian. Make sure your veterinarian understands that this prescription is for air travel.
- Do not feed your pet for four to six hours prior to air travel. Small amounts of water can be given before the trip. If possible, put ice cubes in the water tray attached to the inside of your pet's kennel. A full water bowl will only spill and cause discomfort.
- Try not to fly with your pet during busy travel times such as holidays and summer. Your pet is more likely to undergo rough handling during hectic travel periods.
- Carry a current photo of your pet with you. If your pet is lost during the trip, a photograph will make it easier for airline employees to search effectively.
- When you arrive at your destination, open the carrier as soon as you are in a safe place and examine your pet. If anything seems wrong, take your pet to a veterinarian immediately. Get the results of the examination in writing, including the date and time.

Do not hesitate to complain if you witness the mishandling of an animal — either yours or someone else's — at any airport.

If you have a bad experience when shipping your animal by air, contact The HSUS, the U.S. Department of Agriculture (USDA), and the airline involved. To contact the USDA write to USDA, Animal, Plant and Health Inspection Service (APHIS), Washington, D.C. 20250.

TRAVELING BY SHIP

With the exception of assistance dogs, only a few cruise lines accept pets — normally only on ocean crossings and frequently confined to kennels. Some lines permit pets in private cabins. Contact cruise lines in advance to find out their policies and which of their ships have kennel facilities. If you must use the ship's kennel, make sure it is protected from the elements.

Follow the general guidelines suggested for other modes of travel when planning a ship voyage.

TRAVELING BY TRAIN

Amtrak currently does not accept pets for transport unless they are assistance dogs. (There may be smaller U.S. railroad companies that permit animals on board their trains.) Many trains in European countries allow pets. Generally, it is the passengers' responsibility to feed and exercise their pets at station stops.

HOTEL ACCOMMODATIONS

There are approximately eight thousand hotels, motels and inns across the United States that accept guests with pets. Most hotels set their own policies, so it is important to call ahead and ask if pets are permitted and if there is a size limit.

IF YOUR PET IS LOST

Whenever you travel with your pet, there is a chance that you and your pet will become separated. It only takes a moment for an animal to stray and become lost. If your pet is missing, immediately canvass the area. Should your pet not be located within a few hours, take the following actions:

- Contact the animal control departments and humane societies within a sixty-mile radius of where your pet strayed. Check with them each day.

- Post signs at intersections and in storefronts throughout the area.

- Provide a description and a photograph of your missing pet to the police, letter carriers or delivery people.

- Advertise in newspapers and with radio stations. Be certain to list your hotel telephone number on all lost-pet advertisements.

A lost pet may become confused and wary of strangers. Therefore, it may be days or even weeks before the animal is retrieved by a Good Samaritan. If you must continue on your trip or return home, arrange for a hotel clerk or shelter employee to contact you if your pet is located.

DO YOUR PART TO MAKE PETS WELCOME GUESTS

Many hotels, restaurants and individuals will give your pet special consideration during your travels. It is important for you to do your part to ensure that dogs and cats will continue to be welcomed as traveling companions. Obey local animal-control ordinances, keep your animal under restraint, be thoughtful and courteous to other travelers and have a good trip!

If you have more specific questions or are traveling with a companion animal other than a dog or cat, contact the Companion Animals section of The HSUS.

HELPFUL HINTS

- To transport birds out of the United States, record the leg-band or tattoo number on the USDA certificate and get required permits from the U.S Fish and Wildlife Service.

- Carry a current photograph of your pet with you. If your pet is lost during a trip, a photograph will make it easier for others (airline employees, the police, shelter workers, etc.) to help find your pet.

- While thousands of pets fly without problems every year, there are risks involved. The HSUS recommends that you do not transport your pet by air unless absolutely necessary.

Whenever you travel with your pet, there is a chance that you and your pet will be separated. If your pet is lost, immediately canvass the area and take appropriate action.

CANADA

Lake Superior

Fargo • Duluth •

★ Augusta

Montpelier ★

St. Paul • Eau Claire
Minneapolis •

Lake Huron

Concord ★
Boston

Lake Ontario

Albany •

★ Providence

Rochester •

Milwaukee •
Madison ★

Lansing •

Buffalo •

Hartford ★

Lake Erie

Cedar Rapids •

Chicago •

Ann Arbor •
Detroit

New York •

Omaha • Des Moines •

Indianapolis •

Cleveland •

Harrisburg •

★ Trenton
• Philadelphia
Wilmington
★ Dover

Lincoln

Columbus •
• Dayton

Pittsburgh •

Washington D. C. ★
Annapolis •

Springfield

Cincinnati •

Charleston •

★ Richmond
• Norfolk

Topeka • Kansas City
★

• St. Louis

Louisville •

Jefferson City •

★ Frankfort

Ohio R.

Greensboro •

Raleigh •

Atlantic Ocean

Fayetteville •

Arkansas R.

Mississippi R.

Knoxville •
• Nashville

Charlotte •

Memphis •

Columbia •

Wilmington •

Little Rock •

Birmingham •

★ Atlanta

• Macon

Charleston •

Shreveport •

Montgomery ★

Jackson ★

Savannah •

Houston

Baton Rouge ★

Biloxi •

Mobile •

Tallahassee ★

Jacksonville •

New Orleans •

Galveston •

Orlando •

Tampa •

Gulf of Mexico

Fort Myers •

West Palm Beach •

Miami •

Key West •

Residence Inn by Marriott

1700 South Clementine Street
Anaheim, California 92802
800-331-3131 • (714) 533-3555

Room Rates:	$169 – $229, including breakfast buffet. AAA and AARP discounts.
Pet Charges or Deposits:	$6 per day. $275 deposit.
Rated: 3 Paws 🐾🐾🐾	200 rooms and suites with fully equipped kitchens and some fireplaces, daily maid service, grocery shopping service, heated pool, whirlpool, Sport Court, health club privileges, meeting facilities, complimentary evening beverage.

L ocated near major Southern California attractions, the Anaheim Residence Inn by Marriott will appeal to business travelers and vacationers alike. From spacious accommodations with separate sleeping and living areas, the fully equipped kitchens, grocery shopping service, laundry facilities, room service from any of the local restaurants, work areas and meeting facilities, to the manager-hosted continental breakfast buffet and informal hospitality hour, the inn seems more like a home than a hotel.

For recreation, the retreat offers a heated swimming pool, whirlpool, toddlers' pool, barbecue areas and a Sport Court, where you can play a game of basketball, volleyball or tennis. Your pet can join you for a stroll around the groomed grounds.

Apple Lane Inn Bed and Breakfast

6265 Soquel Drive
Aptos, California 95003
800-649-8988 • (831) 475-6868

Room Rates:	$95 – $150, including breakfast. AAA, AARP and AKC discounts.
Pet Charges or Deposits:	$25 fee. $250 refundable deposit or credit card imprint. Horses welcome.
Rated: 4 Paws	5 guest rooms with private baths.

O ne of Santa Cruz County's oldest farmhouses is also among its first bed-and-breakfast inns.

The Apple Lane Inn is a charming Victorian house and barn, lovingly restored to reflect the original 1872 character and set on three acres, amid fields and apple orchards.

Guests may choose from private guest rooms with romantic decor, antique furniture, plump quilts and picturesque views of the meadows. Before heading out for a day of beachcombing and sightseeing with your four-legged friend, begin your day with an elegant country breakfast of fresh fruit, juice, pastries, a hearty main course and special coffee blends.

If you prefer to linger at the historic inn, owners Doug and Diana Groom invite you to unwind in the front parlor with a glass of wine or a book; play darts, cards, horseshoes or croquet; visit resident animals in the barn; pick apples from the orchard; or relax in the white Victorian gazebo surrounded by the trim lawn, flowering gardens and wisteria arbors.

Regent Beverly Wilshire

9500 Wilshire Boulevard
Beverly Hills, California 90212
800-545-4000 • (310) 275-5200

Room Rates:	$265 and up.
Pet Charges or Deposits:	None.
Rated: 4 Paws 🐾🐾🐾🐾	275 oversized rooms, including 69 suites, business center, heated pool, saunas, whirlpool, health club, valet laundry service, 24-hour room service, coffee shop, restaurant and cocktail lounge.

L ocated in the heart of Beverly Hills, the historic Regent Beverly Wilshire's 275 generously proportioned guest rooms have housed dignitaries, celebrities and discerning travelers since 1928. The attention to detail is evident by the services of the 24-hour personal room attendants, the attentive concierge staff, the oversized and understated rooms, the use of natural fabrics and hues, the opulent bathrooms with their deep soaking tubs and separate showers, the plush terry robes, premium toiletries, dual phone lines and executive-sized desks.

Nothing is overlooked, including your pet. Upon arrival, canine guests receive a dish of biscuits and bottled water to make their stay more comfortable.

For your dining pleasure, select from the creative California-continental cuisine in the Dining Room, have cappuccino overlooking Rodeo Drive in the Café, high tea or cocktails in the European ambiance of the Lobby Lounge or a brandy in The Bar.

Elfriede's Beach Haus

59 Brighton Avenue
Bolinas, California 94924
800-982-2545 • (415) 868-9778

Room Rates:	$75 – $149. AAA, AARP, AKC and ABA discounts.
Pet Charges or Deposits:	$10 per stay. Manager's prior approval required.
Rated: 3 Paws 🐾🐾🐾	3 guest rooms, fireplace, deck and garden.

 uilt in the early 1900s, Elfriede's Beach Haus bed and breakfast charms guests with large, cozy rooms with brass beds, plump down comforters and French doors opening onto the deck.

Breakfast is a celebration of wholesome foods prepared by the Bavarian innkeeper in a kitchen that resembles an artist's studio. Fresh juices and herb teas are specialties. With advance notice Ayurvedic or vegetarian meals can be arranged.

Surrounded by abundant wildlife, yet only minutes from the beach, tennis courts or hiking trails, you will delight in strolling through the lush gardens, taking a "wild edible herb walk" or striking out with your dog for a day of sightseeing in this pet-friendly town, where leash laws do not exist.

Airport Hilton and Convention Center

2500 Hollywood Way
Burbank, California 91505
800-445-8667 • (818) 843-6000

Room Rates:	$120 – $480. AAA and AARP discounts.
Pet Charges or Deposits:	$50 deposit.
Rated: 3 Paws	500 guest rooms and suites, some with fireplaces and mountain views, two pools, exercise room, airport transportation, cocktail lounge, dining room and coffee shop.

T he Burbank Airport Hilton and Convention Center, near Southern California attractions, offers guests hospitality, spacious suites with panoramic mountain views, meeting facilities and convenience.

The hotel is 10 minutes from Universal Studios, 30 minutes from Magic Mountain and 50 minutes from Disneyland. Before or after taking in local attractions, enjoy the hotel's saunas, spas or pools. Or if you are up for a workout, head to the hotel's fitness center.

Airport DoubleTree Hotel

835 Airport Boulevard
Burlingame, California 94010
800-222-TREE • (415) 344-5500

Room Rates:	$79. AAA and AARP discounts.
Pet Charges or Deposits:	$20. Manager's prior approval required.
Rated: 3 Paws 🐾 🐾 🐾	291 rooms and suites, many with bay views; airport shuttle, laundry and valet services, library, fitness center, restaurant and lounge. Bayside walking-jogging path, park nearby.

O verlooking the glistening waters of San Francisco Bay and only minutes from the airport and many famous attractions is the San Francisco Airport DoubleTree Hotel. Each room and suite is highlighted by European decor, featuring amenities such as coffeemakers, hair dryers and data ports.

Guests are encouraged to browse the varied collection of books in the hotel library. Full concierge service and a business center with secretarial services are available. The health and fitness center is equipped for a full workout, which can be supplemented with a jog or walk on the bayside trail with your dog.

Pink Mansion

1415 Foothill Boulevard
Calistoga, California 94515
800-238-7465 • (707) 942-0558
Web Site: www.pinkmansion.com
E-mail: pink@napanet.net

Room Rates:	$135 – $225, including lavish breakfast and afternoon wine-tasting.
Pet Charges or Deposits:	$15 per day.
Rated: 3 Paws	6 guest rooms and suites, some with fireplaces; indoor heated pool.

Combining turn-of-the-century elegance with modern amenities, the Pink Mansion is a restored 1875 home in keeping with the spirit of its last resident, Aunt Alma Simic. Under her care in the 1930s, the house was repainted pink and christened the Pink Mansion. It is now a landmark in Calistoga.

Choose the large, Victorian-style Rose Room Suite with its sunken sitting room and raised hearth fireplace or the Garden Room with its light airiness and panoramic view of Mount St. Helena and the Palisades. The Angel Room is set in the corner of the mansion and features pieces from Aunt Alma's personal collection of angels. The Wine Suite is a secluded haven featuring wine collections, a custom-made "Napa Bed" and a fireplace. The Forest Room is a wonderful retreat with antique furnishings and a view of the forest. The Oriental Room, decorated in mauve tones and Asian antiques, has a small sun deck with views of the forest.

You and your pet will enjoy the large garden areas and landscaped grounds. The Pink Mansion is within walking distance of restaurants and spas and within biking distance of most wineries.

Washington Street Lodging

1605 Washington Street
Calistoga, California 94515
(707) 942-6968

Room Rates:	$105, including continental breakfast.
Pet Charges or Deposits:	$15 per stay. Manager's prior approval required.
Rated: 3 Paws	5 cottages with full or partial kitchens, some with decks.

When looking for a secluded, riverside setting, try one of the private cottages at Washington Street Lodging. Here you will enjoy a cozy, country decor with many extra touches to make you feel right at home. Each of the five cottages offers guests a private bath and a full or partial kitchen. Enjoy a continental breakfast served in your room before heading off for a day of wine-tasting or sightseeing in nearby downtown Calistoga.

Located within walking distance of the Napa River, outstanding restaurants and health spas, the Washington Street Lodging is a great find.

Cypress Inn

Lincoln and Seventh Streets
Carmel, California 93921
800-443-7443 • (831) 624-3871
Web Site: www.cypress-inn.com
E-mail: info@cypress-inn.com

Room Rates:	$110 – $285, including continental breakfast.
Pet Charges or Deposits:	$17 per day. First night's room payment in advance. Pet-sitters available.
Rated: 4 Paws	33 guest rooms, verandahs or ocean views, garden courtyard.

S ince fellow animal lover Doris Day is one of its owners, it's of little surprise that the historic Cypress Inn is open to pets. Built in 1929 in the heart of Carmel-by-the-Sea, the 33-room Inn is known for its classic, stately interior and brilliant white Mediterranean exterior, with Spanish tiled roof and intimate garden courtyard.

Each room is distinct in its character and charm, offering a choice of sitting rooms, verandahs or ocean views. While the accommodations may vary, the staff's sincerity and personal attention to detail is constant here.

Guests awake to a generous continental breakfast served in the warmth of the sunny breakfast room or in the serenity of the garden courtyard. In the evening, relax in the elegant "living room" lobby with its overstuffed sofas, soft music and cozy fire.

Forest Lodge and Suites

Ocean Avenue and Torres Street
Carmel, California 93921
(831) 624-7023

Room Rates:	$149 – $240, including breakfast.
Pet Charges or Deposits:	$5 – $10 per stay.
Rated: 3 Paws	1 deluxe room in the main house, plus 3 cottages with fireplaces and full baths; 1 includes a full kitchen; garden setting, located near town and beach.

T ucked away in the quaint village of Carmel is the charming Forest Lodge and Suites, built in the early 1920s by a Dutch immigrant and horticulturist, Johan Hagemeyer. Two of the cottages, the Garret and the Manor House, were later set up as a studio and workshop for his photography. His work included such famous visitors to Carmel as Salvador Dali and Albert Einstein.

Stunning oak trees and lush, flowering English gardens surround these unique accommodations. The Garret is a spacious loft in the main house featuring a king-sized bed and fireplace. The Cottage-in-the-Glen offers a queen-sized bed and fireplace. The Garden House has 2 queen-sized beds and fireplace. The Manor House features a full kitchen, fireplace, and 2 queen-sized beds.

Spend the day exploring the many quaint shops, galleries and restaurants in the village. Then head down to leash-free Carmel Beach with your dog.

Lincoln Green Inn

Carmelo between 15th and 16th Avenues
Carmel, California 93921
800-262-1262 • (831) 624-1880

Room Rates:	$165 – $205.
Pet Charges or Deposits:	$10 per day. Manager's prior approval required.
Rated: 4 Paws	4 individual cottages with kitchens, full baths, large living areas and ocean views.

E nsconced on picturesque Carmel Point, a mere stone's throw from River Beach, is the Lincoln Green Inn. As you enter the English country garden setting of this romantic, Shakespearean-style inn, you'll discover four steep-peaked, white English cottages with forest green shutters. Each cottage has cathedral ceilings, a large living area and bedroom, Carmel-stone fireplace, kitchen, full bath and ocean views.

Relax on the sun deck and drink in the scenic view of the Big Sur mountains and Carmel Point, or stroll through the wild bird reserve and lagoon adjacent to the property. Take advantage of the no-leash law on Carmel Beach for a picnic or a walk on the sandy shores with your dog.

Quail Lodge

8205 Valley Greens Drive
Carmel, Californla 92923
800-538-9516 • (831) 624-1581

Room Rates: $215 and up.
Pet Charges or Deposits: Sorry, no cats.
Rated: 5 Paws 🐾🐾🐾🐾🐾 100 luxury rooms, suites and cottages; 18-hole golf course and
                            four tennis courts with professional golf and tennis instructors;
                            two pools; croquet court; hot tub; sauna; jogging, hiking and
                            bicycling paths; picnic areas; bicycle rentals.

S et on the sunny side of Carmel among lush fairways, oak-studded meadows, rolling hills and sparkling lakes, the Quail Lodge Resort and Golf Club combines natural beauty with five-star resort elegance. From private decks and patios, each room overlooks the lakes, the golf course or the lush gardens.

Recreational pursuits include golf on the championship course, tennis, swimming, jogging or hiking with your dog. Or spend your day exploring the many shops and galleries in the quaint village of Carmel-by-the-Sea.

Start the day with breakfast at the Country Club dining room, with its scenic views of the resort. For evening dining, the recently renovated and award-winning Covey Restaurant has unveiled a new menu based on the abundance of fresh ingredients found on the Central Coast. With views of the lake with its arched footbridge and lighted fountain, as well as live entertainment Wednesday through Sunday, it's a comfortable place to sit back and enjoy the view.

Vagabond House Inn

Fourth Avenue and Dolores Street
Carmel, California 92921
800-262-1262 • (831) 624-7738

Room Rates: $85 – $165, including continental breakfast.
Pet Charges or Deposits: Manager's prior approval required.
Rated: 4 Paws 🐾 🐾 🐾 🐾   11 rooms with fireplaces, some kitchens and courtyard.

 estled in the heart of Carmel is the Vagabond House, a charming brick and half-timbered English Tudor country inn. Your experience begins as you enter the delightful courtyard with its ancient oak tree, cascading waterfall, hanging plants, camellias, rhododendrons, ferns and flowers creating an almost magical atmosphere.

This is an ideal spot to daydream or relax with an intriguing book and a glass of local wine. Accommodations include guest rooms with fireplaces and traditional country decor. The guest parlor offers a variety of collections, including toys and books from the '20s, '30s and '40s.

The charming courtyard is the setting for your continental breakfast, or you may have it served in your room. Then put on your walking shoes, grab the dog's leash and head out for a day of exploring the village.

Valley Lodge

Carmel Valley and Ford Roads
Carmel Valley, California 93924
800-641-4646 • (831) 659-2261

Room Rates:	$99 – $337, including generous continental breakfast. AAA and AARP discounts.
Pet Charges or Deposits:	$10 per day. Room rate as a deposit.
Rated: 4 Paws 🐾 🐾 🐾 🐾	31 guest rooms and studios and 8 cottages with fireplaces and kitchens; antique furnishings, meeting rooms, pool, sauna, whirlpool, exercise room and landscaped grounds.

When looking for a lush and relaxing setting in the sun belt of the Monterey Peninsula, the Valley Lodge has plenty to offer. Tucked into the rolling hills of sunny Carmel Valley, this quiet country inn makes a peaceful retreat for guests wishing to escape crowds. Choose from a garden patio room, fireplace studios or individual one- and two-bedroom fireplace cottages, individually decorated with classic Shaker furniture and quilted bedspreads, with open-beamed ceilings and modern conveniences. The cottages offer the added bonus of wood-burning stoves and kitchens with microwaves.

Start each morning with fresh brewed coffee and a generous continental breakfast before heading out to explore the shops in Carmel Valley Village or wandering through the shops and galleries of Carmel. If you are feeling adventurous, you can hike through the hills with your dog, play golf or tennis, swim, ride horses or relax in the lush garden setting. The resident lodge dog, "Lucky," will gladly show you around.

Lakeside Chalets

5240 North Lake Boulevard
Carnelian Bay, California 96140
800-294-6378 • (916) 546-5857

Room Rates:	$95 – $145.
Pet Charges or Deposits:	$40 deposit.
Rated: 4 Paws	6 chalet cabins with fireplaces, living rooms, fully equipped kitchens, cable TVs, barbecues and panoramic views. Weekly rates available.

Waterfront chalets with stone fireplaces await you at Lakeside Chalets on the North Shore of Lake Tahoe. Here cozy cabins offer guests and their pets homey, comfortable accommodations with conveniences such as fully equipped kitchens with dishwashers, large master bedrooms and smaller bedrooms with bunk beds.

Relax under the canopy of surrounding pine trees or drop a line in the water for a little fishing. Other water sports include windsurfing, water-skiing, sailing and boating. If you're a winter visitor, you're only minutes away from downhill and cross-country skiing or snowmobiling at Incline, Alpine Meadows, Northstar, Slide Mountain, Mount Rose and Sugar Bowl. For gaming fans, Nevada casinos are only 10 minutes away.

Harris Ranch Inn and Restaurants

Interstate 5 and Highway 19
Coalinga, California 93210
800-942-2333 • (209) 935-0717
Web Site: www.harrisranch.com
E-mail: TheInn@HarrisRanch.com

Room Rates:	$89 – $225. AAA and AARP discounts.
Pet Charges or Deposits:	$10 per day. Manager's prior approval required.
Rated: 5 Paws 🐾🐾🐾🐾🐾	123 rooms and 28 suites; Olympic-sized pool, Jacuzzis, fitness facility, private airstrip, country store, restaurants, bar and lounge.

Built in 1937, the Harris Ranch Inn exudes early California charm and family hospitality. Guests may choose from rooms and suites with a patio or balcony, overlooking the courtyard or the pool or with a view of the ranch lands.

The hacienda setting beckons travelers to lounge in the courtyard by the pool, relax in the spa, work out at the fitness center or explore the spacious, landscaped grounds with your four-legged friend.

When it comes to tempting dining, guests may opt for the Ranch Kitchen, featuring the ranch's renowned beef and ranch-style meals. The Jockey Club, with a decor that pays tribute to the ranch's equestrian history and award-winning thoroughbreds, serves up beef specialties and other country favorites.

Greenwood Pier Inn

5928 South Highway 1
P.O. Box 336
Elk, California 95432
(707) 877-9997
E-mail: gwpier@mcn.org

Room Rates: $110 – $225, including continental breakfast.
Pet Charges or Deposits: $12 per day. Manager's prior approval required.
Rated: 4 Paws 🐾🐾🐾🐾   Rooms, cabins and cottages, many with panoramic views, fireplaces, spas; restaurant and room service.

P erched atop an ocean bluff with myriad rock formations and panoramic views in the old lumber town of Elk, the Greenwood Pier Inn dubs itself a "garden-by-the-edge-of-the-sea that grows flowers for your room."

Though your choice of accommodations is varied in this quirky complex of fairy-tale cottages, no matter which you choose it will include a private bath, fireplace and handmade quilts on a comfortable bed. Guests can relax on the deck with a glass of wine and scan the sea for an occasional whale spout and watch the sea gulls soar through the sky as the seals sun themselves on the rocks below and the fog gently rolls in.

The new Café is open daily, offering creative dinners of local seafood accompanied by fresh veggies from the Inn's garden. The flower-bordered paths and seaside gardens are the perfect settings for celebrations or simply for a stroll.

Eureka Inn

518 Seventh Street
Eureka, California 95501
800-862-4906 • (707) 442-6441
Web Site: www.humboldt1.com/~ekainn
E-mail: ekainn@humboldt1.com

Room Rates:	$89 – $250. AAA, AARP and AKC discounts.
Pet Charges or Deposits:	None.
Rated: 5 Paws 🐾🐾🐾🐾🐾	105 rooms and luxury suites, fireplaces, wet bars, kitchens, formal dining areas, valet laundry, Jacuzzi tub, sauna, heated pool, restaurants and lounges.

T he Eureka Inn is set like a gem in one of California's most magnificent natural environments. Forests of towering redwoods, miles of wave-washed shore and cascading mountain streams offer endless allure.

Since 1922, the Inn has enchanted guests with its elegance, sophistication, European flair and Tudor styling. You can almost hear the footsteps of history on the polished hardwood floors. A National Historic Place, the Inn's lofty ceilings, redwood beams and baronial half-timbering exude classic English manor-house richness.

Relax in the deep leather settees by the inviting fire in the Grand Lobby before enjoying the Inn's tradition of fine dining in a variety of restaurants and lounges, which range from the intimately elegant to the eclectic. Venturing out can mean exploring a fern-shrouded canyon, standing beneath the world's tallest tree or greeting fishing boats as they return to harbor.

Tenaya Lodge at Yosemite

1122 Highway 41
Fish Camp, California 93623
800-635-5807 • (209) 683-6555
Web Site: www.tenayalodge.com

Room Rates:	$109 – $239. AAA and AARP discounts.
Pet Charges or Deposits:	$50 cleaning fee.
Rated: 4 Paws 🐾🐾🐾🐾	242 nonsmoking rooms and suites, some sunken tubs and wet bars; indoor and outdoor pools, sauna, steam room, whirlpool, laundry facilities, restaurant, coffee shop and cocktail lounge.

 osemite's natural splendor has inspired the photographs of Ansel Adams and the writings of John Muir as well as captivated millions of visitors. Just two miles from the national park's south entrance, you will find the Tenaya Lodge. Surrounded by acres of Sierra National Forest, this smoke-free resort invites guests to escape the hustle and bustle of the outside world.

Spend the day exploring the natural wonders of the area with your pet, before escaping to the spa to relieve stress with a relaxing massage. With three restaurants on the premises, the menu varies from informal snacks to fine dining. They'll even pack a picnic for you to savor alfresco on a hike through the redwoods. The Guest Experience Center will arrange outings, too, from mountain biking to a ride on a steam-driven logging train.

Isis Oasis Lodge

20889 Geyserville Avenue
Geyserville, California 95441
800-679-PETS • (707) 857-3524

Room Rates:	$45 – $200, including full breakfast.
Pet Charges or Deposits:	None.
Rated: 3 Paws	Lodge with 12 private rooms and shared baths; retreat house that sleeps up to 15; a four-bedroom house with two baths, full kitchen and fireplaces; and 2 cottages, one with full kitchen and private hot tub.

I f you are looking for a magical retreat for the mind and body when visiting the wine country, try the Isis Oasis Lodge. The Lodge has 12 private rooms with Egyptian motif and shared baths. The Retreat House is a three-bedroom, three-bath house that sleeps up to 15. The Tower is a small cottage with a view and private half-bath and shower. The Vineyard House features four bedrooms, two fireplaces, a full kitchen and scenic views. The Isis Suite is a Victorian bedroom and sitting room with private bath. The Wine Barrel Room, Tipi and Pyramid are alternative-style rooms with a bathhouse.

The Lodge is located on ancient Pomo Indian ceremonial grounds. It has been a gathering place for groups and individuals seeking an extraordinary experience for years.

You will enjoy your time hiking, swimming in the heated pool, relaxing in one of the patio areas, taking wine-tasting tours or visiting with the many resident animals. Located near the river, there is plenty of open space for you and your dog to explore.

Big Dog Inn

15244 Arnold Drive
Glen Ellen, California 95442
(707) 996-4319
E-mail: bigdog@wco.com

Room Rates:	$125 – $175, including breakfast.
Pet Charges or Deposits:	Manager's prior approval required.
Rated: 4 Paws 🐾🐾🐾🐾	Guest cottage and in-house suite, both with private baths.

Nestled among six acres of rolling hills in historic Sonoma Valley, the Big Dog Inn blends history and hospitality in the heart of California's famed wine country.

The cathedral-ceiling guest cottage with sitting room, country furnishings and wood-burning stove offers exquisite views of the Sonoma Valley. The in-house suite features two bedrooms and a private sitting room. The patio, pool and spa areas reward travel-weary visitors with a chance for a relaxing pause after a full day of sightseeing, touring local wineries or shopping. For adventuresome guests, the area boasts miles of hiking, biking and horseback-riding trails for you and your dog to enjoy at Jack London State Park.

Innkeepers Penny and Doug Mahon have raised and shown St. Bernards for more than 30 years and welcome guests to tour the kennel building for an up-close and personal Big Dog Inn experience.

Gray Eagle Lodge

Gold Lake Road
Graeagle, California 96103
800-635-8778 • (916) 836-2511

Room Rates:	$145 – $190, including breakfast, dinner and daily maid service.
Pet Charges or Deposits:	$10 per day. Sorry, no cats.
Rated: 3 Paws 🐾 🐾 🐾	18 cabins. Restaurant, bar and gift shop.

Merely step out the door and the adventure begins at the Gray Eagle Lodge, where miles of trails lead to meadows and ponds, ridges, peaks and alpine lakes galore. And should you anglers come back with a "big one" — a fish or a fish tale — the inn keeps champagne on ice to reward the best fish stories.

Established in 1923, the family-owned-and-operated lodge offers guests their choice of 18 rustic cabins with full baths. There are no cooking facilities, but the room rate includes breakfast and dinner. The dinner menu offers daily selections ranging from pan-seared rainbow trout, to medallions of pork tenderloin to slow-roasted Long Island duckling. For a small fee, the chef will gladly prepare a picnic lunch or even cook up your catch of the day.

This "dog-friendly" lodge is set among the vast Plumas National Forest, which includes the Feather River, several lakes, recreation areas and plenty of room to roam. Gray Eagle Creek is next to the Lodge and affords fishing and rafting fun. Gray Eagle Falls spills into a pond, creating an inviting swimming hole. Add with mountain biking, hiking, two golf courses and horse stables nearby, what more could you ask for? How about no phones or televisions as distractions.

Zaballa House Bed and Breakfast

324 Main Street
Half Moon Bay, California 94019
(415) 726-9123
Web Site: www.whistlere.com/zaballa
E-mail: zaballa@coastside.net

Room Rates:	$75 – $250, including full breakfast.
Pet Charges or Deposits:	$10 per stay.
Rated: 3 Paws	12 guest rooms with private baths, some with whirlpool tubs and fireplaces.

O n historic Main Street, within walking distance of shops and restaurants, stands the historic Zaballa House. Built in 1859, it is the oldest building in Half Moon Bay.

This friendly, 12-room inn offers guests a casual, homey atmosphere. Put your feet up and relax in front of the fire with a book or magazine in the parlor or enjoy the privacy of your room, decorated with antiques, original oil paintings and wallpaper. All rooms offer private baths, some with double-sized whirlpool tubs and fireplaces.

Sample the large breakfast menu before heading out for the day. In the evening, you're invited to relax and socialize with the other guests with complimentary beverages and hors d'oeuvres in the front parlor.

Madrona Manor

1001 Westside Road
P.O. Box 818
Healdsburg, California 95448
800-258-4003 • (707) 433-4231
E-mail: madronaman@aol.com

Room Rates: $135 – $280, including full breakfast.
Pet Charges or Deposits: $30 deposit. Manager's prior approval required.
Rated: 5 Paws 🐾🐾🐾🐾🐾   18 Victorian-style rooms and 3 suites on eight acres; air-condi-
                           tioned, most with fireplaces, some with balconies and decks,
                           swimming pool.

 When looking for accommodations with beautifully landscaped grounds, fine dining and a sense of homey elegance, look no further than the elegant country inn and restaurant at Madrona Manor.

Guest rooms are elegantly decorated with stately antique furniture, many with fireplaces and balconies or decks. The Music Room is a good place to visit with other guests, read a bit, look over the house scrapbook, order a glass of wine or share in the on-going jigsaw puzzle.

Your day begins with a complimentary full breakfast, European in style, with sliced meats, imported cheeses, hot breads, fresh orange juice and local fruits.

Sorensen's Resort

14255 Highway 88
Hope Valley, California 96120
800-423-9949 • (916) 694-2203

Room Rates:	$70 – $275.
Pet Charges or Deposits:	Room rate as deposit. Two-pet limit; allowed only in certain cabins.
Rated: 3 Paws	3 bed-and-breakfast rooms and 27 cottages and cabins with fireplaces or wood-burning stoves and full kitchens.

C lose to more than 100 lakes, streams and some of the best skiing in the Sierras, you'll discover Sorensen's Hope Valley Resort. Here you'll find a romantic hideaway or a hostel for your ski trip with friends and family.

Amenities, activities and down-home hospitality make guests feel right at home. There are plenty of activities to keep you busy, including the classes and guide service from the Horse Feathers Fly-Fishing School, river-rafting tours and ski instructions from the Hope Valley Cross-Country Ski Center.

The cozy Country Café is perfect for a warm brew or a cozy meal.

The Ark

180 Highland Way
Inverness, California 94937
800-808-9338 • (415) 663-9338
Web Site: www.rosemarybb.com/ark.html
E-mail: rosemarybb@aol.com

Room Rates:	$130, including breakfast.
Pet Charges or Deposits:	$10 per stay.
Rated: 4 Paws 🐾 🐾 🐾 🐾	Cottage for 2 to 6 guests, full kitchen.

Tucked away in the forest, a mile up the ridge from the village of Inverness, The Ark is a romantic, private hideaway an hour north of the Golden Gate Bridge, next to the magnificent Point Reyes National Seashore.

Built and named in 1971 by a class of UC-Berkeley architecture students, The Ark offers seclusion in the form of a charming two-room cottage, with a spacious main room with a wood-burning stove, overlooking the forest. The cozy, comfortable furnishings include original works by local artists.

Recreational opportunities abound here with whale-watching, horseback-riding, rafting, kayaking and walking along the marshy headwaters of Tomales Bay, a noted place for bird watching.

Dancing Coyote Beach

12794 Sir Francis Drake Boulevard
Inverness, California 94937
(415) 669-7200

Room Rates:	$100 – $130. AAA, AARP, AKC and American Airlines discounts.
Pet Charges or Deposits:	Manager's prior approval required.
Rated: 4 Paws	4 cottages with galley kitchens, skylights, fireplaces and bay views.

Dancing Coyote Beach delivers privacy and bed-and-breakfast charm, only 80 minutes from the cultural energy of San Francisco. Located in the midst of the Point Reyes National Seashore, Dancing Coyote Beach offers a convenient home base for bicycling, hiking, whale-watching, birding and beachcombing.

Each of the four cottages has a galley kitchen, skylights, fireplace and views of the bay. For dining, enjoy breakfast on your own private deck in the morning sun or a romantic fireside dinner at night, or wander into sleepy Inverness to sample the menus of several fine restaurants.

This place is a quiet retreat, free of the noise of electronics and bustle, where you can stroll along the sandy beach, following the graceful curve of the shoreline.

Rosemary Cottage

75 Balboa Avenue
Inverness, California 94937
800-808-9338 • (415) 663-9338
Web Site: www.rosemarybb.com/rosemary.html
E-mail: rosemarybb@aol.com

Room Rates: $170, including breakfast.
Pet Charges or Deposits: $10 per stay.
Rated: 5 Paws 🐾🐾🐾🐾🐾 Cottage for two to four guests, views of Point Reyes National
                          Seashore. Hot tub.

ocated on the Inverness Ridge, Rosemary Cottage is a romantic French country "pied-à-terre." A wall of windows provides a dramatic forest view of Point Reyes National Seashore. A large deck under an aging oak overlooks the herb garden in this secluded hideaway. You will appreciate the many hand-crafted details, the large, cozy bedroom, high ceilings and wood-burning stove.

Only minutes from the beach, you can enjoy fishing, boating, whale-watching, horseback riding or a walk on the beach with your dog. Miles of hiking trails in the Point Reyes National Seashore begin only 10 minutes from the cottage. Just down the road are the marshy headwaters of Tomales Bay, a great place for bird-watching. For rafting or kayaking, try Papermill Creek. If you would prefer to just relax, stay at the cottage and soak in the garden hot tub.

Tree House Bed and Breakfast

73 Drake Summit
P.O. Box 1075
Inverness – Point Reyes Station, California 94956
800-495-8720 • (415) 663-8720
Web Site: www.treehousebnb.com

Room Rates:	$100 – $125, including continental breakfast.
Pet Charges or Deposits:	None. All pets are welcome.
Rated: 4 Paws 🐾🐾🐾🐾	3 private rooms, with separate entry. Hot tub.

T his secluded and peaceful getaway in legendary West Marin is located on the top of Inverness Ridge, with a view of Point Reyes Station and rolling hills. Enjoy the breathtaking views of the surrounding countryside, postcard-perfect with every season, while relaxing on the deck with wine, oysters and barbecue.

Choose from three guest rooms furnished in antiques and brass beds with fireplaces and views of the valley. A complimentary continental breakfast is served each morning.

Explore the park with its endless hiking and bike trails, almost at your doorstep, or ride horses from the nearby stables.

Joshua Tree Bed and Breakfast Inn

61259 Twenty-nine Palms Highway
Joshua Tree, California 92252
800-366-1444 • (619) 366-1188

Room Rates:	$85 – $220. AAA, AARP, AKC and ABA discounts.
Pet Charges or Deposits:	$10 per day. Horses welcome.
Rated: 3 Paws	10 guest rooms and semi-suites, kitchens and pool.

Minutes from the gateway to the scenic 500,000-acre Joshua Tree National Park is the Joshua Tree Bed and Breakfast Inn. This high-desert retreat strives to make you feel right at home with its charming antique furnishings and gourmet home-cooked breakfasts prepared from scratch.

If you and your dog are feeling adventurous, box lunches are available for the asking, so you can spend the day exploring Joshua Tree National Park with its mines, man-made dam, endless trails for hiking or horseback riding and even geological tours.

For a romantic evening, a candlelight dinner under the stars can be arranged. The desert nights are famous for their clear skies and panoramic views. For an evening of entertainment, the Hi-Desert Playhouse is right next door and is known for first-rate theatrical productions.

San Diego Marriott

4240 La Jolla Village Drive
La Jolla, California 92037
800-228-9290 • (619) 587-1414

Room Rates:	$198 – $650. AARP discount.
Pet Charges or Deposits:	Credit card imprint only.
Rated: 4 Paws	360 rooms and 11 luxury suites; whirlpool, saunas, indoor and outdoor pools, health club, game room, restaurants, cocktail lounge, valet parking; close to major attractions.

Situated in the heart of La Jolla's business district and minutes from major attractions, the San Diego Marriott — La Jolla offers impeccable service and striking elegance. The climate-controlled rooms and luxury suites offer guests amenities that range from the basics to concierge-level upgrades.

Dining options include JW's Sea Grill with indoor and outdoor seating, or Character's Bar and Grill for sports action. The San Diego Marriott — La Jolla prides itself on being a hotel big enough for an impressive reception or business conference, yet small enough for personal service.

Embassy Suites Hotel

8425 Firestone Boulevard
Los Angeles-Downey, California 90241
800-EMBASSY • (310) 861-1900

Room Rates:	$109 – $129, including full breakfast. AAA and AARP discounts.
Pet Charges or Deposits:	$15 per day. $50 nonrefundable deposit.
Rated: 3 Paws 🐾🐾🐾	219 suites, refrigerator and microwave, indoor pool, sauna, steam room, whirlpool, exercise room, secretarial services, complimentary evening beverages, restaurant, laundry service; exercise area for dogs.

L ocated in the heart of Southern California, the Embassy Suites Hotel — Los Angeles-Downey offers guests the convenience and luxury of a first-class hotel at an affordable rate. The spacious two-room suites give you that homey feeling while offering all the added amenities a business traveler or vacationing family needs.

Relax in the lush tropical gardens of the eight-story atrium courtyard with its rock waterfall and koi-filled ponds as you enjoy the manager's evening reception. Awake to a complimentary morning newspaper and a full, cooked-to-order breakfast.

Four Seasons — Regent Hotel

300 South Doheny Drive
Los Angeles, California 90048
800-332-3442 • (310) 273-2222

Room Rates:	$295 and up. AAA discount.
Pet Charges or Deposits:	Small pets only.
Rated: 5 Paws ❀ ❀ ❀ ❀ ❀	285 guest rooms including 106 suites; fax machine, voice mail, multi-line phones and computer hookups, heated pool, whirlpool, exercise room, massage, twice-daily maid service, 24-hour concierge services, exercise area for pets, complimentary limousine service to Rodeo Drive, 24-hour room service and award-winning restaurants.

O verlooking Beverly Hills and greater Los Angeles, the Four Seasons — Regent Hotel features 285 residential-style guest rooms and suites, decorated with floral, Oriental, contemporary or eclectic designs.

All rooms offer amenities such as refrigerated bars, computer hookup, 24-hour room and laundry services and twice-daily maid service. Situated among a lush garden on the fourth floor are the outdoor swimming pool and Jacuzzi, with a tented exercise and massage center.

For award-winning dining, Gardens Restaurant offers contemporary California cuisine. For an informal menu, there's The Café or the Poolside Terrace. Top off your evening at the Windows Lounge, featuring nightly entertainment and cocktails.

Your pets will be treated to dinner service, offering a choice of personal favorites prepared to their specifications, before a pet care specialist takes charge of the dog-walking duties.

Hotel Bel-Air

701 Stone Canyon Drive
Los Angeles, California 90071
800-648-4097 • (310) 472-1211

Room Rates: $285 and up.
Pet Charges or Deposits: $250 fee.
Rated: 5 Paws 🐾 🐾 🐾 🐾 🐾 92 luxury rooms and suites with refrigerators, safes and cable
                         television; landscaped grounds, heated pool, health club, meet-
                         ing rooms, secretarial services, valet laundry services, restau-
                         rant and cocktail lounge with live entertainment.

The magic and charm of the Hotel Bel-Air is evident as soon as you cross over the arched bridge and enter this 1920s mission-style hotel. Situated in the prestigious Bel-Air district in a heavily wooded canyon, the two-story pink stucco structure is crowned by a bell tower and flanked by courtyards and fountains. Housed in several buildings, the different rooms and suites offer a variety of sizes, floor plans and views and enjoy individual entrances from the hotel gardens, fountain courtyards or the pool area. Many rooms feature hot tubs, wood-burning fireplaces, terra cotta floors and exquisite needlepoint rugs. For exercise, there's the oval-shaped pool or the 24-hour fitness center.

If you're looking for solitude, escape to the chef's working garden offering a romantic place to relax with a book or special companion. For meals, sample alfresco dining at the bougainvillea-draped Terrace overlooking Swan Lake or try the award-winning seasonal French-California cuisine of the famed Hotel Bel-Air Restaurant. Top your evening off with a cocktail in The Bar, which features nightly piano entertainment. You will soon discover why the Hotel Bel-Air has been an oasis for celebrities and dignitaries for more than 50 years.

Westin Century Plaza Hotel and Tower

2025 Avenue of the Stars
Los Angeles, California 90067
800-WESTIN-1 • (310) 277-2000
Web Site: www.centuryplazala.com
E-mail: comments@centuryplazala.com

Room Rates: $135 – $280.
Pet Charges or Deposits: $15 per day. $50 nonrefundable deposit.
Rated: 4 Paws 🐾 🐾 🐾 🐾   1,072 rooms and suites with ocean and city views, wet bars, stocked refrigerators, twice daily maid service, 24-hour concierge and room service, laundry and valet service, complimentary Town Car service, international business center, pool, guest passes for the Century Plaza Spectrum Club and the Century City Tennis Club, multilingual staff.

A djacent to Beverly Hills, in the heart of the fashionable West Side of Los Angeles and minutes from major attractions, is the Westin Century Plaza Hotel and Tower. Here you'll find spacious accommodations with private lanais or balconies, magnificent views and amenities galore.

Whether in town on business or pleasure, travelers will appreciate the opportunity to relax by the garden swimming pool, work out the stresses of the day at one of the poolside fitness centers or take a relaxing stroll among the acres of lush gardens with the dog.

Residence Inn by Marriott

1700 North Sepulveda Boulevard
Manhattan Beach, California 90266
800-331-3131 • (310) 546-7627

Room Rates:	$99 – $198, including breakfast buffet. AAA, AARP, Entertainment and Quest discounts.
Pet Charges or Deposits:	$8 per day. $75 – $100 deposit/cleaning fee. Small pets only. Manager's prior approval required.
Rated: 3 Paws 🐾 🐾 🐾	176 suites with fully equipped kitchens, pool, Jacuzzi, exercise room, Sport Court, laundry facilities, meeting facilities, business services, room service, manager-hosted evening hospitality.

Whether traveling on business or pleasure, the Residence Inn by Marriott is the next best thing to being home. The spacious 176 rooms and suites provide you with all the comforts and conveniences you'll need, including fully equipped kitchen, large living room, fireplace, private entrance, efficient work space with computer hookup, multi-line phones and laundry facilities.

Start your day off at the Gatehouse with a complimentary continental breakfast, then move on to the fitness facilities for a workout before heading off for your day of sightseeing. Your dog will love the landscaped grounds and the canine exercise areas. For that extra homey touch, guests are treated to a weekly manager's social hour and barbecue.

Stanford Inn by the Sea

Coast Highway I and Comptche Ukiah Road
P.O. Box 487
Mendocino, California 95460
800-331-8884 • (707) 937-5615
Web Site: www.stanfordinn.com
E-mail: stanford@stanfordinn.com

Room Rates:	$175 – $275, including breakfast.
Pet Charges or Deposits:	$25 per stay.
Rated: 5 Paws 🐾🐾🐾🐾🐾	23-room bed-and-breakfast inn, many with fireplaces. Hot tub, spa and large pool in a beautiful solarium.

S et in historic gardens between coastal forest and the Pacific Ocean is the Stanford Inn by the Sea. A small, certified organic working garden and farm, the 23-room Inn embodies the best of the rugged Mendocino Coast. The Inn offers a champagne buffet breakfast and organic meals, along with amenities found in a fine hotel, while maintaining a cozy, homey feeling.

Rooms paneled with pine or redwood and decorated with antiques, plants and art from local artists make you want to linger by the fire just a little longer before heading out.

Pets are most welcome here. At check-in, your dog will receive biscuits, water and food bowls and bedding. But be forewarned. There are animals living on the premises: two horses, 14 llamas, swans, a goose, ducks, three dogs and 11 cats.

Bay Park Hotel

1425 Munras Avenue
Monterey, California 93940
800-338-3564 • (831) 649-1020

Room Rates:	$76 – $160. AAA and AARP discounts.
Pet Charges or Deposits:	$5 per day.
Rated: 3 Paws	80 rooms, pool, restaurant and lounge.

S et among the Monterey pines at the crest of Carmel Hill, Bay Park Hotel stands midway between the quaint charm of Carmel-by-the-Sea and the history of Monterey, affording views of the bay and the wooded hillside. The rustic allure of its natural wood decor comes packaged with modern amenities such as remote-control TV, air conditioning, clock radios and morning coffee.

Priding itself as a "family-style" operation, the hotel is across the street from a pet-friendly city park as well as the Del Monte Shopping Center. After a day of local adventures, unwind in the spa and full-sized pool.

Victorian Inn

487 Foam Street
Monterey, California 93940
800-232-4141 • (831) 373-1602

Room Rates:	$179 – $349. AAA, AARP and AKC discounts.
Pet Charges or Deposits:	$100 deposit, of which $75 is refundable.
Rated: 4 Paws	68 rooms with fireplaces, private patios, balconies or window seats; hot tub, walking distance to local attractions, "Pooch Package" given upon check-in.

L ocated on Monterey's historic Cannery Row, the Victorian Inn combines the best of old and new in what it calls "an oasis of tranquillity." Guests step into hospitality and classic luxury upon entering any of the 68 guest rooms, which include a marble fireplace and honor bar, with either a private patio, balcony or window seat.

To make you feel welcome, the Inn plays host to an afternoon wine and cheese reception in the parlor, a lavish continental breakfast and, for the canine guests, presents a "Pooch Package" containing a bowl with the Inn's logo, filled with dog cookies, bottled water and a postcard for Fido to send to a friend back home.

Tree House — Best Western Motor Inn

111 Morgan Way
Mount Shasta, California 96067
800-545-7164 • (916) 928-3101

Room Rates: $74 – $160. AAA and AARP discounts.
Pet Charges or Deposits: Small pets only.
Rated: 3 Paws   95 rooms and suites; heated indoor pool, restaurant and cocktail lounge.

Perched in the shadow of Mount Shasta is the Tree House — Best Western Motor Inn, where hospitality complements the rustic elegance of the Inn.

The warm glow of the natural wood paneling in the rooms, gourmet dining, the cozy warmth of the fireplace in the cocktail lounge, the view overlooking the majestic mountain and the serene atmosphere of the Inn all add up to a relaxing stay.

The indoor heated pool is enjoyed year-round. Delight in skiing and snow sports in the winter, and when the weather warms up, there's plenty of fishing areas and water sports to keep you busy.

Hyatt Newporter

1107 Jamboree Road
Newport Beach, California 92660
800-233-1234 • (714) 729-1234
Web Site: www.hyattnewporter.com

Room Rates:	$155 and up. AAA discount.
Pet Charges or Deposits:	$50. Pets up to 50 lbs.
Rated: 4 Paws 🐾 🐾 🐾 🐾	410 rooms and 17 suites, plus 4 private villas with private pools and fireplaces, tennis courts, 9-hole golf course, 3 pools, 3 spas, health club, jogging and bicycling trails, business center, secretarial services, laundry, restaurants and lounges, dog runs and exercise areas; near major attractions.

S et on 26 acres of plush gardens, the Hyatt Newporter overlooks the bay of Newport Beach. Enjoy the panoramic view of the bay from your balcony as the fresh sea air washes over you. At this luxury resort, guests may relax by one of the heated pools, play tennis or a few rounds of golf, jog or bike on the trails or visit the health club. Take some time out for a game of fetch with your dog at the beach or explore the lush gardens of this 26-acre paradise. If amusement parks are for you, you will appreciate the convenient proximity to major area attractions.

The casual atmosphere of the hotel's Jamboree Café features American classic cuisine, while Italian dishes are in store at Ristorante Cantori. Join other guests for cocktails, fun and conversation at the Lobby Bar. Duke's Country Western Saloon is perfect for country dancing and live music.

Andril Fireplace Cottages

569 Asilomar Avenue
Pacific Grove, California 93950
(831) 375-0994

Room Rates:	$70 – $285.
Pet Charges or Deposits:	$8 per day.
Rated: 3 Paws	16 cottages with separate living areas, kitchens, fireplaces, some with decks or yards, and a 5-bedroom ranch house, all in a private setting near the beach. Spa, barbecues.

L ocated on a quiet corner in a residential area near the beautiful Pacific Ocean is the charming Andril Fireplace Cottages. This relaxing hideaway consists of sixteen separate cottages set among the pine trees within walking distance of Asilomar State Beach.

Each cottage offers a wood-burning fireplace, homey, comfortable furnishings, a fully equipped kitchen, color television with cable and a private telephone.

Take advantage of your location with a leisurely stroll along the beach with your dog, explore the numerous tidepools, or merely take a few moments to enjoy the breathtaking sunset.

Estrella Inn at Palm Springs

415 South Belardo Road
Palm Springs, California 92262
800-237-3687 • (760) 320-4117

Room Rates:	$125 – $275. AAA, AARP, Entertainment and Quest discounts.
Pet Charges or Deposits:	$20 and credit card deposit. Limitations on certain breeds. Manager's prior approval required.
Rated: 4 Paws 🐾 🐾 🐾 🐾	69 guest rooms, suites and bungalows; daily California breakfast, three pools and two spas, outdoor barbecues, shuffleboard and volleyball courts, golf and tennis arrangements.

T he Estrella Inn is a desert hideaway that is still one of Palm Springs' best kept secrets, but with $4 million in restorations, the cat will soon be out of the bag. Built in the 1930s and once host to stars of Hollywood's golden era, the entire Inn has been remodeled. Most rooms are adorned with antiques, unusual beds and one-of-a-kind pieces, while others boast a desert feel with Southwestern tile and embellishments, and still others with a roaring '20s theme. The bungalows have fireplaces and full kitchens. Suites are equipped with kitchenettes, and guest rooms have wet bars and refrigerators. All guest quarters have balconies, patios or poolside views.

Outside, three acres of land are separated into three special environments, each with a pool: a rose garden, a fountain court and an original area maintained since the mid-'30s. There's even a pet exercise area.

The Inn is in the heart of historic Palm Springs "village," just one block from famous Palm Canyon Drive and within walking distance of restaurants, bistros, boutiques and art galleries.

Riviera Resort and Racquet Club

1600 North Indian Canyon Drive
Palm Springs, California 92262
800-444-8311 • (760) 327-8311

Room Rates:	$99 – $850. AAA discount.
Pet Charges or Deposits:	$300.
Rated: 3 Paws 🐾 🐾 🐾	476 guest rooms and 36 suites, all with refrigerators, microwaves and coffee-makers, 5 rooms with private outdoor hydrotherapy pools, 2 heated pools, wading pool, exercise room, basketball and volleyball courts, lighted putting green, tennis courts, croquet, business and meeting facilities, data ports, valet laundry, restaurant.

Surrounded by mountains and drenched by the Southern California sun, the Palm Springs Riviera Resort and Racquet Club offers deluxe rooms and luxury suites, all with oversized beds, individual climate control and in-room movies. The staff promises to lavish you and your pet with prompt, courteous service.

Guests may linger poolside, tone up in the fitness center, relax with a massage, try a friendly game of croquet, perfect their stroke on the putting course, join in a game of basketball or volleyball or play a few games of tennis, day or night on the lighted courts. To get a bird's-eye view of the scenic area, take a ride on the famous aerial tram. The spacious grounds offer plenty of opportunity for you and your pet to explore the desert setting.

The Grill features poolside cuisine for lunch and dinner, with live evening entertainment on weekends.

Spyglass Inn

2705 Spyglass Drive
Pismo Beach, California 93449
800-824-2612 • (805) 773-4855
Web Site: www.spyglassinn.com

Room Rates:	$59 – $139. AAA and AARP discounts.
Pet Charges or Deposits:	$10 per day. Designated rooms only.
Rated: 3 Paws 🐾🐾🐾	82 guest rooms and suites, many with ocean views, some with kitchens; miniature golf, shuffleboard, heated pool, whirlpool, restaurant and lounge; near beaches, wineries and Hearst Castle.

Designed for comfort and enjoyment, the oceanfront Spyglass Inn offers guests freshly decorated rooms, many with views of the dramatic coastline, set amidst meticulously landscaped grounds. This quiet refuge beckons relaxation. Take a walk on the beach with your dog and drink in the beauty of the ever-changing tides, swim in the heated pool, soak your cares away in the spa, play a few rounds of miniature golf or a game of shuffleboard before heading out for an afternoon of sightseeing, wine-tasting, fishing, sailing or other water sports.

For dining, the nautical theme of the Spyglass Inn Restaurant is carried out on an oceanfront deck where guests may sit and watch the sun sink into the ocean while enjoying a cocktail before dinner. Live entertainment is offered nightly.

Red Lion Inn

1401 Arden Way
Sacramento, California 95815
800-733-5466 • (916) 922-8041

Room Rates: $79 – $114. AAA and AARP discounts.
Pet Charges or Deposits: $50 deposit. Manager's prior approval required.
Rated: 3 Paws 🐾 🐾 🐾   376 guest rooms and 8 suites, some with patios or balconies;
                         putting green, 3 pools, wading pool, exercise room, guest laun-
                         dry service, restaurants and cocktail lounge.

L ocated just blocks from the California Exposition Center, eight miles from the city center and minutes from the airport, the Red Lion Inn is easy to get to and offers quick access to downtown, the state Capitol and the central Sacramento area.

Here guests will enjoy spacious accommodations, complete with air conditioning, large work areas and meeting facilities for the business traveler, laundry and valet services.

After a day of sightseeing or business meetings, relax by one of the three pools, go for a stroll around the spacious grounds with your dog or enjoy a workout in the fully equipped exercise room.

Princess Resort

1404 West Vacation Road
San Diego, California 92109
800-344-2626 • (619) 274-4630
Web Site: www.princessresort.com
E-mail: princess@princessresort.com

Room Rates:	$140 – $355. AAA discount.
Pet Charges or Deposits:	None.
Rated: 3 Paws 🐾🐾🐾	462 rooms and bungalows with refrigerators and coffeemakers; 5 pools, sauna, whirlpool, 18-hole putting course, lighted tennis courts, marina, health club, recreational program, canoeing, paddleboats, bicycles; secretarial services.

I f you ever dreamed of vacationing on a tropical island, then the San Diego Princess Resort might just be a dream come true. Located in the heart of San Diego's Mission Bay, this island resort is in a world of its own. The exotic setting is ablaze with color, sparkling waterfalls, winding lagoons and pathways weaving throughout the island for you and your dog to explore. The 462 single-story guest rooms and suites offer comfort and panoramic views, making this an ideal place for an exotic family weekend, a romantic getaway or a business meeting.

Guests may practice their putting on the 18-hole putting links, work out at the fitness center, tour the island by bicycle, jog on the 1.3-mile course, play video games, tennis, croquet, volleyball or shuffleboard, swim, sail, or relax with a sauna and massage.

For dining, try the family-style Village Café, the casual elegance of Dockside, dine poolside at Tropics or enjoy the live entertainment at the Barefoot Bar and Grill.

U.S. Grant Hotel

326 Broadway
San Diego, California 92101
800-HERITAGE • (619) 232-3121

Room Rates: $155 and up. AAA, AARP and AKC discounts.
Pet Charges or Deposits: None.
Rated: 5 Paws 🐾🐾🐾🐾🐾 340 guest rooms and suites, restaurant and cocktail lounge.
                         "Pampered Pet Program" for dogs and cats.

Built in 1910 by Ulysses S. Grant Jr. in memory of his father, the 340 rooms and suites of the historic U.S. Grant Hotel have housed 12 visiting presidents. Exquisitely restored and listed with Preferred Hotels Worldwide, the hotel is known for its Queen Anne reproduction furniture, comfortable and spacious rooms and four-star amenities. For fine dining, you need look no further than the Grant Grill, winner of numerous awards for excellence. A companion lounge features a variety of cocktails.

Four-legged guests will enjoy the "Pampered Pet Program," where your cat will be offered a beckoning feast of warm milk, a scratching post, catnip and squeaky toys. Vacationing dogs will be indulged with soft pillows for naps, chef-prepared gourmet dinners, rawhide toys and turn-down service with a dog biscuit.

Airport Westin Hotel

1 Old Bayshore Highway
San Franciso-Millbrae, California 94030
800-228-3000 • (415) 692-3500

Room Rates:	$94 – $190.
Pet Charges or Deposits:	$75 cleaning fee. Pets under 35 pounds.
Rated: 3 Paws	390 rooms, many with bay views, in-room refreshment centers; landscaped grounds, business center, heated indoor pool, saunas, whirlpool, fitness center, restaurant and lounge.

San Francisco's waterfront is home to the Airport Westin Hotel. Located just two minutes from the airport and 15 minutes from downtown, business travelers and vacationers alike appreciate the convenience of this resort-like hotel.

The fitness-minded should check out the hotel's fully equipped fitness center or grab the leash and take your dog for a run on the six-mile jogging trail at Bayfront Park across the street from the hotel.

Campton Place Hotel

340 Stockton Street
San Francisco, California 94108
800-235-4300 • (415) 781-5555

Room Rates: $230 – $1,000. AAA, AARP, AKC and ABA discounts.
Pet Charges or Deposits: $25 per day. Pets up to 40 pounds.
Rated: 5 Paws 🐾🐾🐾🐾🐾 117 rooms, acclaimed restaurant, five-star amenities, convenient to shopping, business, dining and entertainment.

J ust steps from San Francisco's Union Square and a step up from most hotels is one of the truly luxurious hotels in the world — Campton Place. The accommodations at the Campton Place Hotel frequent the list of the "Readers Choice Awards" of Condé Nast Traveler magazine, which has ranked it "One of the top 25 U.S. hotels." The small niceties of a European inn combine with the polished precision of a grand hotel — concierge, newspaper delivery, thick robes, valet parking.

The elegant, five-star restaurant at Campton Place continues to earn extraordinary acclaim. Diners enjoy award-winning cuisine, fine French and American wines and an ambiance graced by Wedgewood crystal and fresh flowers. The adjoining bar provides a cozy setting for afternoon tea or one of the hotel's famous dry martinis.

Clift Hotel

495 Geary Street
San Francisco, California 94102
800-HERITAGE • (415) 929-2300

Room Rates: $255 and up. AAA, AARP, AKC and ABA discounts.
Pet Charges or Deposits: $40 per day.
Rated: 5 Paws 🐾🐾🐾🐾🐾 326 rooms and suites; business center, fitness center, 24-hour
                                          room service and full-service concierge.

I n 1915, Fredrick C. Clift opened a hotel that rose out of the rubble of old San Francisco amid the futuristic fanfare of the Panama-Pacific Exposition, promising the grand tradition of days gone by while embracing America's growing world influence. The Clift Hotel has kept that promise. This 80-year-old "Grande Dame" has been impeccably maintained and continues to exude luxurious comfort.

Amid chandeliers and elegant decor, guests enjoy high-ranking service and amenities. Each room is decorated with fine linens and furnishings, with an attention to detail. With the staff at your service 24 hours a day, virtually everything is available to you with just one phone call — even chocolate cake and milk at midnight.

For award-winning California French cuisine, look no further than the gracious, romantic setting of the French Room. The Redwood Room is an Art Deco lounge and piano bar built from a 2,000-year-old giant redwood tree from Northern California. The redwood walls, 22-foot fluted columns and mural bar make this one of the most beautiful places in the world for cocktails.

Mansions Hotel

2220 Sacramento Street
San Francisco, California 94115
800-826-9398 • (415) 929-9444

Room Rates:	$139 – $250, including breakfast and nightly magic performance.
Pet Charges or Deposits:	None.
Rated: 3 Paws	21 rooms and suites, billiard/game room, historic museum, magic parlor, sculpture gardens and views of the Golden Gate Bridge.

There's magic in the air in more ways than one at the Mansions Hotel and Restaurant in the heart of San Francisco. When you step into the grand foyer with the crystal chandeliers, the creaking of the gumwood walls and Bach's music playing in the parlor, you are whisked back in time. Surrounded by tapestries, paintings and historic memorabilia, every room is different. Some have a terrace with a view of the Golden Gate Bridge, but all guest rooms include a private bath, fresh flowers, California apples and a special arrival gift.

The Mansions restaurant and dinner theater is one of San Francisco's favored dinner spots, offering an assorted menu, from a light buffet to a lavish banquet. There are haunting nightly performances in the Victorian Cabaret by America's most acclaimed illusionists. Listen closely: can you hear the whispers of the resident ghost, Claudia?

Marriott Fisherman's Wharf

1250 Columbus Avenue
San Francisco, California 94133
800-831-4004 • (415) 775-7555

Room Rates:	$139 – $169. AAA discount.
Pet Charges or Deposits:	Small pets only.
Rated: 3 Paws 🐾 🐾 🐾	256 rooms with honor bars, some with refrigerators; sauna, health club, restaurants and cocktail lounge.

S et in the heart of San Francisco's Northern Waterfront District is the renowned Marriott Fisherman's Wharf. With such a central location, you are within walking distance of Ghirardelli Square, the historic chocolate works turned distinctive shopping center, or the cable car lines to Nob Hill or Union Square or you can simply watch the sun set in a fiery display of color as it dips into the bay.

The hotel boasts an exercise area for your pet to stretch its legs, in addition to nearby local parks.

Pan Pacific Hotel

500 Post Street
San Francisco, California 94102
800-327-8585 • (415) 771-8600

Room Rates:　　　　　　　　$205 and up.
Pet Charges or Deposits:　$25 per day. Small pets only.
Rated: 4 Paws 🐾 🐾 🐾 🐾　330 rooms and 19 suites; exercise room, 24-hour room ser-
　　　　　　　　　　　　　　vice, restaurant and cocktail lounge.

S an Francisco's Pan Pacific Hotel is synonymous with luxury and sophistication. Accommodations are augmented by sumptuous bathrooms with deep soaking tubs, soft terry-cloth robes and personal valets to attend to your every need, including a chauffeur-driven Rolls Royce at your disposal.

The Pan Pacific Bar offers a compelling diversion to the bustling city below. The Pacific Restaurant has become a destination in itself, with its relaxing environment, soft piano music, the splash of the fountain and the crackle of the inviting fire.

Westin St. Francis Hotel

335 Powell Street – Union Square
San Francisco, California 94102
800-WESTIN-1 • (415) 397-7000

Room Rates: $199 and up.
Pet Charges or Deposits: Sorry, no cats.
Rated: 5 Paws 🐾🐾🐾🐾🐾 1,200 rooms and suites; in-room bars, valet parking, exercise
                     room, two dining rooms, coffee shop, cocktail lounge.

S ince 1904, the award-winning St. Francis Hotel has been known for its rich heritage. Located in the heart of San Francisco, it has 1,200 impeccably appointed guest rooms and luxurious suites, with meticulous attention to detail.

The St. Francis is located near the city's finest shops, theaters and restaurants. The bustling financial district and Chinatown are also just steps away.

World-famous Victor's offers a distinctive menu and breathtaking views 32 stories above the city. To partake of some of San Francisco's finest seafood, dine at the elegant, oak-paneled St. Francis Grill. Experience high tea and jazz in the opulent Compass Rose. To taste-test some of the more than 50 beers from around the world, stop by Dewey's Pub.

Homewood Suites Hotel

10 West Trimble Road
San Jose, California 95131
800-CALL-HOME • (408) 428-9900

Room Rates: $69 – $179, including continental breakfast. AAA and AARP
                         discounts.
Pet Charges or Deposits: $75 per day. $200 deposit. Pets up to 30 lbs.
Rated: 3 Paws   140 suites, heated pool, whirlpool, sports court, exercise
                         room, laundry facilities, in-room data ports, airport transporta-
                         tion, convenience store, manager's reception.

T he spacious, apartment-style accommodations of Homewood Suites offer guests separate living and sleeping areas, furnished with the amenities of home, such as remote-controlled televisions, VCRs, data ports, voice-mail message systems and fully equipped kitchens. The expanded continental breakfast and evening social hour in the lodge are complimentary for guests.

Swim a few laps in the pool, work out in the exercise center, join in a game at the sports/activity court or head out for a day of thrills at the nearby Great America Theme Park.

Business travelers will appreciate the 24-hour executive center with use of personal computers, modem and copier, secretarial services, free incoming faxes, discounted outgoing faxes and Federal Express drop-off sites.

Residence Inn by Marriott

1071 Market Street
San Ramon, California 94583
800-331-3131 • (510) 277-9292

Room Rates:	$109 – $189, including breakfast buffet. AAA and AARP discounts.
Pet Charges or Deposits:	$5 per day. $75 cleaning fee.
Rated: 3 Paws 🐾 🐾 🐾	106 rooms and suites, all with living rooms and separate sleeping areas, full kitchens, some with fireplaces; two heated pools, whirlpool, Sports Court, airport transportation and pet exercise area.

W hen it comes to comfortable and affordable lodging, Residence Inn by Marriott often garners top honors. The award-winning Inn offers inviting touches such as wood-burning fireplaces, separate sleeping and living areas, breakfast buffet and complimentary hospitality hours. You will enjoy the convenience of daily housekeeping, guest laundry and valet.

Unwind with a swim in the pool, relax in the heated spa, or hit the Sports Court for a game of racket sports, basketball or volleyball. You and your dog will enjoy the landscaped grounds and pet exercise area. There are even dog runs available and across the street is a park to enjoy.

Fess Parker's DoubleTree Resort

633 East Cabrillo Boulevard
Santa Barbara, California 93103
800-879-2929 • (805) 654-4333

Room Rates:	$229 and up. AAA, AARP, AKC and ABA discounts.
Pet Charges or Deposits:	$50.
Rated: 4 Paws 🐾🐾🐾🐾	360 guest rooms with balcony or patio, in-room honor bar, coffeemakers, putting green, pool, sauna, whirlpool, tennis courts, exercise room, shuffleboard and basketball court, data ports, airport transportation, 24-hour room service, coffee shop, cocktail lounge, spacious landscaped grounds; located across from the beach.

L ocated on the beautiful Santa Barbara coastline is Fess Parker's 25-acre resort. Here guests will find a coastal paradise, featuring 360 luxury guest rooms with amenities such as mini-bars, large bathrooms, 24-hour room service and a patio or balcony with a view of the ocean or the majestic Santa Ynez Mountains.

For fine dining, try the Café Los Arcos or Maxi's, both offering California cuisine brimming with fresh seafood.

Indulge yourself in beach activities such as swimming, volleyball and sailing, all just steps from the resort. In addition to the beach, there's also an on-site exercise area for dogs.

Ivanhoe Inn

1406 Castillo Street
Santa Barbara, California 93101
(805) 963-8832
Web Site: www.ivanhoeinn.com
E-mail: ivanhoeinn@aol.com

Room Rates:	$95 – $195.
Pet Charges or Deposits:	None.
Rated: 3 Paws 🐾🐾🐾	1 two-bedroom cottage and 4 guest suites in the main house.

T his lovely Victorian house in Old Santa Barbara is surrounded by a white picket fence entwined with colorful flowers. In the front yard sits a large, flower-filled cart, and in the back, under an old orange tree, resides a small gazebo in a parklike setting, with benches and tables. It has weathered a century of sun and earthquakes but still retains a quiet strength, much as Captain Sven Hansen, a retired Danish sea captain, must have envisioned when he built it sometime in the 1880s.

Upon your arrival the first night you will be served complimentary wine and cheese in your suite. The next morning a picnic basket will appear outside your door with a continental breakfast in it. Since each suite has a kitchen, you can enjoy the privacy of your room, a sunny patio or the garden.

The Ivanhoe is only a few blocks from the beach and four blocks from downtown Santa Barbara, where there are shopping plazas, unique little stores and sidewalk cafes.

San Ysidro Ranch

900 San Ysidro Lane
Santa Barbara-Montecito, California 93108
800-368-6788 • (805) 969-5046

Room Rates: $499 – $1,500.
Pet Charges or Deposits: $75 cleaning fee per pet. Privileged Pet Program.
Rated: 5 Paws 🐾🐾🐾🐾🐾 39 rooms, including 21 luxury cottages with private terraces,
                      fireplaces, ocean views, health club facilities, tennis courts,
                      restaurant, pub, dog runs and exercise areas; near major
                      attractions.

Situated on 500 acres in the foothills of the Santa Ynez Mountains, the San Ysidro Ranch for more than a century has offered guests rustic, elegant accommodations in a country setting, blending the charm of yesterday with the tastes of today. Here you can roam colorful flower gardens, swim in the ocean-view pool, join in a friendly tennis match, try your hand at lawn bowling or pamper yourself with a therapeutic massage, facial or body wrap in the privacy of your cottage.

Animals love the "Privileged Pet Program." They receive complimentary dog bowls, dog cookies and bagels, bottled water, a dog bed and turn-down service with a dog bone every evening. There are dog runs and exercise areas, plus 500 acres of oceanfront property to explore. After only one visit you and your pet will know why many guests throughout the years have called this their favorite retreat.

Westin Hotel

5101 Great America Parkway
Santa Clara, California 95054
800-WESTIN-1 • (408) 986-0700

Room Rates:	$109 – $199. AAA discount.
Pet Charges or Deposits:	None.
Rated: 4 Paws 🐾🐾🐾🐾	520 rooms and suites, business center, heated pool, sauna, whirlpool, 18-hole golf course, tennis courts, exercise facilities, restaurant and cocktail lounge, 24-hour room service.

L ocated in the heart of Silicon Valley, next to Paramount's Great America Theme Park and near the Santa Clara Valley vineyards, the Santa Clara Westin Hotel is a popular destination for both business and leisure travelers.

The 14-story facility offers 500 rooms and 20 suites equipped with all the creature comforts of home and a luxury hotel. Eight Westin Guest Offices outfit business travelers with high-tech office setups and services.

Enjoy the flavor and activities of the area by visiting Northern California's pre-eminent theme park, featuring rides and entertainment. If golf or tennis is more your style, the Santa Clara Golf and Tennis Club is next door and features a par-72 championship golf course and tennis center, both with professional instructors. To keep fit away from home, guests can work out in the hotel's private fitness center with exercise equipment, sauna and heated outdoor pool with whirlpool spa. There are even jogging and hiking trails nearby. For your dog's enjoyment, there is an exercise area at the hotel as well as a park nearby.

Ocean Front Vacation Rental

1600 West Cliff Drive
Santa Cruz, California 95060
800-801-4453 • (831) 266-4453
Web Site: www.oceanfronthouse.com

Room Rates:	$1,549 – $1,849 per week.
Pet Charges or Deposits:	$200 refundable deposit. Manager's prior approval required. Sorry, no cats.
Rated: 4 Paws	3-bedroom, 2-bath home with full kitchen; sleeps up to eight people.

I f you're looking for a real "home away from home" for a relaxing family vacation at the beach or an extended business trip, this furnished oceanfront vacation rental may be ideal.

Many vacationers choose these accommodations because they enjoy cooking for themselves and prefer the homelike surroundings, with enclosed back yard and ocean views. Pets are welcome, but should not to be left alone in the house or yard. A list of pet-sitters is available.

Venture along miles of shoreline flanked by prestigious West Cliff Drive and explore secluded beaches with your pets. Or, if you like amusement parks, head over to the Santa Cruz Beach and Boardwalk for a day of entertainment.

Inn at Heavenly Bed and Breakfast Lodge

1261 Ski Run Boulevard
South Lake Tahoe, California 96150
800-MY-CABIN • (530) 544-4244
Email: mycabin@sierra.net

Room Rates:	$115 – $165. AAA discount.
Pet Charges or Deposits:	$100 deposit. Dogs only. Sorry, no cats.
Rated: 4 Paws 🐾🐾🐾🐾	15-room bed and breakfast; some rooms with kitchenettes, refrigerators and microwaves; private spa room, hot tub, sauna, steam room, separate cabins for parties of up to 16. Pet-sitters available upon request.

S et on 11/2 acres of woods in South Lake Tahoe, Inn at Heavenly Bed and Breakfast Lodge is a log-cabin-style lodge with a knotty-pine interior and exterior, with custom log furniture throughout.

Accommodations vary in size, some with natural stone fireplaces, separate sitting areas, refrigerators and microwaves, but all offering large, homey rooms with patchwork quilts and views of the park. There is a private hot tub room, sauna and steam room available by reservation.

You and your canine pal will enjoy the parklike setting, with barbecue and picnic areas and log swings.

Tahoe Keys Resort

599 Tahoe Keys Boulevard
P.O. Box 20088
South Lake Tahoe, California 96150
800-MY-TAHOE • (916) 544-5397

Room Rates:	$100 – $1,750 per night.
Pet Charges or Deposits:	$25 per stay. $100 deposit.
Rated: 5 Paws 🐾🐾🐾🐾🐾	A private resort with waterfront condos, homes and villas. Front desk and concierge services, indoor and outdoor pool, spa, health club, lighted tennis courts, private beach.

T ahoe Keys Resort is a 750-acre private resort at famed Lake Tahoe. This year-round resort offers waterfront vacation rentals of premier three- to six-bedroom homes, studios, condominiums and a VIP villa, all with views of the water or the surrounding mountains. All accommodations come with complete kitchens and fireplaces.

Tahoe Keys Resort is a complete destination resort at Lake Tahoe, featuring a waterfront restaurant, an indoor/outdoor swimming pool, spa and health club. Guests enjoy bicycling, playing volleyball, basketball or tennis, boating, hiking with their dog and relaxing on the private beach. In the winter, you are just minutes away from several prime cross-country and downhill ski areas.

Harvest Inn

1 Main Street
St. Helena, California 94574
800-950-8466 • (707) 963-9463
Web Site: www.harvestinn.com

Room Rates:	$169 – $399. AAA and AARP discounts.
Pet Charges or Deposits:	$20 per pet per day.
Rated: 4 Paws 🐾🐾🐾🐾	54 rooms with wet bars and refrigerators, many with fireplaces, antique furnishings; surrounded by gardens and vineyards; two swimming pools and whirlpool.

N estled in the heart of Napa Valley are the charming, turn-of-the-century, English Tudor guest cottages of the Harvest Inn. The elegant but inviting guest rooms are reminiscent of the country gentry style of a bygone era. Many accommodations feature brick fireplaces, wet bars and refrigerators and are adorned with period antiques.

Reflecting the abundance of each season, colorful flowers and fruit-bearing trees grace lush lawns surrounding the Inn's 14-acre working vineyard.

Guests often stroll to the many neighboring wineries for tasting and for guided tours. Forests and stately vineyards provide walking and/or jogging paths as part of many extras. Bicycle some of the most exciting routes in the Bay Area or hike the scenic hillsides and meadows of Bothe-Napa Valley State Park. The renowned shops and restaurants of St. Helena are only a few minutes away.

Embassy Suites Hotel

1345 Treat Boulevard
Walnut Creek, California 94596
800-EMBASSY • (510) 934-2500

Room Rates: $119. AAA and AARP discounts.
Pet Charges or Deposits: $50 cleaning fee per pet.
Rated: 4 Paws   249 suites with kitchens and living rooms; heated indoor pool, sauna, whirlpool, exercise room, library, game room, restaurant and cocktail lounge.

W alnut Creek, with its specialty shops, department stores, theaters, restaurants and the Regional Art Center, is home to the Embassy Suites Hotel.

Accommodations feature a large private bedroom, living room with a sofa bed, galley kitchen, mini-bar, refrigerator, microwave and a well-lighted dining/work area.

Relax in the garden atrium or on the outdoor sun deck with your complimentary morning paper, swim a few laps in the indoor pool or work out in the fitness center before heading out for a day of meetings or sightseeing. There is a shuttle service to anywhere within a five-mile radius.

Le Montrose Suite Hotel De Gran Luxe

900 Hammond Street
West Hollywood, California 90069
800-637-7200 • (310) 855-1115

Room Rates: $185 – $475. AAA, AARP and AKC discounts.
Pet Charges or Deposits: $250 deposit. Pets up to 30 lbs.
Rated: 4 Paws 🐾🐾🐾🐾   125 suites with fireplaces, refrigerators and kitchenettes;
                            whirlpool, sauna, pool, tennis court, exercise room, restaurant;
                            near major attractions.

 estled in a quiet residential area one block east of Beverly Hills sits Le Montrose Suite Hotel De Gran Luxe. This celebrity hideaway offers guests a departure from ordinary accommodations. Charming, comfortable suites feature sunken living rooms, cozy fireplaces, refrigerators, color TVs with VCRs, maid service and, for the business traveler, multi-line phones, data ports, voice mail and in-suite fax.

The friendly staff and the attention to detail will remind you of a fine European hotel. Guests may relax in the heated rooftop pool and spa, play tennis, work out in the fitness center or enjoy a massage. Diners may choose the rooftop terrace with its panoramic view or an intimate dinner at the Library Restaurant.

Sheep Dung Estates

P.O. Box 49
Yorkville, California 95494
(707) 894-5322

Room Rates:	$75 – $125.
Pet Charges or Deposits:	None.
Rated: 4 Paws	3 cottages, with mini-kitchens, wood-burning fireplaces, private baths; located on 160 secluded acres.

Don't let the name fool you. Sheep Dung Estates is a unique country hideaway with grand views and meticulous attention to detail. Nestled on 160 acres of the picturesque Anderson Valley Hills, this retreat offers three secluded, comfortably furnished, modern cottages, with queen-sized beds, mini-kitchens and wood-burning fireplaces.

Pond Cottage, Sunset Hill and Terra Cottage are set on 15 to 40 acres each, with views of rolling hills. Mini-kitchens come fully stocked with breakfast fixings of homemade granola, fresh fruits, organic apple juice, wine, cheese, coffee, tea and milk.

After a day of sightseeing and a trip to the vineyards or wandering rambling roads, you can prepare your evening feast and sit on your own private deck and toast the sun with a glass of local wine as it sets beyond the hills.

Redwoods Guest Cottages

8038 Chilnualna Falls Road
P.O. Box 2085 — Wawona Station
Yosemite National Park, California 95389
(209) 375-6666
Web Site: www.redwoodsguestcottages.com
E-mail: yosemitrez@aol.com

Room Rates: $82 – $438.
Pet Charges or Deposits: None.
Rated: 5 Paws 🐾🐾🐾🐾🐾 125 fully equipped rustic cottages and modern homes, spacious decks and fireplaces, located in Yosemite National Park.

 he Redwoods Guest Cottages offers lodging choices ranging from rustic, one-bedroom cottages and cabins to spacious, modern, five-bedroom homes, all nestled among the forest and mountain streams of Wawona.

In winter, visitors revel in spectacular skiing at Badger Pass. Spring brings rebirth to the park's natural bounty, especially the waterfalls at Chilnualna Falls. Summer is the perfect time to rent a horse or take a stagecoach ride at Wawona Stables, play a round of golf at Wawona Golf Course or wet your fishing line in one of the many streams and creeks. In the fall, enjoy the crisp days and colorful changes in the foliage and nights around a campfire. No matter what the season, nature is at your doorstep in Yosemite.

Vintage Inn — Napa Valley

6541 Washington Street
Yountville, California 94599
800-351-1133 • (707) 944-1112

Room Rates:	$180 – $325. AAA and AARP discounts.
Pet Charges or Deposits:	$25 per stay. Credit card guarantee as deposit.
Rated: 4 Paws 🐾🐾🐾🐾	80 rooms with balcony or patio, views of the vineyard, mountain or town, fireplaces and refrigerators; champagne breakfast, massage, heated lap pool, whirlpool spa and tennis courts.

 estled among the vineyards of the Napa Valley on lush, estate-like grounds is the country villa called the Vintage Inn. The Old World charm and contemporary amenities make this a popular choice for vacationers and business professionals.

After settling into your room with its custom furnishings, cozy fireplace and complimentary bottle of wine, stroll through the landscaped grounds and admire the pools, fountains and courtyards with your pet.

Guests are encouraged to enjoy the tennis courts, do a few laps in the heated pool, relax in the spa or treat themselves to a massage. While you are here, visit the adjacent Vintage 1870, a restored winery with unique shops, restaurants and galleries.

Owyhee Plaza Hotel

1109 Main Street
Boise, Idaho 83702
800-233-4611 • (208) 343-4611

Room Rates: $63 – $124. AAA and AARP discounts.
Pet Charges or Deposits: $25 refundable deposit.
Rated: 3 Paws 100 guest rooms and 2 suites with pool and guest privileges at health club.

T he historic Owyhee Plaza Hotel, named for the majestic Owyhee Mountain Range, has been a downtown Boise landmark since 1910. Renovated to reflect the luxury of the 1990s, great care has been taken to preserve the hotel's historic charm. A member of Grand Tradition Hotels, the Owyhee Plaza maintains a reputation for excellence and hospitality.

A variety of convenient services, including valet, room service, courtyard pool and guest privileges at the city's finest health club, are available for guests. Room amenities include coffeemakers, mini-bars, refrigerators and in-room movies.

Gooding Hotel Bed and Breakfast

112 Main Street
Gooding, Idaho 83330
888-260-6656 • (208) 934-4374

Room Rates:	$45 – $50, including full breakfast. Call for discounts.
Pet Charges or Deposits:	$10 per day. $25 refundable deposit. Manager's prior approval required.
Rated: 3 Paws	3 guest rooms and 4 suites.

A small wooden structure, originally known as Kelly's Hotel, was built along the railroad line in 1906 by early settler William B. Kelly. Later, the building was enlarged with a brick addition, and the name was changed to the Gooding Hotel. As the oldest building in town, the Gooding Hotel has led a colorful life. Saved from destruction in the early 1980s, the Gooding Hotel has been lovingly restored and is now on the National Register of Historic Places.

Your day begins with a bountiful breakfast buffet before you head out for a day of golfing, fishing, skiing, snowmobiling or white-water rafting. The Shoshone Ice Caves, Snake River Canyon, Malad Gorge State Park and numerous wineries are here for you to explore.

Heidelberg Inn

1908 Warm Springs Road
P.O. Box 5704
Ketchum, Idaho 83340
(208) 726-5361
Web Site: www.taylorhotelgroup.com
E-mail: bookings@micron.net

Room Rates:	$60 – $130, including continental breakfast. AAA and AARP discounts.
Pet Charges or Deposits:	$5 per day.
Rated: 3 Paws 🐾🐾🐾	30 guest rooms and 8 suites with kitchens. Heated outdoor swimming pool (summer only), indoor hot tub, sauna, laundry facilities.

L ocated in a quiet, residential neighborhood, midway between Ketchum and Sun Valley, the Heidelberg Inn is convenient to the Warm Springs ski lifts and the world-famous Bald Mountain skiing. A golf course and tennis complex are across the street, and restaurants, shopping and night life are just minutes away by free shuttle bus. Sawtooth National Recreation area offers cross-country skiing, fishing, hiking and back-country adventure.

Guest rooms are spacious and comfortable, featuring king- or queen-sized beds; some have kitchenettes. Each room has a refrigerator, microwave, coffee server and TV with VCR, with movie rentals available at the front desk. A continental breakfast is served to your room each morning.

Tyrolean Lodge

260 Cottonwood
P.O. Box 802
Ketchum, Idaho 83340
800-333-7912 • (208) 726-5336
Web Site: www.taylorhotelgroup.com
E-mail: bookings@micron.net

Room Rates:	$65 – $125, including continental breakfast and champagne. AAA and AARP discounts.
Pet Charges or Deposits:	$5 per day.
Rated: 3 Paws	56 guest rooms and 7 suites. Indoor and outdoor hot tubs, pool, exercise room, game room, laundry facilities.

T he Lodge has been remodeled in the classic Austrian style, with comfort and value in the spacious and tastefully appointed guest rooms. Over-sized beds are graced with down comforters and the rooms have color cable TVs; many offer mountain views. Suites are equipped with all of the comforts of home, including wet bars, microwaves, refrigerators and in-room spa baths. A complimentary continental breakfast is served each morning.

At the base of world-famous Mount Baldy, you are just a short walk to the River Run chair lift, as well as being conveniently located for restaurants, shops and night life.

Kingston 5 Ranch Bed and Breakfast

42297 Silver Valley Road
P.O. Box 130
Kingston, Idaho 83839
800-254-1852 • (208) 682-4862
Web Site: www.nidlink.com/~k5ranch
E-mail: k5ranch@nidlink.com

Room Rates:	$65 – $125, including full breakfast. 15% discount if you mention Pets Welcome™ guidebook.
Pet Charges or Deposits:	Pets are not allowed indoors, but are kept in a fenced, grassy run with a Veri Kennel for shelter. No additional pet fee. Horse-boarding available.
Rated: 4 Paws 🐾🐾🐾🐾	3 guest rooms. Fireplace, Jacuzzi tub, outdoor private spa.

S urrounded by majestic mountains and towering pines, the Kingston 5 Ranch is on a small rise overlooking a lush green valley in the Coeur d'Alene mountains. When you step into the new 4,500-square-foot, two-story, New England-style farmhouse, you will be amazed by the spectacular views from every room.

Guest rooms are spacious and beautifully appointed, with four-poster oak beds, comfortable Queen Anne chairs, fluffy down comforters and crystal lamps. Plush carpeting, vaulted ceilings and crackling fireplaces add to the rooms' charms. A private verandah or deck with your own hot tub and sitting area is decorated with wrought-iron tables, chairs and lounge.

Breakfast is served on the deck or in the cozy country dining room, featuring homemade, crisp Belgian waffles, topped with fresh fruits and whipped cream, country cured meats, tasty omelets and hot breads and muffins. Many of the fruits and vegetables used for your breakfast are grown here at the ranch.

Three Rivers Resort

HC 75, Box 61
Kooskia at Lowell, Idaho 83539
800-LOCHSA-3 • 888-926-4430 • (208) 926-4430
Web Site: www.threeriversrafting.com
E-mail: info@threeriversrafting.com

Room Rates:	$49 – $99.
Pet Charges or Deposits:	None.
Rated: 3 Paws 🐾 🐾 🐾	25 guest rooms and 10 suites with kitchens, on 180 acres. Pool, Jacuzzi and hot tubs.

 hree Rivers Resort sits at the confluence of the Lochsa, Selway and Clearwater rivers in Kooskia at Lowell, Idaho. This beautiful vacation spot is in the middle of great fishing, rafting, kayaking and camping territory.

The resort features private, rustic and modern riverfront cabins with fully equipped kitchens. Many of the cabins feature wood-burning fireplaces.

Ride a wave through the Royal Gorge or Arkansas River with the oldest and most experienced outfitters here. If fishing is what you are looking for, there are float trips, wade trips and raft-floating fishing, with full instructions for the new angler.

Pinehurst Resort

5604 Highway 95
New Meadows, Idaho 83654
(208) 626-3323

Room Rates:	$35 – $55.
Pet Charges or Deposits:	$3 per day. Manager's prior approval required.
Rated: 3 Paws 🐾🐾🐾	6 guest cottages with kitchens.

Nestled in the pines along Interstate Highway 95, the entire property at Pinehurst Resort is fronted by the Little Salmon River. This facility is not one with swimming pools, spas and fancy food. Instead, you will experience a serene, historic stay, offering starry skies and some of the most spectacular scenery in the country.

The cottages are only steps from the river and are clean, comfortable and well-decorated, with vintage furniture that reflects the history of the area. The kitchens are furnished with basic necessities and each cottage has its own picnic table. If you're not in the mood for cooking, the Trading Post next door offers a full menu, along with groceries and gas.

Fly-fish for trout in the summer or fish for giant steelhead in spring and fall. The resort has the best private fishing hole on the river.

Back O' Beyond Inn

404 South Garfield Avenue
Pocatello, Idaho 83204
800-232-3820 • (208) 232-3825
Web Site: www.gemstate.net/backbeyond
E-mail: backbeyond@gemstate.net

Room Rates: $65, including full breakfast. AAA and AARP discounts.
Pet Charges or Deposits: Manager's prior approval required.
Rated: 3 Paws 🐾 🐾 🐾   3 guest rooms.

Back O'Beyond is an elegant Queen Anne home, built in 1893, which combines the spirit of the hearty pioneers with the gracious comforts of today.

Each of the three warm and inviting bedrooms is furnished with fresh flowers, candles and down comforters and each offers a private bath. Guests are encouraged to enjoy the parlor with its 14-foot ceilings — a great place to curl up with a good book by the fire. Upstairs is a sitting room that includes a cable TV, fireplace, fax machine, copy machine, computer and phone. A sofa bed is available for children or extra guests.

Old-fashioned tea, lemonade and homemade cookies are served on the porch and patio under century-old shade trees. Awake to a full breakfast served on lace tablecloths, old china and silver.

Bottle Bay Resort

115 Resort Road
Sagle, Idaho 83860
(208) 263-5916
Web Site: www.keokee.com/bottlebay
E-mail: bottlebay@dmi.net

Room Rates:	$60 – $135.
Pet Charges or Deposits:	$5 per day. Refundable deposit must equal to half of stay.
Rated: 3 Paws 🐾 🐾 🐾	6 cabins. Cocktail lounge, kitchen and country store. Boat rentals available.

L ocated on a quiet, wind-protected bay of Lake Pend Oreille, the resort offers a variety of water sports or just lazy, sun-filled days on the sandy beach.

Modern housekeeping cabins with scenic lake views feature queen-sized beds in the sleeping lofts, hide-a-beds in the living rooms and fully equipped kitchens. Two- and three-bedroom lakefront cabins are also available adjacent to the resort. Linens, with the exception of beach towels, are provided. A free boat slip is provided for cabin guests.

Some of the lake's best cutthroat trout fishing is at the mouth of Bottle Bay and the water skiing is great in the calm, protected bay.

Smith House Bed and Breakfast

49 Salmon River Road
Shoup, Idaho 83449
800-238-5915 • (208) 394-2121

Room Rates:	$35 – $55, including deluxe continental breakfast.
Pet Charges or Deposits:	$15 per stay. Refundable deposit.
Rated: 3 Paws	5 guest rooms and 1 cottage. Outdoor hot tub.

O n the Salmon River, downriver from the historic townsite of Shoup, is the Smith House Bed and Breakfast, offering a sense of informality, privacy and cozy comfort at economical rates.

The roar of the mighty Salmon River can be heard from every room. Birdwatchers will enjoy the wide range of native and migratory birds here. You are within a short distance of historical points of interest, hot springs, numerous nature areas for hiking, ski areas, the aquarium and vineyards.

Teton Ridge Ranch

200 Valley View Road
Drawer K
Tetonia, Idaho 83452
(208) 456-2650

Room Rates: $300 – $475.
Pet Charges or Deposits: Manager's prior approval required.
Rated: 5 Paws 🐾🐾🐾🐾🐾 7 guest rooms on 400 acres, 2 spring-fed, stocked ponds.
Restaurant.

 his small, luxurious guest ranch is located in a mountain valley on the west side of the Teton Range in Idaho, 40 miles from Jackson Hole, Wyoming. Situated atop a 6800-foot knoll on 4,000 acres, the ranch overlooks the valley that was once the hunting grounds of the Crow, Blackfoot and Shoshonie Indians.

The 10,000-square-foot log lodge is constructed of mammoth lodgepole logs, heavy beams and polished plank flooring. The cathedral ceiling living room and dining room with adjacent library have matching stone fireplaces and porches. There are five suites, each with a majestic view of the Tetons, featuring individual porches, woodstoves, large Jacuzzis and steam showers. In the summer a two-room apartment with bath is also available for guests.

The ranch has no formal structured dude ranch program, but rather tailors the vacation wants of each individual guest or group. Riding, fishing, skiing, floating, soaring and cycling are available.

Meadow Lake Resort

100 Saint Andrews Drive
Columbia Falls, Montana 59912
800-321-4653 • (406) 892-7601
Web Site: www.meadowlake.com
E-mail: mdwlake@meadowlake.com

Room Rates: $89 – $129. AAA and AARP discounts.
Pet Charges or Deposits: $15 per day.
Rated: 5 Paws 🐾 🐾 🐾 🐾 🐾 24 guest rooms and condominiums on 330 acres. 18-hole golf
                          course, indoor and outdoor pool and spas, hot tubs, tennis
                          court, recreation center, fitness center, restaurant and lounge.

Meadow Lake Resort, located in northwest Montana's Flathead Valley, is just minutes from Glacier National Park, the Big Mountain ski area and Flathead Lake. Internationally recognized for its quality, service and luxury accommodations, Meadow Lake Resort offers deluxe guest rooms at the Inn, as well as condominiums and vacation homes.

When the snow falls, the golf course turns into miles of cross-country skiing — just slip on your skis and head out your back door. You can also enjoy yourself on one of Meadow Lake's outside skating areas. Skate rentals are available at the recreation center. Ten minutes from the resort is the Olympic-sized Mountain Trails Ice Skating Center.

Hotel Albert Bed and Breakfast

No. 2 Yellowstone Trail
P.O. Box 300186
De Borgia, Montana 59830
800-678-4303 • (406) 678-4303

Room Rates:	$56 – $64, including full breakfast. AAA, AARP, AKC and ABA discounts.
Pet Charges or Deposits:	$5 per stay. Manager's prior approval required. Sorry, no cats. Small dogs only.
Rated: 3 Paws 🐾 🐾 🐾	4 guest rooms.

Hotel Albert Bed and Breakfast looks like something out of a Western movie set, with its false front and elk antlers over the wooden-railed upper porch. Built in 1911 to serve the early travelers on the railroad of the historic Mullan Trail, recent renovations meet the needs of today's travelers on Interstate 90, while maintaining the atmosphere of old Montana.

There are extensive trails and roads in the surrounding national forest for mountain biking, bird-watching, hiking, cross-country skiing, snowmobiling or just enjoying the scenery. Lookout Pass ski area is just 18 miles west.

Querencia Bed and Breakfast on the Yellowstone

Mile Post 36.74 Highway 89 South
P.O. Box 184
Emigrant, Montana 59027
(406) 333-4500
E-mail: querencia@mcn.net

Room Rates: $90 – $125, including full breakfast.
Pet Charges or Deposits: None.
Rated: 3 Paws 🐾 🐾 🐾   5 guest rooms and 1 suite.

E legantly rustic and warmly hospitable, Querencia Bed and Breakfast offers guest rooms with private entrances from spacious decks, each with magnificent views of the Absaroka and Crazy Mountains.

A complete kitchen is available to guests, as is the riverside grill and picnic area. The gathering area features an antique wood stove and stone hearth, the perfect interior to share the day's adventures and plan tomorrow's. The library holds a sampling of Montana's best literature and folklore.

Winter is spectacular scenery and quiet solitude on the Yellowstone. Large numbers of eagles are visible from Querencia between November and March. Summer is bright cool mornings and peaceful walks along the river. The fishing is as fabulous as the scenery, and surprisingly uncrowded.

LH Ranch Bunk and Biscuit

471 Mullan Trail
Gold Creek, Montana 59733
(406) 288-3436

Room Rates:	$75 – $85, including breakfast. AAA, AARP, AKC and ABA discounts.
Pet Charges or Deposits:	None.
Rated: 3 Paws	2 guest rooms with a 2-acre fenced yard and hot tub.

T his log home, built on a historical ranch, offers stunning views from all sides. Relax on the deck with a book from their library or slip into the warm spa and enjoy the scenic splendor surrounding you.

Picturesque Gold Creek runs in the back of this home, where activities such as gold-panning, fishing for rainbow, brown and cutthroat trout, woodland exploring for wild flowers and bird-watching can be enjoyed. Bordering the national forest, picnic lunches, horseback riding and hiking are right out your front door.

Deer Crossing Bed and Breakfast

396 Hayes Creek Road
Hamilton, Montana 59840
800-763-2232 • (406) 363-2232
Web Site: www.wtp.net/go/deercrossing
E-mail: deercross@bitterroot.net

Room Rates:	$70 – $100, including full breakfast.
Pet Charges or Deposits:	$25 refundable deposit. Manager's prior approval required. Horses welcome.
Rated: 4 Paws 🐾🐾🐾🐾	3 guest rooms, 2 suites and 1 bunkhouse. Access to the Bitterroot National Forest; corrals and water for horses.

T his is your invitation to experience Western hospitality at its finest. Deer Crossing Bed and Breakfast is located along the Lewis and Clark Trail, on 25 lush acres of tall pines and pasture, overlooking the Bitterroot Valley. Here you will be treated to the sight of elk, fox, coyote and a wide assortment of birds, from tiny hummingbirds to majestic bald eagles.

Guest accommodation choices include a stay in one of the large guest rooms, a spacious suite including a large tub and window overlooking the fields, or the bunkhouse, where you can experience the feel of the Old West.

Relax on the deck with a steaming hot cup of coffee and watch the sunrise over the Sapphire Mountains, followed by a hearty ranch breakfast on the porch or in the country kitchen. Enjoy world-class fly-fishing, horseback riding or hiking, or just relax and savor the breathtaking views and quiet. Kick off your boots, hang up your hat and make yourself at home.

Barrister Bed and Breakfast

416 North Ewing Street
Helena, Montana 59601
800-823-1148 • (406) 443-7330
E-mail: Barrister@rcisys.net

Room Rates:	$85 – $100, including full breakfast and evening social. AAA discount.
Pet Charges or Deposits:	None.
Rated: 3 Paws 🐾🐾🐾	5 guest rooms. Refrigerators, microwaves, honor bar, washer and dryer.

R elax in this 1874 Victorian mansion, centrally located in Montana's capital city. Enjoy more than 2,000 square feet of common area, featuring a parlor, formal dining room, den and TV room, library, office and enclosed sun porch.

The original home boasts six ornate fireplaces, original stained glass windows, high ceilings and carved staircases. Guest rooms are spacious and carefully decorated to provide an intimate atmosphere as well as comfort. A full breakfast is included, served in the dining room or on the sun porch.

Kalispell Grand Hotel

100 Main Street
Kalispell, Montana 59901
800-858-7422 • (406) 755-8100
Web Site: www.vtown.com/grand
E-mail: info@vtown.com

Room Rates:	$44 – $115, including continental breakfast. AARP discount.
Pet Charges or Deposits:	None.
Rated: 3 Paws 🐾 🐾 🐾	38 guest rooms and 2 suites. Exercise room.

L ocated just 30 minutes from Glacier National Park in Montana's magnificent Flathead Valley, this historic accommodation offers a glimpse into the past with its original high, pressed-tin ceilings, Terazzo floor and grand oak staircase. Complimentary continental breakfast is an every morning occasion in the Grand Lobby. Each evening you are invited to enjoy wine, coffee, tea and cookies.

You'll climb the royal oak stairway to enjoy your room furnished with the warmth of Victorian cherry wood. Guest rooms vary in size, including family suites and jetted tub suites. All of the rooms feature private baths with showers, cable television with remote controls and telephones equipped with data ports.

River Inn on the Yellowstone

4950 Highway 89 South
Livingston, Montana 59047
(406) 222-2429
Web Site: www.wtp.net/go/riverinn
E-mail: riverinn@alpinet.net

Room Rates:	$40 – $90, including full gourmet breakfast.
Pet Charges or Deposits:	Manager's prior approval required. Call for deposits.
Rated: 3 Paws 🐾 🐾 🐾	3 guest rooms, I cabin and I wagon.

T his lovely, 100-year-old farmhouse rests on the west bank of the Yellowstone River, surrounded by five acres with at least 500 feet of riverfront property to meander or fish.

The interior has a warm, Western-style with fir floors and a view from each window. Original art works meet eclectic furnishings, ranging from both hemispheres and several centuries.

All three bedrooms are upstairs and have their own private baths and scenic views. French doors open onto a rock patio, where breakfast is served on warm mornings, just a few steps from a fine fishing hole. A small rustic cabin and a restored turn-of-the-century sheepherder's wagon offer additional lodgings for the adventurous.

Elkhorn Mountain Inn

1 Jackson Creek Road
Montana City, Montana 59634
(406) 442-6625

Room Rates:	$50 – $55, including continental breakfast. AAA and AARP discounts.
Pet Charges or Deposits:	$5 per day. Manager's prior approval required.
Rated: 3 Paws	20 guest rooms and 3 suites.

Your hosts at the Elkhorn Mountain Inn are not just innkeepers, but a local family. They know the area, things to do, short-cut directions, local entertainment and events and the best dining facilities.

The Inn was designed around locally hand-crafted furnishings, with select color schemes and accessories. It offers great accommodations and real Montana hospitality at affordable rates.

Lake Upsata Guest Ranch

135 Lake Upsata Road
P.O. Box 6
Ovando, Montana 59854
800-594-7689 • (406) 793-5890
Web Site: www.upsata.com
E-mail: rhowe@upsata.com

Room Rates:	$190 – $220, including 3 meals, horseback riding, fly-fishing and all activities.
Pet Charges or Deposits:	Manager's prior approval required.
Rated: 3 Paws 🐾🐾🐾	8 guest cabins with refrigerators.

L ocated on a scenic lake in the mountains of western Montana, Lake Upsata Guest Ranch has something for everyone — fly-fishing, horseback riding, children's programs, swimming, boating, canoeing, kayaking and ghost towns to explore.

Each of the well-appointed cabins offers picturesque lake views from your private porch. Three hearty meals a day are included in a home-style setting. The "Continental Divide" breakfast is a full buffet of cereals, breads, fruits, yogurts and juices, in addition to a hot special like eggs to order or French toast. You select your lunch for the next day, which is ready to go after breakfast. Dinners are friendly and hearty — some nights it's a barbecue, or it could be a buffalo roast or fresh rainbow trout.

Mystical Mountain Inn

126 Indian Prairie Loop
Stevensville, Montana 59870
(406) 642-3464
E-mail: Mystical@over-the-rainbow.com

Room Rates:	$50 – $105, including full breakfast. AAA, AKC and ABA discounts.
Pet Charges or Deposits:	$5 per day. $50 refundable deposit. Manager's prior approval required.
Rated: 3 Paws 🐾🐾🐾	5 guest rooms and I suite on 15 acres. Exercise room, Jacuzzi, hot tubs, home theater with Surround-Sound.

T his spacious home is located 28 miles south of Missoula, Montana, in the Bitterroot Valley, on 15 acres of pastured and pine-covered property. Mystical Mountain Inn has two ponds — one stocked with rainbow trout for catch-and-release fishing — and is within walking distance of the mountain wilderness. On-site wildlife viewing of deer, an occasional elk, eagles and moose is an everyday pastime.

The Inn is well designed for privacy and comfort. On the main floor in the living room, a magnificent stone fireplace continues to the vaulted ceiling. Directly above the living room, at the top of the stairs, is a library with a wide selection of books and magazines for guest use. The bedrooms are spacious, comfortable and inviting. Social hour hors d'oeuvres (high tea on weekends) and a full country breakfast are included in your room rate.

Windmill Inn of Ashland

2525 Ashland Street
Ashland, Oregon 97520
800-547-4747 • (541) 482-8310

Room Rates:	$46 – $250, including continental or full breakfast.
Pet Charges or Deposits:	None.
Rated: 4 Paws 🐾🐾🐾🐾	145 guest rooms and 85 luxury suites, some with kitchens, seasonal outdoor swimming pool and whirlpool, fitness room, tennis courts, laundry facilities, jogging path, bicycles, helicopter landing pad.

Nestled in the foothills of Southern Oregon's Cascade Mountains, in the famed town of Ashland, is Windmill Inn of Ashland, one of the Northwest's premier resort destinations. Whether you choose one of the comfortable guest rooms with a panoramic view of the Cascade Mountains, or a spacious two-bedroom suite, all guests receive the same attention to detail and excellent service.

Your day begins with complimentary morning coffee, juice, muffins and the morning newspaper delivered to your door. For your recreational pleasure, the Inn has a seasonal heated swimming pool and whirlpool, a fitness room, tennis courts, a jogging path, bicycles for guests to enjoy and beautifully landscaped, spacious grounds for you and your pet to explore.

The influence of the theater and arts can be seen throughout the town. The area also offers horseback riding, river rafting on the Rogue or Klamath rivers and salmon, steelhead or trout fishing. Ashland also has many award-winning wineries and several nearby golf courses and parks for you to enjoy.

Greenwood Inn

10700 Southwest Allen Boulevard
Beaverton, Oregon 97005
800-289-1300 • (803) 643-7444

Room Rates:	$87 – $148, including continental breakfast.
Pet Charges or Deposits:	$10 per day. $100 refundable deposit.
Rated: 4 Paws	250 guest rooms and 26 suites, some with kitchens, decks, fireplaces and private whirlpools; 2 heated swimming pools, sauna, whirlpool, exercise room, restaurant and cocktail lounge.

F rom the lush landscaping to the inviting Northwest architecture — every detail welcomes you to the Greenwood Inn. Clearly, your comfort is their first consideration here, with custom furnishings, refrigerators, tasteful prints and original Northwest art. Oversized work stations, two-line phones and computer hook-up capabilities appeal to the professional.

Unexpected touches include guest shuttles to nearby business parks, shopping and local attractions, use of a local athletic club and the on-site exercise room, two outdoor pools and Jacuzzi.

Riverhouse Resort

3075 North Highway 97
Bend, Oregon 97701
800-547-3928 • (541) 389-3111

Room Rates:	$57 – $175. Packages available.
Pet Charges or Deposits:	None.
Rated: 4 Paws	220 guest rooms and suites, indoor and outdoor heated pools, spa, sauna, exercise room, jogging trails, golf course, restaurants, entertainment and dancing.

L ocated on the banks of the picturesque Deschutes River is the Riverhouse Resort, offering guests a wide selection of room accommodations that include kitchens, fireplaces and spa tubs.

Relax in the saunas and heated whirlpool, stay with shape with the exercise room and indoor pool or enjoy a scenic jog along the river. The Riverhouse even has a championship golf course, River's Edge, open year-round.

With three restaurants on the property and others nearby, you have a wide variety of dining choices. After dinner, enjoy some of the Northwest's finest entertainment in the popular Fireside Nightclub.

Sea Dreamer Inn

15167 McVay Lane
Brookings, Oregon 97415
800-408-4367 • (541) 469-6629

Room Rates:	$50 – $80, including full breakfast.
Pet Charges or Deposits:	$10 per stay. Call for deposit requirements. Manager's prior approval required.
Rated: 3 Paws 🐾🐾🐾	4 guest rooms, two with private baths, two with shared baths.

 uilt of redwood in 1912, this country Victorian commands a view of Southern Oregon's famous lily fields, gently sloping to the ocean. The oldest home of its kind in Curry County, the Sea Dreamer Inn is surrounded by spacious grounds amidst pine, fruit trees and flowers that bloom year-round.

Awaken to the smell of fresh coffee and baking breads. Breakfast is served in the Inn's formal dining room. You will enjoy magnificent sunsets and whalewatching from the front porch. There is a warm, cozy fire for those chilly nights and rainy winter days.

Hallmark Resort

1400 South Hemlock
Cannon Beach, Oregon 97100
888-448-4449 • 800-345-5676 • (503) 436-1566
Web Site: www.hallmarkinns.com

Room Rates:	$59 – $229. AAA, AARP, AKC and ABA discounts.
Pet Charges or Deposits:	$8 per day. Limit 2 pets.
Rated: 4 Paws 🐾🐾🐾🐾	132 rooms and suites, fireplaces, ocean views, fully equipped kitchens, spa units, recreation center with heated pool, wading pool, two swirl spas, dry sauna and exercise room.

O verlooking the famous Haystack Rock and the majestic Pacific Ocean, the Hallmark Resort commands dramatic views of the Northwest coastline. Located at the base of the coastal mountain range, Cannon Beach is blessed with a dramatic shoreline and moderate climate.

Guest accommodations range from cozy rooms for two to luxurious two-bedroom suites with fully equipped kitchens, designed for a family of six. Most rooms include a gas fireplace and spacious deck.

Relax or work out in the indoor recreation center, complete with heated pool, two whirlpool spas, dry sauna and exercise room. Things to see and do and experience are nearly endless in the Cannon Beach area. Take a leisurely stroll on seven miles of pristine beach and maybe even build a sand castle or two.

Coos Bay Manor

955 South 5th Street
Coos Bay, Oregon 97420
800-269-1224 • (541) 269-1224

Room Rates:	$65 – $100, including full breakfast. AARP discount.
Pet Charges or Deposits:	$10 per stay.
Rated: 3 Paws 🐾🐾🐾	5 rooms, 3 with private baths.

Built in 1912, the historic Colonial-style Coos Bay Manor offers guests their choice of five charming, individually decorated rooms. The house has a unique open-air balcony that surrounds the second floor, detailed woodworking throughout and large rooms with high ceilings.

The Victorian Room is full of lace, ruffles, romance and elegance, featuring a sitting area overlooking the rolling hills. An Old West theme and a queen-sized feather bed are enjoyed in the Cattle Baron's Room. The Country Room is old-fashioned, warm and inviting, just like Grandma's house, with a brass queen-sized bed and handmade quilts.

Each morning a full gourmet breakfast is served in the dining room.

Big K Guest Ranch

20029 Highway 138 West
Elkton, Oregon 97436
800-390-2445 • (541) 584-2295

Room Rates:	$195 – $250, including all meals.
Pet Charges or Deposits:	$10 per day. Manager's prior approval required.
Rated: 4 Paws 🐾🐾🐾🐾	20 private cabins, some suites with fireplaces and Jacuzzis, game room, exercise room, fly-casting pond, fishing excursions, skeet-shooting, horseshoes, scenic river float trips, bicycle rentals, picnic facilities, horseback riding and hiking trails.

 his working ranch is set on 2,500 remote, wooded acres along the 10-mile scenic Umpqua River. Guests may choose from 20 spacious country pine cabins with fireplaces and Jacuzzis. Home-style dining, in this unique country atmosphere, is included in the price of your room.

Professional guides are available to escort you along the Umpqua, to angle for salmon, steelhead, smallmouth bass and shad. Trail rides and hiking treks take you through meadows and forests of tall conifers and oaks to view deer, elk, turkey, osprey and eagles.

Valley River Inn

1000 Valley River Way
P.O. Box 10088
Eugene, Oregon 97401
800-543-8266 • (541) 687-0123

Room Rates:	$135 – $300; special family amenities.
Pet Charges or Deposits:	None. Complimentary pet packs.
Rated: 4 Paws	248 guest rooms and 9 suites, many with balconies; swimming pool, saunas, whirlpool, jogging path, bicycles, restaurant and lounge.

With so much to see and do, it's nice to come home to the casual elegance of the Valley River Inn's towering wooden beams, brick and copper fireplaces and spacious rooms and suites. Perched on the lush banks of the Willamette River, this Mobil Four-Star hotel offers all the amenities you would expect from any upscale resort.

Your pet will appreciate the complimentary "Pet Pack," which includes a toy, a bone and directions to local pet stores, parks and veterinary hospitals.

Sweetwaters Restaurant and Lounge serves Pacific Northwest cuisine, created from fresh seasonal ingredients and locally grown foods. Sunday brunch is a must.

Salishan Lodge

7760 North Highway 101
Gleneden Beach, Oregon 97388
800-452-2300 • (541) 764-2371
Web Site: www.dolce.com

Room Rates: $135 – $279. AAA and AARP discounts.
Pet Charges or Deposits: $15 per day.
Rated: 5 Paws 🐾 🐾 🐾 🐾 🐾 205 guest rooms and 3 luxury suites, many with fireplaces and
                         balconies with ocean or forest views, nature trails, putting
                         green and 18-hole golf course, tennis club, beach, heated
                         indoor pool, saunas, whirlpool, massage, wine cellar and
                         restaurant.

A n acclaimed and treasured hideaway of the Pacific Northwest, Salishan
is quietly woven into Mother Nature's spectacular surroundings. You
will immediately feel at one with Salishan — just steps from the mountains and sea, gently tucked into this secluded setting.

Guest rooms are native wood structures of pine and cedar, built in harmony
with the naturally landscaped surroundings, and decorated with original
Northwest art. Most rooms include a fireplace and private balcony overlooking
the forest, links or bay. Treat yourself to a fireside massage in the privacy of your
room.

Vegetables from area market gardeners, hook-and-line caught fish from local
day boats, and shellfish raised and harvested in nearby bays are prepared and
flavored in a tempting Pacific Northwest cuisine at Salishan Lodge.

Columbia Gorge Hotel

4000 Westcliff Drive
Hood River, Oregon 97031
800-345-1921 • (541) 386-5566

Room Rates: $150 – $365, including their "World-Famous Farm Breakfast."
Pet Charges or Deposits: $15 per day. "Pet Package" upon check-in.
Rated: 5 Paws 42 guest rooms, with river or garden views, fireplaces, award-
                               winning restaurant.

H igh atop a cliff overlooking the extraordinary Columbia River Gorge is the Columbia Gorge Hotel with its acres of manicured gardens. Built in 1921 by a Portland lumber baron, the hotel has maintained its legendary reputation for hospitality for more than 75 years.

This 11-acre oasis offers a wide selection of distinctive guest rooms. Each features antique furnishings and a view of either the gardens rimming Phelps Creek or the spectacular Columbia River Gorge. The most unique rooms have polished brass or canopy beds, and some of the larger suites have fireplaces. Each evening the turn-down service will leave a fresh rose and sweet chocolate as a final treat for the day.

Upon check-in, four-legged guests will receive a special "Pet Package" consisting of a doggy toy, a chew bone, doggy treats and a special dish with the hotel's logo, to make their stay more enjoyable.

Sunset Vacation Rentals

P.O. Box 505
Manzanita, Oregon 97130
800-883-7784 • (503) 368-7969
Web Site: www.doormat.com

Room Rates:	$99 – $250.
Pet Charges or Deposits:	$5 per day. $50 refundable deposit. Manager's prior approval required.
Rated: 4 Paws 🐾🐾🐾🐾	2- to 4-bedroom vacation homes, sleeping up to 12 guests, many oceanfront or with ocean views, with fully equipped kitchens, cable television and VCR, barbecue, telephone, linens, laundry facilities and supplies, cleaning service upon departure, 24-hour assistance and self check-in.

Most of the vacation homes available through Sunset Vacation Rentals have fully equipped kitchens, a barbecue for cookouts, all your linens, laundry facilities and supplies, as well as 24-hour assistance, self check-in and cleaning service upon departure.

When visiting nearby Rockaway, choose from Elbows, a two-story home with knotty-pine interior and spectacular ocean views, or Chuck's Sunset, an oceanfront cozy cabin that sleeps up to six guests, located along a freshwater creek.

For those heading to Twin Rocks, the Captain's Inn is a spacious, three-bedroom, two-bath home located 100 yards from the beach. Nedonna Beach is home to the Crow's Nest, a cozy beach house for up to six guests, only 80 yards from the beach, or D's Cottage, a cute and cozy cottage-style beach house with fabulous ocean views located
in Arch Cape.

Shilo Inn

2111 Biddle Road
Medford, Oregon 97504
800-222-2244 • (541) 770-5151
Web Site: www.shiloinns.com

Room Rates:	$49 – $69, including continental breakfast. AAA and AARP discounts.
Pet Charges or Deposits:	$7 per pet, per day.
Rated: 3 Paws 🐾🐾🐾	48 guest rooms, some with refrigerators and microwaves; laundry facilities, spa, sauna and steam room.

In Medford, home of the Rogue River National Forest, you will find the affordable Shilo Inn. Your comfortable accommodations will include amenities such as in-room coffeemakers, refrigerators, microwaves, wet bars and guest laundry facilities. Enjoy your complimentary continental breakfast of fresh fruit, muffins, pastries, hot tea and freshly brewed coffee before heading out for your day.

While in the area, be sure to visit the Rogue River National Forest, which offers acres of parkland to explore with your dog. Here you will find Mount Ashland, the highest point in Oregon's Cascade Range, and the headwaters of the Applegate River in the Siskiyou Mountains. This environment includes conifer forests, open woodlands, rocky ridgetops and many botanical specimens native to the Pacific Northwest.

Benson Hotel

300 Southwest Broadway
Portland, Oregon 97205
888-5-BENSON • (503) 228-2000

Room Rates: $190 – $800.
Pet Charges or Deposits: $50. Small pets only.
Rated: 5 Paws 🐾🐾🐾🐾🐾 286 guest rooms and 55 suites with fireplaces and whirlpools,
                           exercise room, health club, restaurant and cocktail lounge.

Currently listed on the National Register of Historic Places, The Benson Hotel has been a Portland landmark since 1912. From its location in the heart of the city's vibrant downtown, the hotel is convenient to everything Portland has to offer.

The Benson provides modern luxury in a classic setting. Whether you select a Grand Suite with a baby grand piano, fireplace and Jacuzzi, a penthouse with a panoramic view of the city, or a specially appointed elegant guest room, you will appreciate the comfort and ambiance.

No visit to The Benson Hotel is complete without dining at the landmark London Grill and Trader Vic's. The menus and decor of each restaurant have been updated, but the elegant fare, excellent service and superb culinary staff have remained the standard for quality for decades.

Fifth Avenue Suites Hotel

506 Southwest Washington
Portland, Oregon 97204
800-711-2971 • (503) 222-0001
Web Site: www.5thavenuesuites.com

Room Rates: $145 – $190.
Pet Charges or Deposits: None.
Rated: 5 Paws 🐾 🐾 🐾 🐾 🐾 221 deluxe guest rooms and suites, Aveda spa, restaurant.

 arved out of a 1912 building in downtown Portland that once housed a department store, this 10-story, 221-unit hotel is intimate in spite of its size. A wood- and mirror-trimmed, arcaded passageway gives views into the lobby with its soaring ceiling and tall white pillars.

With its cozy seating arrangements and lamps scattered throughout, the lobby feels like your grandmother's living room — assuming your grandmother had plenty of money and good taste. Complimentary wine-tasting every evening, and coffee, tea and juice in the morning, complete the home-like atmosphere.

All guest rooms are beautifully appointed, light and airy, with curtained sliding French door partitions. Color schemes feature soft apricot carpeting paired with saffron and cream tones. Upholstered pieces are overstuffed and the beds have padded headboards and thick brocade bedspreads.

Phoenix Inn

4370 Commercial Street
Salem, Oregon 97302
800-445-4498 • (503) 588-9220

Room Rates:	$65 – $105, including continental breakfast. AAA, AARP, AKC and ABA discounts.
Pet Charges or Deposits:	$10 per day.
Rated: 3 Paws	88 suites, indoor pool, Jacuzzi, fitness center, restaurant and lounge.

Conveniently located just south of downtown Salem, the Phoenix Inn offers guests spacious mini-suites complete with microwaves, refrigerators, wet bars, plush love seats and large worktables for those traveling on business.

The continental breakfast buffet is always complimentary at the Phoenix Inn. While reading your newspaper or watching the morning news, enjoy a selection of fruits, juices, coffee, cereals and pastries in the breakfast room.

Edgewater Cottages

3978 Southwest Pacific Coast Highway
Waldport, Oregon 97394
(541) 563-2240

Room Rates: $65 – $140.
Pet Charges or Deposits: $5 – $10 per pet, per day. Manager's prior approval required.
Rated: 4 Paws 9 oceanfront or oceanview cottages and housekeeping units with kitchens, fireplaces and sun decks.

O n the sandy shores of Alsea Bay, Edgewater Cottages offers guests a change of pace from the usual vacation accommodations. These ocean-front cottages and housekeeping units have fully equipped kitchens, cozy fireplaces and wonderful sun decks.

Cottages range from intimate oceanview studios for two, to the Beachcomber, the largest unit, which offers three bedrooms, a living room with a large fireplace and a game room.

Old Welches Inn Bed and Breakfast

26401 East Welches Road
Welches, Oregon 97067
(503) 622-3754

Room Rates:	$75 – $175, including full breakfast.
Pet Charges or Deposits:	Credit card deposit. Manager's prior approval required. Sorry, no cats.
Rated: 4 Paws 🐾🐾🐾🐾	4 nonsmoking guest rooms, one with private bath; a private two-bedroom cottage with a fireplace and fully equipped kitchen, all with mountain or river views.

L ocated along the Salmon River in the Welches Valley, the heart of the Mount Hood Recreational Area, is the Old Welches Inn Bed and Breakfast. Built in 1890, the Inn was the first hotel and summer resort established on Mount Hood.

Choose from four guest rooms, all named after various wildflowers found in Oregon. Accommodations feature sleigh beds with fluffy comforters, heirloom furniture and views of the Salmon River. For those who want more privacy, the Lilybank Cottage is located behind the Inn. This private, two-bedroom cottage, residing under a 500-year-old Douglas fir tree, has a fully equipped kitchen, a river-rock fireplace and a fenced yard for the dog.

Old Brook Inn

530 Old Brook Lane
Anacortes, Washington 98221
800-503-4768 • (360) 293-4768

Room Rates: $80 – $90, including continental breakfast.
Pet Charges or Deposits: None.
Rated: 4 Paws   2 guest rooms with private baths and beautiful views of the woods or the bay.

S heltered in a valley of woods and green meadows, only three miles outside Anacortes, this enchanting inn is nestled within an heirloom orchard planted in 1868. The Inn takes its name from the small brook that meanders alongside it and winds throughout the tranquil ten acres.

Both guest rooms have scenic views of either the surrounding woods and orchards, or beautiful Fidalgo Bay. In the morning awake to a complimentary continental breakfast of fruit, hot muffins or coffee cake served in the dining room overlooking the orchard.

For the vigilant bird watcher, you will see hawks, eagles, osprey, kingfishers and great blue herons. The sightseeing doesn't end there. The San Juan Islands, only a short ferry ride away, are known as a vacation paradise.

Island Country Inn

920 Hildebrand Lane Northwest
Bainbridge Island, Washington 98110
800-842-8429 • (206) 842-6861
Web Site: www.NWCountryInns.com/Island
E-mail: nwcinns@seanet.com

Room Rates: $71 – $149, including continental breakfast. AAA, AARP, AKC
                         and ABA discounts.
Pet Charges or Deposits: $10 – $20 per day. Credit card imprint required.
Rated: 3 Paws 🐾 🐾 🐾   40 guest rooms and 6 suites, kitchens, pool and Jacuzzi.

J ust 35 minutes by ferry from Seattle there's a quiet retreat — the Island Country Inn, the only hotel on Bainbridge Island. Guest rooms and suites feature queen- or king-sized beds, wet bars and kitchens. A complimentary continental breakfast is included in your room rate. Guests are encouraged to enjoy the heated outdoor pool in season, the spa and patio area.

Historic Bainbridge Island is one of Puget Sound's most beautiful — tall timber, quiet farms, lovely homes and gardens, bays and harbors filled with pleasure boats. There's golf here, parks and playgrounds, a winery, shopping, art galleries, restaurants and hiking and biking trails to enjoy.

Stewart Lodge

805 West First Street
Cle Elum, Washington 98922
(509) 674-4548

Room Rates: $45 – $60, including continental breakfast. AAA discount.
Pet Charges or Deposits: $5 per stay.
Rated: 3 Paws 🐾 🐾 🐾   36 guest rooms, some refrigerators, laundry facilities, heated
                             swimming pool, outdoor spa.

 ilming site of the hit television series "Northern Exposure," the town of Cle Elum is home to the Stewart Lodge.

This rustic-style inn features appealing guest rooms with a country decor, unique pine furnishings, quilted spreads and comfortable wingback chairs.

Home by the Sea Cottages

2388 East Sunlight Beach Road
Clinton, Washington 98236
(360) 321-2964

Room Rates:	$165 – $175, including breakfast basket.
Pet Charges or Deposits:	None.
Rated: 5 Paws 🐾🐾🐾🐾🐾	A cottage with wood-burning fireplace, living room, small kitchen and full bath. Plus a private suite in the beachfront main house with kitchen, dining and living rooms, wood-burning stove, private deck and Jacuzzi.

L ocated on beautiful Whidbey Island, only steps from the beach, you will find the Home by the Sea Cottages. Guests may choose from two types of accommodations.

The Cape Cod Cottage is a 1940's-style beach cottage located just steps from Useless Bay. The main floor has a cozy cedar living room with a large wood-burning fireplace and views of Deer Lagoon. Upstairs there are two bedrooms, each with full-sized beds and views of the pasture and farmlands. The small country kitchen is great for relaxing with your morning cup of coffee and your complimentary breakfast basket, filled with homemade specialties using local products when in season.

The Sandpiper Suite is located in the main house on the beach. It has its own private garden entrance and a private outdoor Jacuzzi and deck that are perfect for those relaxing weekend getaways. With both properties so close to the beach, you and your dog can enjoy long walks on the driftwood-strewn beach.

Victorian Bed and Breakfast

602 North Main Street
P.O. Box 761
Coupeville, Washington 98239
(360) 678-5305

Room Rates:	$85 – $100, including full breakfast.
Pet Charges or Deposits:	Manager's prior approval required. Credit card as deposit.
Rated: 4 Paws 🐾🐾🐾🐾	2 guest rooms with private baths and a secluded cottage with full kitchen and bath.

Plan to be pampered during your stay here. Enjoy a gourmet breakfast, relax in the courtyard and stroll historic Coupeville. Built in the late 1800s, the Victorian Bed and Breakfast is a charming Italianate Victorian home on Whidbey Island.

The Jenne and the Blue Goose Rooms, both with comfortable, queen-sized beds and private bathrooms, are located upstairs. For the ultimate in privacy, stay in the Cottage Hideaway, with a full kitchen and private bathroom. It has a queen-sized bed and a trundle bed, perfect for a child.

Weinhard Hotel

235 East Main Street
Dayton, Washington 99328
(509) 382-4032

Room Rates:	$65 – $125, including continental breakfast. AAA discount.
Pet Charges or Deposits:	None.
Rated: 4 Paws 🐾🐾🐾🐾	15 guest rooms, rooftop garden, lobby Espresso Café; non-smoking hotel.

s you enter through the brick archway of the Weinhard Hotel, with its antique coach lights and ornate, massive oak door, you are taken back in time to the late 19th century, when this beautiful old building was the town saloon and lodge hall. Now this elegant Victorian, nestled in the heart of historic Dayton, is a blending of modern comfort and elegance.

The unique guest rooms feature an exquisite collection of Victorian-American furniture with all the modern conveniences you expect to find in a fine hotel. Guests are invited to enjoy the gracious splendor of the Victorian roof garden with its potted flowers and comfortable, Adirondack-style chairs, while tasting a flavorful latté from the Weinhard Espresso Café.

Love's Victorian Bed and Breakfast

31317 North Cedar Road
Deer Park, Washington 99006
888-929-2999 • (509) 276-6939

Room Rates:	$75 – $98, including full breakfast.
Pet Charges or Deposits:	Call for deposit requirements.
Rated: 4 Paws	2 guest rooms with private baths.

Set on five wooded acres overlooking a pond, this gracious, gabled Victorian resides, complete with gingerbread trim and a wraparound porch. When you cross the threshold, you will be transformed back in time. Love's Victorian Bed and Breakfast is an ornate home that reflects the turn-of-the-century style.

The two guest rooms are the Turret Suite, with a gas fireplace, a sitting area, private bath and a balcony overlooking the pond, and Annie's Room, named after Leslie's grandmother, with period wallpaper, lace curtains and a private bath.

The main-floor hot tub beckons visitors to relax and enjoy a view of the moon and stars through the overhead transom window.

South Fork Moorage – Guest Houseboats

2187 Mann Road
Fir Island, Washington 98238
(360) 445-4803

Room Rates:	$80 – $115.
Pet Charges or Deposits:	Small pets only. Manager's prior approval required.
Rated: 4 Paws 🐾🐾🐾🐾	2 nonsmoking houseboats for up to 4 guests, each with a fully equipped galley, wood-burning stove, barbecue, front and back decks.

Floating in a quiet cove on the Skagit River are the South Fork Moorage – Guest Houseboats. Spend some time relaxing on the deck as the magic of the river and the gentle movements of a charming houseboat lull your worries away.

These unique, cozy houseboats are moored off the coast of Fir Island. Each houseboat has a fully equipped kitchen, separate sleeping areas, a cozy wood-burning stove and wonderful observation decks.

Drop your line off the deck and try your hand at catching dinner, or venture out onto the river for canoeing, boating or swimming. There are spectacular fields on the island, which offer a blaze of color from tulips in the spring.

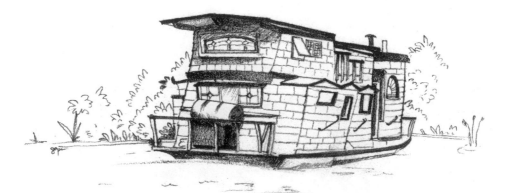

Kalaloch Lodge

157151 Highway 101
Forks, Washington 98331
(360) 962-2271

Room Rates:	$99 – $200.
Pet Charges or Deposits:	$10 per day. One night's room rate as deposit.
Rated: 4 Paws	58 guest rooms and 2 suites, some with ocean views, fireplaces, kitchens.

Perched on a bluff overlooking the Pacific Ocean sits one of the most memorable resorts in Olympic National Park. It's Kalaloch Lodge, and it has the charming characteristics of an oceanside fishing village.

Here you'll discover cozy oceanfront log cabins with Franklin fireplaces, and charming guest rooms that suit any vacationer's lifestyle.

There are plenty of activities to keep you busy, with hiking, fishing, clamming, beachcombing and exploring the endless tidepools. Since the lodge is located within a national park, leash laws do apply.

Tucker House Bed and Breakfast with Cottages

260 B Street
Friday Harbor, Washington 98250
800-965-0123 • (360) 378-2783

Room Rates:	$75 – $210, including full breakfast.
Pet Charges or Deposits:	$15 per day. $15 nonrefundable deposit. Manager's prior approval required. Small dogs only. Sorry, no cats.
Rated: 4 Paws 🐾 🐾 🐾 🐾	2 bed-and-breakfast rooms with shared bath, wraparound porch and lovely gardens, plus 3 private cottages with full baths, kitchenettes, wood-burning stoves, electric heaters and sun decks; outdoor hot tub for all guests.

B uilt in 1898, the Tucker House Bed and Breakfast with Cottages is a charming Victorian home has been turned into a bed and breakfast. Upstairs are two bedrooms decorated in antiques, with queen-sized beds and a shared bath.

Three private cottages offer queen-sized beds, kitchenettes, wood-burning stoves and large sun decks. Each morning a full breakfast is served for all guests in the solarium of the main house. Their signature dish is their famous home-made cinnamon bread.

The State Ferry Landing and the waterfront are only two blocks from the Tucker House Bed and Breakfast with Cottages.

West Winds Harmony Cottage

685 Spring Street, No. 107
Friday Harbor, Washington 98250
(360) 378-5283
Web Site: www.karuna.com/westwinds

Room Rates:	$150 – $225.
Pet Charges or Deposits:	None.
Rated: 4 Paws 🐾 🐾 🐾 🐾	Private one-bedroom, one-bath, two-story cottage for up to four, with extra queen-sized bed downstairs in living room, full kitchen, wood-burning stove, covered decks, views of the mountains and water.

F our wooded acres with views of the Strait of Juan de Fuca, summer residence for hundreds of orca whales, is the setting for West Winds Harmony Cottage. This private one-bedroom, two-story cottage sleeps up to four with the extra queen-sized bed downstairs in the living room.

Harmony Cottage has a fireplace and a fully equipped kitchen. French doors open onto the covered deck surrounding the entire house — wonderful for outside dining.

The Orca Whale Watch Park is a mile down the coastline — a lovely morning walk with a chance to see eagles perched in trees, ready to swoop down for their salmon breakfast. This enchanting cottage offers complete tranquillity for mind and spirit. The sunsets over the water are extraordinary.

Wharfside Bed and Breakfast Aboard the "Jacquelyn"

Slip K-13, Port of Friday Harbor
Mailing address:
P.O. Box 1212
Friday Harbor, Washington 98250
(360) 378-5661

Room Rates: $90 – $95, including full breakfast.
Pet Charges or Deposits: $10 per day.
Rated: 4 Paws 🐾🐾🐾🐾 2 guest staterooms, sky-lit main salon with wood-burning fireplace.

 summer island adventure or a romantic winter retreat is yours aboard the "Jacquelyn," docked in Port of Friday Harbor. This 60-foot, ketch-rigged motorsailer is fully seaworthy, but remains docked as a year-round floating bed-and-breakfast inn.

On board are two spacious, private staterooms with elegant hardwoods, double and queen-sized beds with down comforters, dual-control mattress warmers, electric heaters and private full baths. There is a special area near the dock for your dog to get its daily exercise.

The sky-lit main salon is furnished with antiques and art, warmed by a wood-burning fireplace. Each morning a sumptuous array of breakfast specialties are freshly prepared in the galley.

Alta Crystal Resort

68317 State Route 410 East
Greenwater, Washington 98022
800-277-6475 • (360) 663-2500

Room Rates: $89 – $179.
Pet Charges or Deposits: $15 per day. Manager's prior approval required.
Rated: 5 Paws 🐾🐾🐾🐾🐾 25 chalets and cabins on 22 acres, with fully equipped kitchens, wood stoves or fireplaces, outdoor hot tub, swimming pool and recreation area.

Located near the entrance to Mount Rainier National Park and the Crystal Mountain ski area, Alta Crystal Resort is the perfect choice for a group retreat, family vacation or ski trip.

The spacious log cabins and chalets offer wood-burning stoves or fireplaces and fully equipped kitchens, complete with all the modern appliances.

With a creek, a pond, hiking trails and 22 acres of woods and open fields, you and your dog will have plenty of room to explore. Resident dogs Beta Max and Fortuna, the co-managers of the property, will show your dog all their favorite places.

Country Inn

107 South Second Street
La Conner, Washington 98257
(360) 466-3101

Room Rates:	$93 – $117, including continental breakfast.
Pet Charges or Deposits:	$25, plus credit card as deposit.
Rated: 4 Paws 🐾🐾🐾🐾	28 guest rooms.

T ucked away on the Swinomish Channel, in the farming and fishing community of Skagit Valley, is the home of the Country Inn. This cozy inn welcomes you with comfortable rooms, each with a fireplace and all the modern amenities you would expect to find in a luxury inn. Your complimentary breakfast is served each morning in the library.

The history and charm of La Conner is evident, from the Victorian houses with their widow's walks, to the unique shops and restaurants and the artists' center with authentic Indian crafts. Be sure to take in all the town's landmarks, such as the picturesque Rainbow Bridge.

Cinnamon Rabbit Bed and Breakfast

1304 Seventh Avenue West
Olympia, Washington 98502
(360) 357-5520

Room Rates:	$55 – $80, including full breakfast.
Pet Charges or Deposits:	Small pets only. Manager's prior approval required.
Rated: 3 Paws	2 guest rooms, hot tub, spacious grounds with organic garden, walking distance to beach.

Built in 1935, on the southern end of Puget Sound, this Dutch Colonial-style home offers guests their choice of two cozy bedrooms. The lovely grounds are edged in flowers and include an organic vegetable garden.

In the morning you are treated to a breakfast featuring delicious homemade waffles with fresh blueberries and raspberries. Low-fat or vegetarian meals can be prepared — just ask your hosts and they will gladly oblige.

For those who are feeling adventurous, the beach is within walking distance, as is Capitol Lake Park. The area also offers canoeing, white-water rafting, golf, swimming, tennis, mountain biking and hiking. Located within driving distance are historic sights, several antique shops, the aquarium, nature areas, vineyards and Olympic National Forest, where you and your dog can explore more than 632,000 acres of parkland.

Puget View Guesthouse

7924 61st Avenue Northeast
Olympia, Washington 98516
(360) 413-9474

Room Rates:	$89, including deluxe continental breakfast.
Pet Charges or Deposits:	$10 per day. Manager's prior approval required.
Rated: 4 Paws	A private two-room guest cottage, deluxe continental breakfast served at your door, deck with barbecue, ocean and mountain views.

P uget View Guesthouse is a secluded cottage on the shore of Puget Sound. Since 1984, guests have come to appreciate its peaceful beauty and comfortable hospitality. Tall firs, Olympic Mountains and island views surround you in this 1930s log house.

The cottage interior is complete with queen-sized bed, private bath, sitting room with sofa sleeper, dining area, refrigerator and microwave. A "continental plus" breakfast is served at your door. Outside, enjoy your deck and barbecue, lounge in the hammock or walk the beach.

Log Cabin Resort

3183 East Beach Road
Port Angeles, Washington 98363
(360) 928-3325

Room Rates:	$48 – $119.
Pet Charges or Deposits:	$6 per day.
Rated: 3 Paws 🐾 🐾 🐾	28 lakeside lodge rooms and rustic cabins, restaurant and general store.

Y ou'll be secluded among giant old-growth firs and cedars, with nearby trails to spectacular waterfalls, snow-capped mountains and the deep blue water of Lake Crescent. To the south, Mount Storm King rises above the lake. This popular vacation and recreation paradise displays the variety for which Olympic National Park is so famous.

The resort offers a variety of accommodations: lakeside chalets, comfortable lodge rooms and rustic cabins, as well as full hookup RV sites.

Whatever you like to do — hiking, boating, water sports, or just a lakeside picnic — you'll find it here, in a picturesque environment. Or try your luck fishing for the elusive Beardslee trout, the ultimate trophy.

Inn at Ludlow Bay

One Heron Road
Port Ludlow, Washington 98365
(360) 437-0411

Room Rates:	$138 – $450, including continental breakfast.
Pet Charges or Deposits:	$50 refundable deposit. Manager's prior approval required.
Rated: 4 Paws	34 spacious rooms and 3 suites, ocean views, fireplaces, oversized Jacuzzi tubs, boat moorage at marina, waterfront dining and fireside bar.

L ocated on a finger of the Olympic Peninsula on the Hood Canal is the Inn at Ludlow Bay. Here guests are surrounded by spectacular views of the waterfront and the picturesque Olympic and Cascade Mountains.

Guest rooms offer scenic views, fireplaces, oversized Jacuzzi tubs, plush terrycloth bathrobes and comfortable beds with down-filled comforters. For those arriving at the Inn by boat, priority boat moorage can be arranged at Port Ludlow Marina.

The sandy shores surrounding the inn are perfect for beachcombing, fishing, boating or kayaking in the Hood Canal. The scenic array of state parks is perfect for day excursions, hiking, mountain biking and sightseeing.

Palace Hotel

1004 Water Street
Port Townsend, Washington 98368
800-962-0741 • (360) 385-0773
Web Site: www.olympus.net/palace
E-mail: palace@olympus.net

Room Rates:	$59 – $139, including continental breakfast. AAA, AARP, AKC and ABA discounts.
Pet Charges or Deposits:	$20 per stay.
Rated: 4 Paws	13 guest rooms and 3 suites, fireplaces, Jacuzzi or clawfoot tubs, efficiencies and kitchens, laundry facilities, restaurant.

T he historic town of Port Townsend is home to the charming 1889 Victorian-style Palace Hotel. Each spacious guest room in this beautifully restored hotel is uniquely decorated in a Victorian theme and furnished in period antiques.

Many of the rooms have views of Port Townsend Bay or historic downtown and offer Jacuzzi or old-fashioned clawfoot tubs and cozy fireplaces. Guests are treated to a continental breakfast of fresh pastries and fruit delivered to their room each morning.

Swan Hotel and Conference Center

Monroe and Water Streets
Port Townsend, Washington 98368
800-776-1718 • (360) 385-1718
Web Site: www.waypt.com/bishop
E-mail: swan@wapt.com

Room Rates:	$79 – $129, including continental breakfast. AAA, AARP, AKC and ABA discounts.
Pet Charges or Deposits:	$10 per pet, per day.
Rated: 4 Paws 🐾🐾🐾🐾	2 penthouses, 4 suites and 4 studio cottages, kitchenettes.

T he Swan Hotel, located in the historic district, offers visitors downtown convenience in newly redecorated condominium-style suites and cottages.

The one-bedroom suites feature queen-sized beds, full baths with tubs, living rooms with cable TV and queen-sized sofas that convert into beds. Each suite offers a kitchenette with a dining table and chairs, distinctively furnished with fine marine art and antiques. Decks offer views of the Straits of Juan De Fuca and Admiralty Inlet.

The penthouses occupy the top two floors of the main building, with decks offering unparalleled views of the Cascade and Olympic mountains.

Adjacent to the main building are four "historic" cottages, newly remodeled with hardwood floors, new built-in queen-sized beds, full bathrooms and kitchenettes.

Lake Quinault Lodge

345 South Shore Road
P.O. Box 7
Quinault, Washington 98575
800-562-6672 (Oregon & Washington only) • (360) 288-2900

Room Rates:	$65 – $140. AAA, AARP and seasonal discounts.
Pet Charges or Deposits:	$10 per pet, per day.
Rated: 4 Paws	92 guest rooms with fireplaces, lake or mountain views, restaurant and cocktail lounge.

N estled in the heart of Olympic National Forest lies a sanctuary with a sweeping view of a pristine lake, known as Lake Quinault Lodge. Built in 1926, the lodge is set on Lake Quinault, with the Olympic Mountains in the background.

Tastefully appointed guest rooms offer a restful retreat for those visiting the Northwest. The heated indoor pool and dry sauna are a great diversion after a day of hiking, canoeing, sea cycling or any of the other outdoor activities at the lodge.

The Roosevelt Dining Room, with its Native American art decor, features a savory selection of regional cuisine.

Alexis Hotel

1007 First Avenue
Seattle, Washington 98104
800-426-7033 • (206) 624-4433

Room Rates: $210 – $550, including evening wine-tasting.
Pet Charges or Deposits: None.
Rated: 5 Paws 🐾 🐾 🐾 🐾 🐾 66 guest rooms and 43 suites, kitchens, 2 tennis courts, exercise and spa facilities, steam room, whirlpool, 24-hour room service, restaurant and cocktail lounge.

 ocated in downtown Seattle, the Alexis Hotel, has elegantly welcomed guests from around the world since 1901. Its graceful refinement and warm hospitality make it a premier hotel.

The guest rooms are warm and rich, with an eclectic mix of tradition highlighted by a scattering of antiques. Some of the elegant, spacious suites feature wood-burning fireplaces, jetted tubs and graciously appointed sitting and dining rooms, perfect for the discriminating traveler.

At the Alexis you can expect the red-carpet treatment for both you and your pet. This "pet friendly" hotel has always welcomed pets, but they go out of their way to assure that "all" of their guests have an enjoyable stay. In their opinion, bringing your pet makes the hotel feel more like home. So when you call for room service, be sure to add a doggy bone for Fido or a saucer of warm milk for Fluffy to your order.

Four Seasons Olympic Hotel

411 University Street
Seattle, Washington 98101
(206) 621-1700

Room Rates: $295 – $365.
Pet Charges or Deposits: None.
Rated: 5 Paws 🐾 🐾 🐾 🐾 🐾 450 guest rooms and suites, fully equipped health club with
                           pool, whirlpool, sauna and massage, three restaurants.

L ovingly restored to its 1924 Italian Renaissance glory, the Four Seasons Olympic Hotel reflects the splendor of another age. Here you will enjoy the comfort and elegance of the city's most spacious accommodations, all conveniently close to the key cultural, business and retail centers.

Each year the hotel wins top national and international honors from the lodging industry for its superb service and state-of-the-art restaurants. The Four Seasons Olympic Hotel also offers some of the city's best shopping, featuring more than a dozen exclusive salons and luxury retail shops. The hotel is within minutes of the Fifth Avenue Theater, Seattle Art Museum, Pike Place Market and the waterfront.

Guests of the hotel can maintain their exercise regimens in the on-site health club, which includes a lap pool and cardiovascular equipment.

Residence Inn by Marriott – Fairview Avenue North

800 Fairview Avenue North
Seattle, Washington 98109
(206) 624-6000

Room Rates:	$110 — $290, including continental breakfast. AAA and AARP discounts.
Pet Charges or Deposits:	$10 per pet, per day. Call for deposit requirements.
Rated: 4 Paws 🐾🐾🐾🐾	234 studio, one- and two-bedroom suites, with fully equipped kitchens, some balconies with river views, indoor lap pool, spa, steam room, sauna and exercise facilities.

A long the banks of Lake Union, the Residence Inn by Marriott offers visitors to the Seattle area the comfort and conveniences of home. Residence Inn is designed with a residential look and feel, from the inside out.

Choose from a studio or a one- or two-bedroom suite with fully equipped kitchen, a spacious, elegantly appointed living area and views of the lake.

Each morning a buffet-style breakfast awaits you by the waterfall in the seven-story garden atrium lobby.

Salish Lodge and Spa

6501 Railroad Avenue Southeast
P.O. Box 1109
Snoqualmie, Washington 98065
800-826-6124 • (206) 888-2556
Web Site: www.salish.com

Room Rates: $169 – $269. AAA discount.
Pet Charges or Deposits: $50 per stay. Manager's prior approval required.
Rated: 5 Paws 🐾 🐾 🐾 🐾 🐾 90 guest rooms and 4 suites, complete spa facilities, rooftop
                         hot tub, heated therapy pools and restaurant.

S et in the middle of the Snoqualmie Valley, the Salish Lodge and Spa blends naturally into its surroundings. This harmonious fusion of the rustic and the sophisticated assures guests absolute comfort. You'll enjoy Four Diamond luxury enhanced by the spectacular sights and sounds of Snoqualmie Falls.

Every well-appointed guest room has a wood-burning fireplace, an oversized whirlpool tub, custom designed furniture, pillowed window seats and fluffy goose-down comforters. Spend a day in the tranquil spa, featuring massage, aromatherapy and skin and body renewal treatments. The rooftop hot tub is perfect for gazing at the stars and feeling as if there is no one else in the world.

The only thing that could possibly compare with the picturesque scenery surrounding the lodge is the fabulous cuisine. From breakfast to dinner, the culinary brilliance is evident.

Cavanaugh's River Inn

700 North Division Street
Spokane, Washington 99202
800-THE-INNS • (509) 326-5577
Web Site: www.cavanaughs.com

Room Rates:	$75 – $225. AAA and AARP discounts.
Pet Charges or Deposits:	None.
Rated: 3 Paws 🐾🐾🐾	245 guest rooms and 4 guest suites, pools, Jacuzzi, tennis courts and volleyball.

C avanaugh's River Inn is a full-service resort-style hotel located in a beautifully landscaped setting along the north bank of the Spokane River.

Superb hospitality and restful lodging at affordable prices are offered in tastefully appointed guest rooms and suites. Deluxe rooms feature king-sized beds, poolside access and river views.

Cavanaugh's offers two outdoor pools, one covered for year-round use, a children's wading pool, tennis and volleyball courts, a horseshoe pit and a children's playground. Enjoy a run along the two-mile loop path through Riverfront Park, then relax in the saunas and whirlpool. Access is convenient to the Centennial Trail across the river.

Royal Coachman Inn

5805 Pacific Highway East
Tacoma/Fife, Washington 98424
800-422-3051 • (253) 922-2500

Room Rates:	$65 – $125. AAA, AARP, AKC and ABA discounts.
Pet Charges or Deposits:	$25 refundable deposit.
Rated: 3 Paws	88 guest rooms and 6 suites, Jacuzzi and kitchenettes, laundry facilities, health club privileges, restaurant and cocktail lounge.

T he stone-covered exterior of the Royal Coachman Inn, with its medieval turrets, is located 20 minutes south of SeaTac Airport with easy access to Interstate 5.

Choose from a comfortable, spacious guest room or a suite offering all the comforts and conveniences of home. The Inn features a private library room with a cozy fireplace for meetings or large gatherings.

Health club privileges are available for guests of the Inn so you won't miss your daily workout while on vacation, and there is a whirlpool on the property.

Llama Ranch Bed and Breakfast

1980 Highway 141
Trout Lake, Washington 98650
(509) 395-2786

Room Rates:	$79 – $99, including full breakfast.
Pet Charges or Deposits:	Free boarding for your pet llama.
Rated: 3 Paws	5 guest rooms, laundry facilities.

I n a peaceful valley on a 97-acre ranch is the Llama Ranch Bed and Breakfast. Guests may choose from five private guest rooms with picturesque views of the ranch or the mountains.

One guest room has a king-sized bed and a queen-sized hide-a-bed, plus a private kitchen. Four other guest rooms, with queen-sized beds, which a common kitchen, living room, dining room and laundry facilities, making these accommodations the perfect choice for a private retreat for a small group or families with children. There are plenty of open spaces and wooded areas, allowing you and your dog to enjoy the great outdoors.

Guests of the ranch are treated to walks, hikes or even a picnic with the llamas. You will soon learn that besides their beauty and dignity, llamas' calm nature affects the people around them, producing a relaxing, serene atmosphere.

Alderbrook Resort

East 7101 Highway 106
Union, Washington 98592
800-622-9370 • (360) 898-2200

Room Rates:	$69 – $179. AAA and AARP discounts.
Pet Charges or Deposits:	$8 per day. $25 deposit.
Rated: 4 Paws 🐾🐾🐾🐾	18 housekeeping cottages, fully equipped kitchenettes, fireplaces and courtyards. Plus 80 guest rooms and 2 suites with private lanais and courtyards. Beachfront, heated indoor swimming pool, Jacuzzi, 4 tennis courts, marina and boat dock, playground, 18-hole golf course, restaurant and lounge.

A visit to Alderbrook Resort puts you in the midst of more than 525 wooded acres on the shores of beautiful Hood Canal, a fjord-like inlet of Puget Sound. Framed by the towering, snowcapped Olympic Mountains, Alderbrook Resort offers you unlimited recreation and fine accommodations.

No matter what your favorite recreation is, chances are you will find it here. You can play tennis, relax in the heated indoor pool and Jacuzzi, bicycle or hike through the miles of forest and trails, rent a pedal boat and tour the local area, or a power boat and water-ski the entire canal.

Guests have their choice of two-bedroom housekeeping cottages with fully equipped kitchenettes, brick fireplaces and private courtyards, or guest rooms and suites with private lanais.

Swallow's Nest Guest Cottages

6030 Southwest 248th Street
Vashon Island, Washington 98070
800-ANY-NEST • (206) 463-2646

Room Rates:	$75 – $170.
Pet Charges or Deposits:	$5 per pet, per day. Call for deposit requirements. Manager's prior approval required.
Rated: 4 Paws 🐾🐾🐾🐾	5 private cottages with full kitchens, golf privileges, hot tub.

L ocated only a short ferry ride from Seattle, Tacoma, or the Olympic Peninsula, the Swallow's Nest Guest Cottages offer you a sojourn to a peaceful, country retreat at affordable rates.

Five charming cottages in three separate locations sit atop a bluff, looking out at Puget Sound, Mount Rainier and the Cascades. Large picture windows overlook orchards, pastures and the woods. The cottages are comfortably furnished with plants, televisions, cooking facilities, books, magazines and a supply of tea, cocoa and fresh coffee.

The community of Vashon offers kayaking, boating, fishing and swimming. The island has many good restaurants, antique shops, art galleries and parks to enjoy. Bicyclists will enjoy the miles of paved roads and outstanding views, which also provide a great way for you and your dog to explore the island.

Alpen Haus Hotel Resort

Junction of Highways 89 and 26
P.O. Box 3258
Alpine, Wyoming 83128
800-343-6755 • (307) 654-7545
Web Site: www.cyberhighway.net/~alpenhau/
E-mail: alpenhau@cyberhighway.net

Room Rates:	$45 – $99, including continental breakfast. AAA and AARP discounts.
Pet Charges or Deposits:	$5 per day.
Rated: 3 Paws 🐾 🐾 🐾	45 guest rooms and 2 suites with refrigerators and lounges.

T he Alpen Haus Hotel Resort, designed in the Alpine style, is enhanced with decorative paintings by famed artist Gerhard Lipp of Austria. His paintings not only adorn the outside of the buildings, but he has done extensive painting in the bar, shops and guest rooms.

Nestled in Star Valley at the base of the Targhee Mountain Range, the area offers some of the best float trips, horseback rides and fishing in the summer, and cross-country skiing and snowmobiling in the winter. Downhill skiing is 36 miles away at Jackson Hole.

A. Drummond's Ranch Bed and Breakfast

399 Happy Jack Road
Cheyenne, Wyoming 82007
(307) 634-6042
Web Site: www.cruising-america.com/drummond.html
E-mail: adrummond@juno.com

Room Rates:	$65 – $150, including full breakfast.
Pet Charges or Deposits:	$10 per day for dogs and cats. Horses welcome. $15 boarding fee.
Rated: 5 Paws 🐾🐾🐾🐾🐾	4 guest rooms and 1 suite on 120 acres. Refrigerators, microwaves, fireplaces, hot tubs, spas. Indoor riding arena.

T his award-winning, quiet, gracious retreat is more than just a place to spend the night. Guests are given the opportunity to explore the area with innkeepers Kent and Taydie Drummond as their guides for hiking, mountain biking, cross-country skiing, four-wheeling, or even taking a llama to lunch. For those less adventurous, soaking in a private hot tub under the stars gives a visit to Cheyenne a new dimension.

Nestled on the south side of a hill, looking south to the Colorado Rockies, this setting creates a calming effect on all who stay. The Carriage House loft offers a private deck, hot tub, gas fireplace, steam sauna/shower and stocked pantry closet-kitchen. Complimentary homemade snacks, fresh fruit and beverages are always available. Breakfasts are tailored to the guest of the day and served on fine china with silver and crystal.

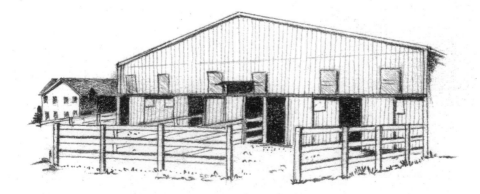

Porch Swing Bed and Breakfast

712 East 20th Street
Cheyenne, Wyoming 82001
(307) 778-7182

Room Rates:	$43 – $66, including full breakfast.
Pet Charges or Deposits:	Manager's prior approval required.
Rated: 3 Paws 🐾🐾🐾	3 guest rooms.

t the Porch Swing, long ago is not far away. This charming 1907 two-story cottage is filled with antiques. Relax on the back-porch swing and listen to water splash into the garden pond or crank up the old Victrola and listen to music of bygone days.

Breakfast is by the fire, with tempting specials of yeast waffles with pure maple syrup and fresh strawberries, spicy cheese grits, orange pecan French toast or German pancakes with Swiss honey, to name a few.

Summer gardens are colorful and fragrant here, with a variety of perennials, culinary and aromatic herbs, wildflowers and annuals. The Porch Swing is within easy walking distance of downtown shopping, museums and restaurants.

Hunter Peak Ranch

Painter Route
P.O. Box 1731
Cody, Wyoming 82414
(307) 587-3711

Room Rates:	$80 – $110. Call for weekly rates.
Pet Charges or Deposits:	$5 per day or $25 per week. Refundable deposit required. Manager's prior approval required.
Rated: 3 Paws 🐾🐾🐾	4 guest cabins.

L ocated on the Upper Clark's Fork River at an elevation of 6,700 feet, the Hunter Peak Ranch lies adjacent to the North Absaroka and Beartooth Wilderness areas. This is some of the most magnificent country you will ever see.

The ranch was homesteaded in 1909 and started taking guests in 1912. The original structure is built out of hand-hewn logs, with a beautiful river rock fireplace, and now houses the lodge room and dining room of this family-owned business. The modern housekeeping cabins and suites feature fully equipped kitchens and comfortable furnishings.

Ranch activities include pack trips, horseback riding, fishing, hiking, swimming, ice skating and snowmobiling.

MacKenzie Highland Ranch

3945 U.S. Highway 26
Dubois, Wyoming 82513
(307) 455-3415
E-mail: Dmackenz@wyoming.com

Room Rates:	$80 – $180.
Pet Charges or Deposits:	Refundable deposit depends on pet. Horses welcome.
Rated: 3 Paws	3 guest cabins and 2 houses.

MacKenzie Highland Ranch is located inside the Shoshone National Forest and near the southern entrance to Yellowstone National Park, as well as the northern entrance to Grand Teton National Park. This small, family-run guest ranch specializes in independent living. The prices are reasonable and the location is ideal. They will rent you a cabin or a house and help you pursue your own agenda.

The Wind River runs through the ranch, offering excellent trout fishing, and, at an altitude of 8,000 feet, breathtaking views of the mountains. You can rent horses by the day or week or bring your own horses for exploring the scenic trails. Activities abound here with white-water rafting on the Snake River and snowmobiling in winter.

Pinnacle Buttes Lodge and Campground

3577 U.S. Highway 26 West
Dubois, Wyoming 82513
800-934-3569 • (307) 455-2506

Room Rates:　　　　　　　　70 – $160. AAA discount.
Pet Charges or Deposits:　Sorry, no cats. $50 refundable deposit.
Rated: 3 Paws 🐾 🐾 🐾　　　10 guest rooms and 3 cabins with pool and Jacuzzi.

T he owners of the Pinnacle Buttes Lodge and Campground offer you a friendly family atmosphere at affordable rates, with 10 guest rooms and 3 cabins with kitchens.

Outdoors there is a hot tub and a swimming pool for guest use, a convenience store for snacks and groceries and a little café serving home-cooked breakfasts, lunches and dinners. The menu ranges from hamburgers to chicken Alfredo, with delicious homemade pastries as their specialty.

Trips to Yellowstone are a pleasant drive from the Pinnacles, and Jackson Hole is a 11/2-hour drive over Togwotee Pass, with some of the most beautiful scenery you will see. Float or white-water trips down the Snake River, horseback rides, pack trips and Jeep rides or 4-wheeling are enjoyed on this peaceful side of the mountain.

Snow King Resort

400 East Snow King Avenue
P.O. Box SKI
Jackson, Wyoming 83001
800-522 KING • (307) 733-5200
Web Site: www.snowking.com

Room Rates: $90 – $190, including complimentary airport shuttle.
Pet Charges or Deposits: $50 per stay. $50 refundable deposit.
Rated: 4 Paws 🐾🐾🐾🐾   204 guest rooms, suites and condominiums. Whirlpool, sauna,
                              exercise room and pool. Restaurant. Ski packages available.

 he largest year-round facility in Jackson Hole, Snow King Resort is a full-service ski-in/ski-out hotel, offering a selection of rooms, suites and condominiums tailored to your needs. Enjoy complete convenience, comfort and privacy in a fully furnished one- to four-bedroom condominium, including kitchen facilities.

Out your front door you will enjoy skiing, hiking and horseback riding, the Alpine Slide, miniature golf and the Snow King Center, with its indoor ice rink. The outdoor pool is heated for year-round swimming. Two large whirlpools are relaxing places to lounge after a day of mountain activities.

Window on the Winds Bed and Breakfast

10151 Highway 191
P.O. Box 996
Pinedale, Wyoming 82941
888-367-2395 • (307) 367-2600
E-mail: lmclain@wyoming.com

Room Rates:	$60 – $95, including full breakfast.
Pet Charges or Deposits:	None.
Rated: 3 Paws	4 guest rooms, hot tub.

L ocated at the base of the Wind River Mountains, home of the Bridger Teton National Forest and a major route to the Grand Teton and Yellowstone National Parks, you will find this rustic retreat with a bit of luxury.

When you enter the grand room you will be awed by the breathtaking views and sunset off the balcony. Guests enjoy a hot tub in the sun room, set among roses, redbud trees, flowers and culinary herbs.

The second floor is reserved for guests and features the grand room, four bedrooms and two baths, shared suite-style. The comfortable bedrooms have lodgepole pine queen-sized beds with down comforters and pillows. Each morning awaken to a healthy full breakfast featuring a dish or two from the oven, fresh fruit, homemade Swiss-style Muesli and yogurt, along with pitchers of juice, hot coffee and tea.

Piney Creek Inn Bed and Breakfast

11 Skylark Lane
P.O. Box 456
Story, Wyoming 82842
(307) 683-2911
Web Site: www.pineycreekinn.com
E-mail: si@wilderwest.com

Room Rates:	$50 – $150, including full breakfast and afternoon snacks.
Pet Charges or Deposits:	Manager's prior approval required. Sorry, no cats.
Rated: 3 Paws 🐾🐾🐾	3 guest rooms and 2 cabins, with fireplace and Jacuzzi tub.

Nestled in the beautiful Big Horn Mountains of northern Wyoming, this comfortable, secluded log home provides a peaceful, relaxing atmosphere. Sit on the deck and enjoy the tranquillity of the forest or venture out and experience the colorful surroundings. For the Old West buff, historic sites are only minutes away.

Guest rooms are rustic and restful, with vaulted ceilings and sliding glass doors that lead out onto the deck. A hot tub on the back patio offers relaxation among the pine trees and sparkling skies. Don't be surprised if deer walk by as you enjoy a hearty breakfast, which can include freshly baked pastries, muffins and homemade jam.

Calumet and Arizona Guest House

608 Powell Street
Bisbee, Arizona 85603
(520) 432-4815

Room Rates:	$60 – $70, including full breakfast.
Pet Charges or Deposits:	None.
Rated: 3 Paws 🐾🐾🐾	6 guest rooms.

T his Spanish Mission-style guest house offers spacious guest rooms, lofty crowned ceilings from which unusual chandeliers are suspended, oak and maple flooring, fireplaces, leaded, beveled glass windows and antique furnishings.

Included in your room rate is a gourmet, all-you-care-to-eat breakfast featuring fresh fruits, pancakes, bacon, eggs, hash browns, homemade breads and more.

Cedar Hill Bed and Breakfast

175 East Cedar Street
Globe, Arizona 85501
(520) 425-7530

Room Rates: $40 – $50, including full breakfast. AARP discount.
Pet Charges or Deposits: None.
Rated: 3 Paws 🐾 🐾 🐾   2 guest rooms.

T his historic bed and breakfast is an extension of an old-fashioned concept of hospitality — sharing one's house with new acquaintances. The warmth of this home and friendly welcome are what Cedar Hill Bed and Breakfast is all about.

The property is well landscaped, with fruit trees and flower beds. Guest rooms are comfortably furnished and situated off the front porch, with large windows. Guests may enjoy both a front porch with a porch swing or the back patio with shade trees, which is fenced for pets. A full breakfast is served each morning.

White Mountain Lodge

140 Main Street
Greer, Arizona 85927
888-493-7568 • (520) 735-7568

Room Rates: $65 – $150, including full breakfast.
Pet Charges or Deposits: $20 per stay. Manager's prior approval required.
Rated: 3 Paws 🐾 🐾 🐾   7 cabins.

reer has become a year-round vacation recreation center in the heart of the White Mountains, at the headwaters of the Little Colorado River. Nestled in a remote mountain valley at the 8,525 foot level, the White Mountain Lodge offers hospitality in true Southwest fashion. The Lodge, the oldest building still standing in Greer, was built in 1892 as a family home.

In bed and breakfast tradition, each bedroom is individualized, with an emphasis on country accents. The main rooms of the house provide a comfortable atmosphere that invites guests to lounge and appreciate their time at this mountain retreat.

An exceptional, complimentary full breakfast of fresh fruit and juices, homemade coffee cakes, rolls and breads is paired with a delicious main course each morning.

Arizona Golf Resort

425 South Power Road
Mesa, Arizona 85206
800-528-8282 • (602) 832-3202

Room Rates:	$79 – $350. AAA and AARP discounts.
Pet Charges or Deposits:	None.
Rated: 3 Paws 🐾 🐾 🐾	89 guest rooms and 98 suites on 150-acre resort. Tennis, bicycles, basketball, swimming, spas and fitness center.

 his resort is unique and tucked away from the busy city, in the heart of many activities. Western towns, horseback riding, river-rafting and the breath-taking Superstition Mountains nearby provide an Old West adventure.

A championship golf course resides on this 150-acre oasis, surrounded by tropical palms and flowers. The guest rooms and suites are masterfully decorated, many with private patios and balconies overlooking the green fairways.

Sky Ranch Lodge

P.O. Box 2579
Sedona, Arizona 86339
888-708-6400 • (520) 282-6400

Room Rates:	$75 – $165.
Pet Charges or Deposits:	$10 per day.
Rated: 4 Paws 🐾🐾🐾🐾	94 guest rooms and cottages, some with fireplaces, kitchenettes and decks; swimming pool, Jacuzzi and garden.

L ocated on top of Table Mountain in the heart of Sedona's Red Rock panorama, Sky Ranch Lodge offers country hospitality in a setting of secluded comfort. Featuring six acres of landscaped ponds, creek and garden, Sky Ranch offers views up to 75 miles in all directions, with sunrises and sunsets filling the sky.

The Lodge offers a variety of accommodations, featuring decks, kitchenettes, beamed and vaulted ceilings and pool and Jacuzzi in a splendid garden setting.

J Bar J Ranch Bed and Breakfast

P.O. Box 524
Wickenburg, Arizona 85358
800-537-2173 • (520) 684-9142
E-mail: jbarj@primenet.com

Room Rates: $65 – $85, including full breakfast.
Pet Charges or Deposits: One night's refundable deposit. Manager's prior approval
                           required. Horses welcome.
Rated: 3 Paws   5 guest rooms.

This hacienda, built in 1994, was designed as a guest/horse ranch offering 5 rooms, all with private baths and entries.

Guest rooms are furnished with queen-sized beds and decorated in Southwestern motif. A Great Room with fireplace, wet bar, refrigerator, microwave, TV and reading area is available for guests to enjoy. A large patio area offers panoramic views of the desert and mountains.

Awake each morning to breakfast that is included in your room rate. Bring your own horses, or the innkeepers can arrange for you to enjoy one of their registered Arabian or quarter horses.

Little Nell

675 East Durant Avenue
Aspen, Colorado 81611
888-843-6355 • (970) 920-4600

Room Rates: $250 – $4,800. AARP discount.
Pet Charges or Deposits: None.
Rated: 5 Paws 🐾🐾🐾🐾🐾 92 guest rooms, including 15 suites. AAA Five-Diamond and
                         Mobil Five-Star award-winner; pool, whirlpool, Jacuzzi, hot
                         tubs, spa.

T he Little Nell is Aspen's premier hotel, located at the base of Aspen Mountain and just steps away from the famous shopping district. The Little Nell blends the virtues of an intimate country inn with the personalized service and amenities of a grand hotel.

No two rooms are alike, but all are equipped with gas-burning fireplaces, down-filled sofas and lounge chairs, built-in bar/refrigerator units, VCR's and oversized beds with down comforters. The rooms also feature Belgian wool carpets, marble bathrooms and breathtaking views of the town or mountain.

The Little Nell Restaurant, established nationally for its superb American Alpine cuisine, offers breakfast, lunch and dinner daily.

Loews Giorgio Hotel

4150 East Mississippi Avenue
Denver, Colorado 80222
800-345-9172 • (303) 782-9300

Room Rates: $199 – $1,000. AAA and AARP discounts.
Pet Charges or Deposits: None.
Rated: 5 Paws 🐾🐾🐾🐾🐾 183 guest rooms and 17 suites. 24-hour room service, health
                        club, restaurant.

 Rising above Denver's Mountain Tower Complex in the city's bustling southeast corridor, Loews Giorgio is a 4-star, 4-Diamond hotel that promises travelers extraordinary hospitality.

From the moment you step into the lobby, classic Italian beauty surrounds you, accented with original art, rare antiques and quarried marble. Guest rooms are tastefully decorated with minibars, three telephones, robes and coffeemakers.

The Tuscany Lounge offers complimentary coffee, steaming espresso and cappuccino. Fresh dolci are available all day and into the evening. At midday, an enticing menu offers a light luncheon. Cocktails and a grand selection of Italian liqueurs are served until late.

Annabelle's Bed and Breakfast

276 Snowberry Way
Dillon, Colorado 80436
(970) 468-8667

Room Rates:	$55 – $95, including full breakfast and treats for your pet. AAA discount.
Pet Charges or Deposits:	None.
Rated: 3 Paws 🐾 🐾 🐾	3 guest rooms and 1 suite. Dog-sitting available on request.

L ocated in a quiet residential area with property backing onto Keystone land, Annabelle's is an ideal retreat if you want to enjoy Summit County outdoor adventure. Hiking, biking and ski trails are right out the back door, with Keystone Ski Resort only 10 minutes away. The resorts of Copper Mountain, Breckenridge, Arapahoe Basin and Loveland are a 20-minute drive, and Vail is 30 minutes away. Catering to the needs of families, Annabelle's can provide roll-away beds for children, a crib, baby "stuff," and baby-sitting services. Each room is furnished with TV, VCR and telephone.

Breakfast fare is delicious here, with choices of Belgian waffles piled high with strawberries, cheese blintzes, homemade muffins or breads, espresso or cappuccino. Picnic lunches are also available.

Casa Milagro Bed and Breakfast

13628 County Road 3
Parshall, Colorado 80468
888-632-8955 • (970) 725-3640

Room Rates:	$105 – $200, including full breakfast and afternoon snacks.
Pet Charges or Deposits:	$10 per horse or llama. Horses and llamas welcome. Sorry, no cats or dogs.
Rated: 3 Paws 🐾 🐾 🐾	2 guest rooms and 1 suite with hot tubs and fireplaces.

T his comfortable hideaway log home in the pine trees above the Williams Fork River offers all the convenience and comfort of home. The guest rooms and common areas are pleasantly decorated with Southwestern arts and crafts, down comforters and fluffy pillows.

You will awaken each morning to a gourmet Southwestern breakfast of baked chili rellenos with homemade tortillas, Dutch apple-peach pancakes with real maple syrup or whipped cream, and homemade cinnamon rolls or biscuits. Afternoon treats include warm homemade bread or cookies just out of the oven.

Enjoy premier cold-water fishing on the Colorado River, just a few miles north, or hiking or mountain biking around Lake Evelyn. In the winter there is snowshoeing, cross-country skiing and snowmobiling near the house. Six major ski areas are only 45 minutes away for downhill skiing and snowbiking — then retreat to the peace and quiet of Casa Milagro.

Antlers at Vail

680 West Lionshead Place
Vail, Colorado 81657
800-843-8245 • (970) 476-2471

Room Rates: $90 – $785.
Pet Charges or Deposits: $10 – $15 per pet, per day.
Rated: 5 Paws 🐾🐾🐾🐾🐾 68 studio, one-, two- and three-bedroom condominiums with
                          fully equipped kitchens, fireplaces, maid service, laundry and
                          dry-cleaning service, outdoor swimming pool, sun deck and
                          Jacuzzi.

Set along the banks of Gore Creek, only steps from the center of Lionshead, Antlers at Vail offers exceptional lodging at a great value. Choose a condominium ranging from a studio to a three-bedroom, complete with fully equipped kitchens, cozy gas fireplaces, comfortable living rooms with sofa sleepers and private balconies.

No matter what time of year you visit, there are plenty of activities to keep you entertained. Antlers is less than 100 yards from the gondola base and ski school of Vail Mountain. The splendor of summer, with mild temperatures and fresh mountain air, offers the opportunity to enjoy the outdoor swimming pool and sun deck, or to soak in the Jacuzzi. Whitewater rafting, horseback riding, golf, tennis, fishing, mountain biking and hot-air ballooning are also available to fill your days.

Vintage Hotel

100 Winter Park Drive
Winter Park, Colorado 80482
800-472-7017 • (970) 726-8801
E-mail: skimj@frontier.net

Room Rates:	$80 – $525. AAA and AARP discounts.
Pet Charges or Deposits:	Credit card refundable deposit.
Rated: 3 Paws 🐾🐾🐾	118 guest rooms with refrigerators, microwaves, pool, sauna and hot tubs. On-site ski shop.

 he Vintage Hotel has been host to thousands of Winter Park vacationers since opening in 1986. The finely appointed guest rooms offer spectacular views of the majestic Rocky Mountains with their lush, pine-covered mountainsides.

From traditional hotel rooms to studios featuring kitchenettes and fireplaces and spacious one- and two-bedroom suites, a wide range of accommodations are available to suit your specific lodging needs.

Open all year, the outdoor heated pool and hot tubs are a welcome treat after a day on the mountain. Guests at Vintage Hotel can enjoy the warm coziness of a classic alpine retreat here.

Genoa House Inn

P.O. Box 141
Genoa, Nevada 89411
(702) 782-7075

Room Rates:	$105 – $150, including full breakfast and complimentary wine. Call for discounts.
Pet Charges or Deposits:	Credit card refundable deposit. Manager's prior approval required. Sorry, no cats. Doggie biscuits delivered with master's coffee tray in the morning.
Rated: 3 Paws	3 guest rooms.

A. C. Pratt, a newspaper publisher, built this Victorian home in 1872 for his family. Today the house is listed on the National Register of Historic Places and has been fully restored to reflect the charm and tranquillity of an earlier time. Snuggled against the Sierra foothills, Genoa is a vision of the Old West, with panoramic views of lush Carson Valley and the surrounding mountains.

Refreshments are served when you arrive. Early in the morning, coffee is delivered to your door, followed by a full breakfast, served either in your room or in the sunlit dining room.

Genoa's local activities include ballooning, bicycling and touring the Victorian homes and antique buildings with their various businesses, from Nevada's oldest saloon to nearby Walley's Hot Springs.

Horseshu Hotel

Horseshu Hotel
1385 Highway 93
P.O. Box 508
Jackpot, Nevada 89825
800-432-0051 ▪ (775) 755-7777
Web Site: www.ameristars.com

Room Rates:	$27–$97. AAA discount.
Pet Charges or Deposits:	None.
Rated: 3 Paws 🐾🐾🐾	110 guest rooms and 10 Jacuzzi suites, seasonal pool and year-round Jacuzzi, gambling, restaurant.

L ocated along U.S. Highway 93 on the Idaho border, within sight of the rugged Gollaher and Middlestack mountains, the Horseshu has evolved from a small roadside stop into a showcase of traditional Western hospitality. Here you will find exciting casino action, good food and quality accommodations at old-fashioned prices.

In keeping with the Western theme, casino patrons can sit back and enjoy decor reminiscent of a saloon in Dodge City. The hotel features 110 spacious rooms and 10 Jacuzzi suites, with a country inn decor that complements the rustic Frontier Kitchen and its famous country cooking.

Stonehouse Country Inn

P.O. Box 77
Paradise Valley, Nevada 89426
(702) 578-3530
Web Site: www.sprynet.com/sprynet/stonehouse
E-mail: stonehouse@sprynet.com

Room Rates:	$50 – $85, including full breakfast.
Pet Charges or Deposits:	Manager's prior approval required. Horses welcome.
Rated: 3 Paws	6 guest rooms.

Paradise Valley is a historic and scenic setting, surrounded by the Santa Rosa Mountains, working cattle ranches and the town of Paradise Valley. Here you will find the Stonehouse Country Inn, a lovely, three-story country home surrounded by majestic cottonwood trees.

Spacious guest rooms feature views from every window overlooking the scenic beauty of wildlife, meadows and ranch life. You will awaken to a mouth-watering, home-cooked breakfast.

Horses are welcome and kept in a safe shelter with fencing, at no additional charge.

The Ranchette

2329 Lakeview Road
Albuquerque, New Mexico 87105
800-374-3230 • (505) 877-5140
Web Site: www.viva.com/nm/ranchette

Room Rates:	$55 – $85, including full breakfast.
Pet Charges or Deposits:	$100 refundable deposit. Manager's prior approval required. Horses welcome.
Rated: 3 Paws 🐾🐾🐾	3 guest rooms.

it outside under the arbor in the hot tub, on the chaise lounge or in the swing, and you will appreciate the unobstructed, panoramic views of the Sandia and Manzano mountains from this unique bed and breakfast inn.

The Ranchette offers lovely indoor and outdoor living areas, a cozy fireplace and a grand piano in the formal dining room, with space to play games. There are walking paths adjacent to the property and indoor/outdoor facilities for horses traveling with their owners.

All guest rooms are furnished with terrycloth robes, writing desks, easy chairs, original art and antiques. A gourmet vegetarian breakfast is prepared each morning.

Alexander's Inn Bed and Breakfast

529 East Palace Avenue
Santa Fe, New Mexico 87501
888-321-5123 • (505) 986-1431

Room Rates:	$75 – $160, including continental breakfast.
Pet Charges or Deposits:	None.
Rated: 4 Paws 🐾🐾🐾🐾	5 guest rooms and 4 spacious suites, some with private baths, living rooms and fireplaces; landscaped yard with hot tub. Mountain bikes and guest privileges at a nearby health club.

 or a romantic stay in Santa Fe, nestle into this delightful bed and breakfast in the town's historic residential east side. Quiet and peaceful, yet just a short walk from the famous central plaza and the multitude of galleries on Canyon Road, this 1903 Craftsman-style home has been lovingly decorated.

Hand stenciling, dried flowers and family antiques create a warm, relaxing and nurturing atmosphere. The country cottage feel is enhanced by dormer windows and carefully restored architectural details. Sunlight streams through stained glass windows or lace curtains onto gleaming hardwood floors. Fresh flowers grace every room throughout the house.

A scrumptious breakfast of homemade muffins and granola, whole-grain breads, yogurt and fresh fruits is enjoyed in the cozy kitchen, warmed by a roaring wood stove, or on the verandah overlooking the garden.

Inn of the Turquoise Bear

342 East Buena Vista Street
Santa Fe, New Mexico 87501
800-396-4104 • (505) 983-0798
Web Site: www.turquoisebear.com
E-mail: bluebear@roadrunner.com

Room Rates: $90 – $250, including continental breakfast.
Pet Charges or Deposits: $20 per day. Manager's prior approval required.
Rated: 4 Paws   10 guest rooms and 1 guest suite.

T his rambling adobe house, constructed in Spanish-Pueblo Revival style from a core of rooms that date to the mid-1800s, is considered one of Santa Fe's most important historical buildings. With its signature portico, tall pine trees, magnificent rock terraces and gardens filled with lilacs and wild roses, the Inn offers guests a retreat close to the center of Santa Fe.

An acre of terraced gardens, with old stone benches, meandering flagstone paths and soaring ponderosa pines, is enclosed by adobe walls and coyote fences. Guest rooms with Kiva fireplaces and Viga ceilings are reached through private entrances and romantic courtyards. Fluffy robes, fresh flowers and fruits are enjoyed in each of the Southwestern-style guest rooms at Inn of the Turquoise Bear. The public rooms invite quiet conversation, reading, relaxing and listening to soft music. Complimentary off-street parking is available.

Inn on the Alameda

303 East Alameda Street
Santa Fe, New Mexico 87501
800-289-2121 • (505) 984-2121

Room Rates:	$144 – $334, including continental breakfast. AAA and AARP discounts.
Pet Charges or Deposits:	None.
Rated: 4 Paws	58 guest rooms and 9 guest suites; fitness facility andwhirlpool spas.

S ituated on tree-lined Alameda Street across from Santa Fe's River Park, the Inn's location is perfect for quiet morning walks or jogs. Inside its adobe walls, the Inn offers a secluded setting with private, flower-filled courtyards.

Each of the guest rooms and suites is designed with an emphasis on detail, comfort and Southwestern style. Many rooms include balconies, patios, Kiva fireplaces, handmade furniture and local artwork.

Each morning, enjoy a lavish continental breakfast, featuring seasonal fresh fruits and juices, delectable freshly baked pastries, muffins, bagels, breads and granolas. Then revitalize with a workout in the fitness facility, followed by a soak in one of the two open-air whirlpool spas.

Zuni Mountain Lodge

40 Perch Drive
Thoreau, New Mexico 87323
(505) 862-7616

Room Rates:	$45 – $65, including full breakfast and dinner. AAA, AARP, AKC and ABA discounts.
Pet Charges or Deposits:	None.
Rated: 3 Paws	6 guest rooms and 4 guest suites. State and national parks and forests are within walking distance. Spacious fenced yards with 4 large enclosed verandahs.

J ust up the mountainside from Bluewater Lake is the Zuni Mountain Lodge. With 10 guest rooms, the Lodge provides all the comforts of modern living amidst the rugged beauty of the mountains, with spectacular lake and mountain scenery.

Comfortably furnished public areas provide places for quiet meditation and relaxation, or a place to view the very latest on cable or video in the spacious lounge. An intimate dining room seats 24 people, while the kitchen prepares the most delicious meals in two counties. Landscaped lawns and gardens surround an outdoor gazebo.

Boulder Mountain Lodge

P.O. Box 1397
Boulder, Utah 84716
800-556-3446 • (435) 335-7460

Room Rates:	$69 – $134.
Pet Charges or Deposits:	$9 per day.
Rated: 4 Paws 🐾🐾🐾🐾	18 guest rooms and 2 suites, with refrigerators and microwaves.

 Boulder Mountain Lodge is an oasis of calm, comfort and discreet luxury in the middle of Utah's widest, most remote sandstone canyon country. The tiny town of Boulder, Utah, was the last community in America to receive its mail by mule train. Boulder today still feels remote and undiscovered. Above the Lodge, Boulder Mountain and the Aquarius Plateau rise like an alpine island of lakes, aspens and evergreens over a sea of sandstone canyons.

This intimate complex of detached buildings is grouped around an 11-acre lake, the Lodge's own bird sanctuary. The architecture is Western eclectic at its best: reddish stucco, rose sandstone blocks, massive timbers, dramatically pitched, rusted metal roofs. The rooms and suites are furnished with understated elegance, traditional quilts and craftsman-quality wooden furniture, against a restful backdrop of white plaster and exposed beams.

Jackson Fork Inn

7345 East 900 South
Huntsville, Utah 84317
800-255-0672 • (801) 745-0051

Room Rates: $60 – $120, including continental breakfast.
Pet Charges or Deposits: $20 per stay. Manager's prior approval required.
Rated: 4 Paws 🐾 🐾 🐾 🐾   8 guest rooms. Restaurant.

L ocated in scenic Ogden Valley Recreation Area, minutes from Nordic Valley, Powder Mountain ski resorts and Pineview Reservoir is the Jackson Fork Inn. This charming inn was once a rustic dairy barn, but has now been transformed into a lovely inn and dinner house. The name of the inn came from the old hayfork used to unload hay in the loft area of the barn, once considered to be the most modern dairy barn in the area, complete with indoor plumbing. The original fork proudly hangs outside the barn today.

Each of the guest rooms is uniquely decorated, and five rooms have Jacuzzi tubs for two. Mornings at the Inn bring a wonderful, self-serve continental breakfast. The dinner house is open for dinner and Sunday brunch. The dinner menu ranges from such delights as fettuccine or filet mignon, to mahi mahi and lobster.

Canyon Ranch Motel

668 Zion Park Boulevard
Springdale, Utah 84767
(801) 772-3357

Room Rates:	$58 – $72.
Pet Charges or Deposits:	Manager's prior approval required.
Rated: 3 Paws 🐾🐾🐾	22 guest rooms. Pool and Jacuzzi.

T he Canyon Ranch Motel is not a motel in the normal sense of the word. It is not an impersonal, noisy building enclosed by parking lots. It is various small buildings consisting of 4 units, 2 units and individual cottages, which surround a large, central, shady lawn area. You will find the Canyon Ranch's park-like setting very peaceful and charming.

Guest rooms are available in several configurations. One bed or two, with or without a kitchen. All are either new or newly remodeled cottages, with the necessary comforts of home.

Apart from Zion National Park, which is right at your doorstep, you are a short drive from Bryce National Park, Grand Canyon National Park — North Rim, Cedar Breaks National Monument and Lake Powell.

Fillenwarth Beach

87 Lakeshore Drive
P.O. Box 536
Arnolds Park, Iowa 51331
(712) 332-5646
Web Site: www.fillenwarthbeach.com

Room Rates:	$42 – $444, including cocktail cruises.
Pet Charges or Deposits:	None.
Rated: 3 Paws	41 guest rooms, 52 suites and cottages. Free cocktail cruises, sailing, tennis, indoor and outdoor pool and playground.

F illenwarth Beach is more than just a place to stay. Many activities are offered only to guests, and at no charge. Enjoy waterskiing, sail in a 28-foot racing sailboat, take out a canoe or paddleboat or sit back and delight in a scenic lake cruise on one of the 49-foot yachts.

Accommodations vary considerably at Fillenwarth Beach. Choose from individual cottages, duplexes, studios and apartments. Each unit has air conditioning, heating, a kitchen with microwave, a patio area and color cable TV with VCR and free tapes. All linens are provided except beach towels. Daily maid service is included.

A very short drive around the Iowa Great Lakes will take you to seven golf courses, summer stock theaters, antique shops, the Lakes Art Center, galleries, museums, a state park and fitness trails, including the paved 14.5-mile multipurpose trail from Spirit Lake to Milford. Shopping, dining and dancing are plentiful.

Brass Lantern

2446 Highway 92
Greenfield, Iowa 50849
888-743-2031 • (515) 743-2031
Web Site: www.brasslantern.com
E-mail: schaefer@brasslantern.com

Room Rates:	$95 – $195, including full breakfast.
Pet Charges or Deposits:	Manager's prior approval required. No pets allowed indoors. Fenced area provided. Sorry, no cats.
Rated: 3 Paws 🐾 🐾 🐾	2 guest suites with indoor pool and kitchenette.

T he Brass Lantern, the only bed and breakfast in Iowa with an indoor pool, features 40-foot heated pool available year-round.

Guest rooms open onto the pool terrace and include access to a fully equipped kitchenette. Both suites are spacious and well-appointed, with brass or four-poster beds and comfortable furnishings. A full breakfast is included in your room rate.

Varner's Caboose Bed and Breakfast

204 East Second Street
Montpelier, Iowa 52759
(319) 381-3652

Room Rates: $60, including full breakfast.
Pet Charges or Deposits: $20 refundable deposit. Manager's prior approval required.
Rated: 4 Paws   1 caboose.

C ome stay in a real Rock Island Lines caboose, set on its own track, at the original home of the Montpelier Depot.

The caboose is a self-contained unit, with bath, shower and complete kitchen. It comfortably sleeps four, with a queen-sized bed and two singles in the cupola. The accommodations are comfortable and convenient, with central air conditioning and heat, color TV and plenty of off-street parking. A fully prepared country breakfast is left in the caboose kitchen for guests to enjoy at their leisure.

Located close to the Mississippi River, it is just 2 blocks from Clarks Ferry Campground for picnic areas, a children's playground and a boat launch. The village of Buffalo, 5 miles upriver, has a good sand beach, and Wild Cat Den State Park, 3 miles away, offers great hiking and area roads that are good for biking.

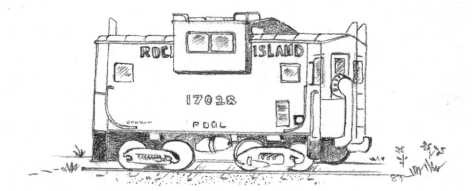

Thayer's Historic Bed 'n' Breakfast

60 West Elm Street
P.O. Box 246
Annandale, Minnesota 55302
800-944-8595 • (320) 374-8222

Room Rates:	$33 – $135, some rates including full breakfast. AAA, AARP, AKC and ABA discounts.
Pet Charges or Deposits:	$20 per stay.
Rated: 3 Paws 🐾🐾🐾	11 guest rooms with whirlpools, Jacuzzis and hot tubs.

 usic pours out of a jukebox and patrons of the well-stocked Depot Lounge enjoy board games and lively conversation. Others relax in the stately dining room, and overnight guests enjoy four-poster beds in perfectly restored rooms.

Though you will find modern amenities like a sauna, hot tubs and other touches of pleasure, the feeling here seems only seconds away from the parlors at the turn of the century. There is laughter, banter and song billowing out of Thayer's on any given night.

Timber Bay Lodge and Houseboats

8347 Timber Bay Road
P.O. Box 248
Babbitt, Minnesota 55706
800-846-6821 • (218) 827-3682
Web Site: www.timberbay.com
E-mail: timber@uslink.net

Cabin Rates:	$100 – $185.
Houseboat Rates:	$450 – $900 per weekend.
Pet Charges or Deposits:	$7 per day. Call for refundable deposit.
Rated: 3 Paws 🐾 🐾 🐾	12 private cabins.

I f you enjoy camping, boating and fishing, you'll love Timber Bay Lodge and Houseboats. Explore 20-mile-long Birch Lake with its many miles of forested shoreline and rocky islands. Take your small boat to the base of the foaming rapids of the Stony River or paddle a canoe up the Kawishiwi River. At night anchor in a secluded bay and sleep with the sounds of wind in the pines and the gentle motion of your floating home.

The houseboats range in size from 30 feet to 44 feet, accommodating 2 to 10 people. The boats are completely modern with hot and cold running water, propane gas stove, oven and refrigerator, pollution-free toilet and shower. Furnishings include pillows, blankets, cooking utensils, deck furniture, a charcoal grill and even the ice chest.

The deluxe log-sided, knotty-pine cabins feature wood-burning fireplaces, color TVs, showers and decks. The interiors are comfortably furnished and contain full housekeeping facilities, including stoves, refrigerators, microwaves, linens, grills and deck furniture.

Manor on the Creek Country Inn Bed and Breakfast

2215 East Second Street
Duluth, Minnesota 55812
800-428-3189 • (218) 728-3189
Web Site: www.visitduluth.com/Manor

Room Rates: $119 – $199, including full breakfast.
Pet Charges or Deposits: $10 per stay. Manager's prior approval required. Sorry, no cats.
Rated: 5 Paws 🐾 🐾 🐾 🐾 🐾 3 guest rooms and 5 suites.

E xperience the grand style that lumber baron Charles A. Duncan enjoyed in 1907. Here you have all the charm and personality of a Bed and Breakfast with the extra privacy, space and amenities of a country inn. This distinctive 15,000 square-foot, Neo classical/Arts and Crafts style mansion and carriage house are built on 2 private acres.

Once inside, you are surrounded by warm woods of burled African mahogany and quarter-sawn white oak, with ornate oval arched ceilings. Guest rooms feature king- and queen-sized beds, lovely antique furnishings, fireplaces, balconies and a screened porch overlooking acres of scenic, wooded Oregon Creek.

Manor on the Creek is located in the east end of town, minutes from downtown, Lakewalk and Canal Park.

Voyageur Lakewalk Inn

333 East Superior Street
Duluth, Minnesota 55802
800-258-3911 • (218) 722-3911
E-mail: voyageur@visitduluth.com

Room Rates: $35 – $149, including continental breakfast.
Pet Charges or Deposits: None.
Rated: 3 Paws   40 guest rooms and 1 guest suite.

I n the heart of the historic art district, the Voyageur Lakewalk Inn offers clean, comfortable lakefront rooms. You'll be within walking distance of some of the most interesting entertainment, shopping and dining experiences Duluth has to offer — Canal Park, Fond-du-Luth Casino, Fitger's Brewery Complex and countless restaurants, museums, art galleries and antique shops.

The new lodge rooms have whirlpools which invoke the feeling of the "great north woods" with roughhewn log furniture, pine walls, fireplaces and wonderful views of Lake Superior. The penthouse suite offers floor-to-ceiling windows overlooking Lake Superior, leather furnishings, fireplace, deck and a full kitchen.

Glencoe Castle Bed and Breakfast

831 13th Street East
Glencoe, Minnesota 55336
800-517-3334 • (320) 864-3043

Room Rates:	$85 – $175, including full breakfast. Military and senior discounts.
Pet Charges or Deposits:	None.
Rated: 3 Paws 🐾🐾🐾	2 guest rooms, 1 suite.

This 5,000-square-foot Queen Anne/Gothic Victorian "Castle" boasts quite a history. The three-story, turn-of-the-century home contains elaborately designed wood floors and carved woodwork, a formal visitor's parlor and chaperone's bench, and numerous stained and leaded glass windows. The fireplace in the parlor is an architectural showpiece, with a stained glass window where the chimney should be, while the dining room contains a mural painted on all four walls.

Guest rooms are furnished in early '90s decor and share a bath. The master suite has a brass and marble California king-sized, soft-sided waterbed, a fireplace and a large private bath with Jacuzzi tub and separate shower.

Clearwater Lodge

774 Clearwater Road
Grand Marais, Minnesota 55604
800-527-0554 • (218) 388-2254
Web Site: www.canoe-bwca.com
E-mail: clearwater@canoe-bwca.com

Room Rates:	$68 – $140, including full breakfast.
Pet Charges or Deposits:	$10 per day or $60 per stay. Call for refundable deposit.
	Manager's prior approval required.
Rated: 3 Paws 🐾 🐾 🐾	6 cabins, 2 suites and 3 rooms.

C learwater Lodge, the only resort on Clearwater Lake, was built in 1926 by pioneer Charlie Boostrom, and is the largest original whole-log structure in northeastern Minnesota. On the National Register of Historic Places, it has retained the look and feel of earlier times. The lounge area has a large fireplace surrounded by one of the finest collections of diamond willow furniture along the trail. The Lodge has a wide, verandah-like porch, where guests can enjoy the majestic views.

As the name suggests, Clearwater is an exceptionally clear lake that is home to lake trout, smallmouth bass, loons, otters, turtles, eagles, osprey and other abundant wildlife.

Nestled at lake's edge are six log cabins, each with a unique personality. The cabins sleep from two to ten people and normally rent by the week, except during May, early June and September.

Gunflint Pines Resort

217 South Gunflint Lake Road
Grand Marais, Minnesota 55604
800-533-5814 • (218) 388-4454
Web Site: www.gunflintpines.com
E-mail: play@gunflintpines.com

Room Rates:	$90 – $130. Call for weekly rates.
Pet Charges or Deposits:	$8 per day in summer; $10 per day in winter.
Rated: 3 Paws	6 cabins.

Nestled in the pine-crested high country of northern Minnesota and at the doorstep of a federal wilderness area is Gunflint Pines Resort. The resort has both modern, A-frame housekeeping cabins and complete campground facilities.

Each cabin is fully carpeted, with your choice of three or four bedrooms, 1 1/2 baths and a fully equipped kitchen. A fireplace and large picture window overlooking Gunflint Lake complete the vacation atmosphere.

Gunflint Lake and connecting waterways offer the fisherman abundant opportunity to catch walleyes, lake trout, smallmouth bass and northerns. Try a leisurely canoe paddle to Little Rock Falls and have a picnic. Photography and wildlife watching can also be rewarding here. Or just sit back and revel in nature's beauty at its finest.

Country Inn by Carlson

2601 South Highway 169
Grand Rapids, Minnesota 55744
800-456-4000 • (218) 327-4960

Room Rates:	$60 – $74, including continental breakfast. AAA and AARP discounts.
Pet Charges or Deposits:	None.
Rated: 3 Paws 🐾 🐾 🐾	46 rooms. Indoor heated pool and whirlpool.

 ere you will find cozy rooms, a complimentary breakfast and great rates. You'll feel the country charm throughout, in the fireplace, hardwood floors and personal touches of home.

Country Inn by Carlson offers small-town hospitality while offering area attractions such as the Judy Garland House, Forest History Center, golf and cross-country skiing.

Mountain Inn

P.O. Box 58
Lutsen, Minnesota 55612
800-686-4669 • (218) 663-7244

Room Rates:	$49 – $119, including continental breakfast.
Pet Charges or Deposits:	$15 per stay.
Rated: 3 Paws 🐾🐾🐾	30 guest rooms and 1 suite. Refrigerators, microwaves, whirlpool, Jacuzzi and sauna.

n Lutsen Mountain, removed from the bustle of shoreline traffic, guests of the Mountain Inn will find beautifully appointed guest rooms or mini-suites with microwaves, refrigerators and bar sink combinations. All rooms include continental breakfast.

The hardest part of staying at the Mountain Inn is deciding what to do first. The Mountain Inn is situated in the heart of the Lutsen area and provides easy access to the finest in outdoor recreation.

Solbakken Resort

4874 West Highway 61
Lutsen, Minnesota 55612
800-435-3950 • (218) 663-7566

Room Rates:	$39 – $229. AAA discount.
Pet Charges or Deposits:	$5 per day. Manager's prior approval required.
Rated: 3 Paws	18 guest units including the lodge, condos, cabins or lake homes. Full kitchens, whirlpool, sauna.

Small, peaceful and quiet, Solbakken Resort's shoreline is ledge rock that slopes into Lake Superior. Bird migrations usually begin in early to mid-May here, where a variety of birds and majestic eagles nest in the Superior National Forest. An array of wildflowers begin to bloom in late May through summer, right up to the October frosts. This is a place to relax and recharge.

Guest accommodations include kitchenettes and cabins that are tucked along the shoreline, close enough so the sound of the waves lulls you to sleep. Lodge suites offer scenic lake views and each has its own fireplace and fully equipped kitchen. The Joan House and Olof House are two- and three-bedroom lakefront homes with wood-burning stoves, antiques and handmade quilts.

Superior Shores Resort

10 Superior Shores Drive
Two Harbors, Minnesota 55616
800-242-1988 • (218) 834-5671
Web Site: www.superiorshores.com
E-mail: supshores@norshor.dst.mn.us

Room Rates:	$49 – $399. Call for discounts.
Pet Charges or Deposits:	$25 refundable deposit. Manager's prior approval required.
Rated: 5 Paws 🐾🐾🐾🐾🐾	57 guest rooms, 87 suites and lakefront homes with kitchens; tennis courts, 2 pools, whirlpool, Jacuzzi and hot tub. Restaurant and lounge.

Imagine taking all that Lake Superior's North Shore has to offer. The massive rock formations and pebbled beaches. The pines and the birches. The turbulent majesty of the "Big Lake." Now imagine an extraordinary resort placed right in the middle. A resort with beautiful lodge suites, gorgeous townhouses, stone fireplaces, fully equipped kitchens and warm pine woodwork, along with down comforters. Well, you can stop imagining, because we've just introduced you to Superior Shores Resort.

The resort is open year-round, providing guests four seasons of activities. Premier downhill skiing is an hour's drive away at Lutsen Mountain, with more than twenty runs. Over 500 kilometers of cross-country ski trails await you on the North Shore. During the summer months numerous rivers and streams are home to brook and brown trout. Or pass the time on one of six different golf courses.

Anderson House

333 Main Street West
Wabasha, Minnesota 55981
800-535-5467 • (612) 565-4524
Web Site: www.theandersonhouse.com

Room Rates: $50 – $139. AARP discount.
Pet Charges or Deposits: Manager's prior approval required.
Rated: 5 Paws 🐾🐾🐾🐾🐾 18 guest rooms and 6 suites.

T here is a feeling of time having stopped as you wander through the antique-filled rooms with their high beds, marble-topped dressers, handmade quilts, Victorian, paintings and framed marriage certificates. The Anderson House offers a selection of uniquely decorated rooms, including whirlpool suites and standard and European rooms.

Shoes left outside the door are meticulously shined here. Cold feet call for a hot brick, carefully presented in a quilted envelope, for your bed. You're ailing? A mustard plaster, with instructions for use, will be delivered for your cold. In the summer, flowers from the garden will adorn your room. If you're here at Christmastime, you'll find Christmas trees all over the house. On New Year's Day, champagne will be delivered to your room. The motto here is service, comfort and excellent food.

Oh, by the way — when you make a room reservation at the Anderson House, you may also request one of the ten cuddly Anderson House cats as a room companion at no extra charge. The cats are usually in high demand, so make your reservation well in advance.

Stockman Inn

1402 South Jeffers Street
North Platte, Nebraska 69101
800-624-4643 • (308) 534-3630

Room Rates:	$42 – $65, including coffee. AAA and AARP discounts.
Pet Charges or Deposits:	None.
Rated: 3 Paws 🐾 🐾 🐾	130 guest rooms. Pool and exercise room, restaurant and lounge.

T he Stockman Inn is a good choice for those seeking affordable lodging in Nebraska. Located only minutes from Buffalo Bill's Ranch State Historical Park, 3 public golf courses and the world's largest railroad yard, the Inn provides 24-hour courtesy airport transportation.

Tastefully appointed guest rooms feature king-sized and queen-sized beds, cable TVs with remote control and free HBO. The Stockman offers an outdoor pool, exercise room, laundry services and room service from the Fireplace Restaurant.

Clarion Hotel – Carlisle

10909 M Street
Omaha, Nebraska 68137
800-526-6242 • (402) 331-8220
Web Site: www.4w.com/clarion
E-mail: clarcarol2@aol.com

Room Rates:	$69 – $150, including continental breakfast. AAA discount.
Pet Charges or Deposits:	$35 refundable deposit. Manager's prior approval required.
Rated: 3 Paws 🐾🐾🐾	137 guest rooms and 5 suites. Indoor pool, restaurant and lounge.

Guest rooms are clean, comfortable and quiet, featuring deluxe beds or king-sized beds. Each room or suite includes color cable television with remote control and work desk with ergonomic office chair, speaker phone, data port and office supplies, coffee and tea brewers, fluffy terry robes and upscale personal toiletries. A complete business center and secretarial services are available for the business traveler.

The High Plains Grill's unique menu is based on the bounty of the Heartland. Rotisserie cooking adds the value of a healthy twist to many Midwest favorites.

Buckboard Inn

1191 First Avenue Northwest
Beach, North Dakota 58621
888-449-3599 • (701) 872-4794

Room Rates: $31 – $41, including continental breakfast. AAA discount.
Pet Charges or Deposits: None.
Rated: 3 Paws   39 guest rooms.

T he Buckboard Inn has comfortable and convenient accommodations, with refrigerators, microwaves and color TVs. There is plenty of room for you and your pet to go on long walks around the Inn.

Located nearby is Theodore Roosevelt National Park, where you can enjoy hiking, cross-country horseback riding, camping and canoeing on the Little Missouri River.

Deadwood Gulch Resort

Highway 85 South
P.O. Box 643
Deadwood, South Dakota 57732
800-695-1876 • (605) 578-1294
Web Site: www.deadwoodgulch.com

Room Rates:	$45 – $135. AAA and AARP discounts.
Pet Charges or Deposits:	$10 per stay. No large pets. Manager's prior approval required.
Rated: 3 Paws 🐾 🐾 🐾	100 guest rooms and 2 suites, with color TV, hot tubs and pool.

T he Deadwood Gulch Resort provides the perfect headquarters from which to explore the scenic byways and monumental treasures of the beautiful Black Hills. From horseback riding, fishing and hiking, to snowmobiling, downhill and cross-country skiing, it is all right here.

A gurgling creek and pine-clad hills greet guests to the 100-room resort, which features an indoor hot tub, a heated outdoor pool, casino action, a full-service bar and trolley service.

Fort Randall Inn

Highways 18 and 281
Pickstown, South Dakota 57367
800-340-7801 • (605) 487-7801

Room Rates:	$34 – $60. AAA discount.
Pet Charges or Deposits:	Manager's prior approval required.
Rated: 3 Paws 🐾🐾🐾	17 guest rooms and 1 suite.

O nly a quarter-mile from the water, the Fort Randall Inn offers large, comfortable rooms with queen-sized beds and cable TV at affordable rates. The suite features a deck overlooking Lake Francis Case, three bedrooms, three bathrooms, a large living room and four TVs and will sleep 12 to 14 people comfortably.

There is excellent year-round fishing in Lake Francis Case, and also fast-water fishing below the Fort Randall Dam. Boating and water-skiing are popular summer sports here. Both sail and motor boats are common sights in the summertime. A beautiful 9-hole golf course and a clubhouse complete with dining room and bar are open from April 15 through October 15.

Basin Park Hotel

12 Spring Street
Eureka Springs, Arkansas 72632
800-643-4972 • (501) 253-7837
Web Site: www.basinpark.com

Room Rates:	$69 – $145, including continental breakfast. AAA and AARP discounts.
Pet Charges or Deposits:	None.
Rated: 3 Paws	33 guest rooms and 28 suites.

E xperience Ozark tradition with its quaint, tree-lined streets, a montage of antique and gift stores, fine restaurants, art galleries, museums and cultural attractions, all within reach of historic downtown Basin Park Hotel.

Guest rooms mirror the heritage of the town, while offering modern conveniences. Many include two- and three-room suites with parlors, Jacuzzi spas, panoramic views and fine furnishings.

The Balcony Restaurant overlooks downtown Eureka Springs, offering live music on the weekends.

Crescent Hotel

75 Prospect Avenue
Eureka Springs, Arkansas 72632
800-342-9766 • (501) 253-6905
Web Site: www.crescent-hotel.com

Room Rates:	$69 – $145, including continental breakfast. AAA and AARP discounts.
Pet Charges or Deposits:	None.
Rated: 3 Paws 🐾🐾🐾	60 guest rooms and 8 suites. Spa, pool and formal gardens.

 his historic hotel is a landmark in Eureka Springs and the Ozark Mountains. Eureka Springs is a festive city, bustling with activity. The Christ of the Ozarks towers over America's Victorian Village and trolley carts transport passengers to and from their destinations.

The New Moon Spa in the Crescent Hotel offers indoor and outdoor traditional or Swedish massage, facials, mud wraps, salt glove and aromatherapy. The spa offers a fully equipped gym and weight room with personal trainers. Take yoga, aerobic and tai-chi classes. Acupressure therapy and Reike are also available here.

Roadrunner Inn

3034 Mundell Road
Eureka Springs, Arkansas 72632
888-253-8166 • (501) 253-8166

Room Rates:	$28 – $44, including coffee and muffin breakfast. AAA and AARP discounts.
Pet Charges or Deposits:	Manager's prior approval required.
Rated: 3 Paws	12 guest rooms with kitchenettes.

O verlooking Beaver Lake, atop a 300-foot ridge, the Roadrunner Inn offers spectacular views from each guest room. The location is secluded and quiet — a nature lover's dream. The entire four acres is certified as a Backyard Wildlife Habitat by the National Wildlife Federation and the Arkansas Game and Fish Commission. Guests enjoy views of the lake and the wildlife as well as the natural setting from their room or deck.

The Inn is conveniently located ten miles west of historic Eureka Springs, with its Victorian houses, health spas, great shopping and dining.

Fools Cove Ranch

P.O. Box 10
Kingston, Arkansas 72742
(501) 665-2986

Room Rates:	$55 – $75, including full breakfast.
Pet Charges or Deposits:	Manager's prior approval required.
Rated: 3 Paws	3 guest rooms and 1 suite; hot tub on deck, nature trails.

A nother mountain hamlet that offers a chance to leave it all behind. Located on Scenic State Highway 21, Kingston is centrally located for those wanting to explore the Buffalo National River and its historic Boxley and Lost Valleys, Withrow Springs State Park and the Kings River.

This rustic country farm offers a full country breakfast, served either on the porch or in the country kitchen. Optional lunches or dinners are available with advance notice.

Gaston's White River Resort

1777 River Road
Lakeview, Arkansas 72642
(870) 431-5202
Web Site: www.gastons.com
E-mail: gastons@mtnhome.com

Room Rates:	$57 – $150.
Pet Charges or Deposits:	None.
Rated: 3 Paws 🐾🐾🐾	74 guest cottages. Refrigerators, microwaves, pool, tennis, airstrip, restaurant and private club.

The White River has a worldwide reputation as one of the best trout streams to be found anywhere. Only Gaston's in the Arkansas Ozarks can offer you more than two miles of river frontage with breathtaking scenery — a photographer's and nature lover's dream come true.

The cottages are air conditioned, comfortable and spotlessly clean. Many feature full kitchens, patios, large redwood decks and wood-burning fireplaces.

At Gaston's White River Resort you will find a playground for kids, swimming pool, tennis court, game room, nearby golf course and a nature trail along the river.

Scott Valley Resort and Guest Ranch

223 Scott Valley Trail
Mountain Home, Arkansas 72653
(870) 425-5136
Web Site: www.scottvalley.com

Room Rates:	$115 – $130, including 3 meals a day, horseback riding and other activities.
Pet Charges or Deposits:	$6 per day.
Rated: 4 Paws 🐾 🐾 🐾 🐾	28 units, plus Hilltop Hideaway. Pool, whirlpool spa, game room, tennis.

mid 625 scenic acres of breathtaking meadows, woodland, rocky cliffs and spring-fed streams is the Scott Valley Resort and Guest Ranch, three-year winner of "Family Resorts of the Year," by Family Circle Magazines. Rates not only include all activities on the ranch, but also your meals, where down-home good cooking is all you can eat for breakfast, lunch and dinner.

Here in the serenity of the Ozarks you have your choice of active recreation or you can just "not lift a finger" during your entire stay. Mount up and go into the forest with your helpful wrangler for a trail ride on a gentle, well-trained horse suited for your own riding pleasure — one that you will come to think of as "yours" before your vacation is over. If horseback riding isn't your thing, water sports such as jet-skiing, sailing and scuba div-ing are available at Lake Norfork at no extra charge. For those interested in fishing, there is world-class trout fish-ing on the famous White River, and the Guest Ranch will supply a com-plimentary boat. Canoes are also offered at no cost for scenic adventure trips down the White River.

Windy Heights Bed and Breakfast

607 Country Heights
Lakin, Kansas 67860
(316) 355-7699
E-mail: djaeger@pld.com

Room Rates:	$50 – $60, including full breakfast.
Pet Charges or Deposits:	$10 per stay. Small pets only. Manager's prior approval required.
Rated: 3 Paws 🐾 🐾 🐾	4 guest rooms.

 This relaxing bed and breakfast is located on a 9-hole golf course, which is available for play during the summer. Or if rest is the only thing on your itinerary, take a nap on the porch swing.

Le Jardin Sur Le Bayou

256 Lower Country Drive
Bourg, Louisiana 70343
(504) 594-2722

Room Rates: $85, including a gourmet breakfast and garden tour.
Pet Charges or Deposits: Call for deposit. Pets welcomed upon arrival.
Rated: 5 Paws 🐾 🐾 🐾 🐾 🐾 Private upstairs suite with sitting room and private bath.

Enjoy Cajun hospitality on this 26-acre registered wildlife sanctuary featuring century-old live oaks and native plants teeming with hummingbirds and butterflies. Stroll quiet garden paths under an oak canopy, pause at bridges and enjoy goldfish ponds, swing, or just sit on a garden bench and watch the extensive variety of birds.

Inside the inn awaits a comfortable and tastefully decorated private upstairs suite, set back from a quiet country road, offering central air and heat, cable television, telephone, refrigerator and use of screened breezeway and laundry facilities. Owners and innkeepers Dave and Jo Ann Cognet create magical breakfasts each morning that are served in the garden, overlooking the fish ponds.

This highly recommended bed and breakfast inn is located just one hour from New Orleans. Consider staying at least two nights to enjoy the home cooking and garden tour.

Maison des Anges Bed and Breakfast

508 Academy Street
Houma, Louisiana 70360
(504) 873-7662

Room Rates: $55 – $80, including a full breakfast.
Pet Charges or Deposits: $10 per day. First-night room rate as deposit.
Rated: 4 Paws   5 guest rooms with semi-private and private baths, king-, double and twin-sized beds, telephone, cable television with remote control, laundry facilities and small fenced courtyard.

Built in 1904 for J.C. Cunningham, former mayor of Houma, the Maison des Anges Bed and Breakfast was the first Victorian-style home in Houma. Located near the downtown area, the inn is within walking distance to the Mardi Gras parade route and other historical points of interest. Except for the more recent addition to the home, the building was constructed of virgin cypress, including the interior and exterior walls. Each post of the porch was turned from one solid timber and bears the stencil "St. Louis Cypress Co." under the original green paint.

The house features five guest rooms, two of which may be combined into a two-bedroom suite, with private and semi-private baths with the original claw-foot bathtubs and hand painted tiles. The rooms feature the original doors, with functioning transoms and rolled glass panes, including the 9-foot windows facing the front of the property. There is a spacious, common sun room with cable television and a VCR for guests to use, plus a large fully equipped kitchen, spacious dining room where you can enjoy your complimentary breakfast, as well as a comfortable smoking area. The small fenced courtyard is perfect for exercising your dog.

Bois des Chênes Bed and Breakfast Inn

338 North Sterling
Lafayette, Louisiana 70501
(318) 233-7816

Room Rates:	$95 – $125, including full breakfast.
Pet Charges or Deposits:	$10 per stay. $50 deposit. Manager's prior approval required. Sorry, no cats.
Rated: 4 Paws 🐾 🐾 🐾 🐾	7 suites with private baths, furnished with antiques, television, small refrigerators, some private sitting rooms and wood-burning fireplaces, complimentary breakfast and wine.

S ituated near the center of Lafayette is the award-winning Bois des Chênes Bed and Breakfast Inn, part of the Charles Mouton Plantation House. This magnificent plantation managed to survive the Civil War and is now on the National Register of Historic Places. Over the years, it has become an important entity in the culture and history of the city.

Built in 1820, this Acadian-style plantation house has been lovingly restored and graced with period antiques of mainly Louisiana French origin, as well as American pieces to complement this unique architectural design. Guests may choose their accommodations from the Main Plantation House, which offers two charming suites with sitting rooms and private baths. One suite offers a cozy, wood-burning fireplace. The 1890 Carriage House is at the rear of the plantation and features three suites upstairs and two downstairs, all with private baths and period antiques, yet still affording modern conveniences such as a television and refrigerator.

Guests are served a delicious Louisiana-style breakfast, and later treated to complimentary wine and a tour of the Mouton Plantation House. The resident dog, Tuppence, will be glad to welcome your dog to the inn.

Chimes Bed and Breakfast of New Orleans

1146 Constantinople Street
New Orleans, Louisiana 70115
800-729-4640 • (504) 488-4640

Room Rates:	$61 – $126, including continental breakfast.
Pet Charges or Deposits:	$5 per stay. Manager's prior approval required.
Rated: 3 Paws 🐾 🐾 🐾	3 air-conditioned guest rooms and 2 large suites with private entrances opening onto the courtyard.

Uptown in the largest historical neighborhood in the United States is The Chimes Bed and Breakfast of New Orleans. This 1876 inn offers guests individually decorated rooms reflecting the flavor of New Orleans, with private entries, beautiful antique iron beds, claw-foot bathtubs, high ceilings, wooden or slate floors and a friendly atmosphere. The first-floor rooms have large French doors that open onto an old brick courtyard full of tropical plants to shade you while you relax or read in the hammock.

Begin your day with a lavish continental breakfast served in the large dining room. Only minutes from the famed French Quarter, the inn's neighborhood of ante-bellum homes will take you back in time. It is a charming route for you and your dog to take for a leisurely stroll. You can even get a little help with dog-walking duties if you ask.

Three blocks from St. Charles Avenue, The Chimes is minutes away from major New Orleans attractions including the Audubon Zoological Gardens, antique shops and the famous restaurants, jazz clubs and art galleries.

New Orleans Accommodations Reservation Service

P.O. Box 8163
New Orleans, Louisiana 70005
888-240-0070 • (504) 838-0071

Room Rates: $55 – $350, some include full or continental breakfast.
Pet Charges or Deposits: Sorry, no cats. Manager's prior approval required.
Rated: 3 to 5 Paws 🐾 🐾 🐾 Bed and breakfast inns, condos, homestays and apartments. Call for individual amenities.

I f you are looking for something different from the usual hotel accommodations when visiting the New Orleans area, try booking your reservations through the New Orleans Accommodations Reservation Service. You will learn of hosted or unhosted accommodations in outstanding homes, inns, apartments and guest cottages. Each property is carefully evaluated before allowing it to become a part of the service. Most accommodations are air-conditioned and are located near public transportation to get you to the French Quarter and the downtown area in minutes.

Rates quoted are for double occupancy and are based on the type of accommodation, location, private or shared baths. Make sure to tell them that you are bringing your dog and mention any special amenities you may need, such as a park nearby or an exercise yard. And, of course, all major credit cards are accepted.

Butler Greenwood Plantation

8345 U.S. Highway 61
St. Francisville, Louisiana 70775
(504) 635-6312
Web Site: www.butlergreenwood.com
E-mail: butlergree@aol.com

Room Rates:	$100 – $110, including continental breakfast and tour of main house.
Pet Charges or Deposits:	Manager's prior approval required.
Rated: 4 Paws 🐾🐾🐾🐾	6 cottages with air conditioning, ceiling fans, television, VCR, fireplaces, kitchens, library, bathrobes, full bath, barbecue grill, laundry facilities, swimming pool, Jacuzzi, tennis court, canoes, golfing, Ping-Pong, bird watching and gardens.

Built in 1796, this well-loved working plantation boasts a main ante-bellum house with six charming cottages, all set among 2,200 acres. The extensive grounds have hundreds of ancient, moss-draped oak trees and ante-bellum gardens. All guests receive a guided tour of the grounds and main house with historical information by direct descendants of the original builder.

The 19th-century cottages include the Cook's Cottage with claw-foot tub, fireplace and a porch swing overlooking the duck pond. The Gazebo is a six-sided building with three 9-foot-tall antique stained-glass church windows and a king-sized bed. The Pond House sleeps six and has a hammock on the shaded porch overlooking the pond. The Treehouse is at the edge of a steep, wooded ravine with a three-level deck, king-sized cypress four-poster bed and a fireplace. The Dovecote is three stories with sloped, shingled sides; it sleeps six, has a fireplace, a Jacuzzi and a deck on the ravine.

Take advantage of the spacious acreage to take your dog on a long hike and observe nature at its finest.

Lake Rosemound Inn

10473 Lindsey Lane
St. Francisville, Louisiana 70775
(504) 635-3176

Room Rates:	$75 – $105, including full breakfast.
Pet Charges or Deposits:	Manager's prior approval required.
Rated: 4 Paws 🐾🐾🐾🐾	4 guest rooms and 2 luxurious suites with Jacuzzi tubs, ceiling fans, television, fireplaces, private entrances, clubhouse room with ice cream parlor, set on three lakefront acres.

P erched on three beautiful acres and bound on two sides by Lake Rosemound, one of the most picturesque areas in Louisiana, is charming Lake Rosemound Inn. This romantic inn features the Rosemound and Feliciana Suites, with Jacuzzi tubs, and the Sunrise and Sunset rooms with magnificent views of the lake.

Guests may choose to relax in the Clubhouse Parlor, complete with dart boards, television, stereo, a Brunswick pool table and the Inn's famous "help yourself" ice cream parlor. The common kitchen is complete with grill, refrigerator and microwave. All rooms have television, telephone, queen-sized beds and private baths.

Start your morning with a big country breakfast before you head out to the dock for a day of fishing, stroll along the shoreline with your dog, bike the rolling hills or take in the abundant wildlife that graces the property.

Daniele Hotel

216 North Meramec
Clayton, Missouri 63105
800-325-8302 • (314) 721-0101

Room Rates:	$129 – $295. Call for discounts.
Pet Charges or Deposits:	Sorry, no cats.
Rated: 3 Paws 🐾🐾🐾	82 guest rooms and 6 suites, outdoor pool and health club, laundry facilities, complimentary limousine service, restaurant.

ocated in the heart of Clayton, the Daniele is an elegant, European-style hotel with personalized service. Guest rooms are private, intimate and relaxing.

At the popular health club, you will enjoy complimentary workouts with expert trainers. Continue relaxing by the Olympic-sized pool and enjoy your favorite snack or cocktail.

The staff is available 18 hours a day to fulfill your needs or to chauffeur you to Clayton destinations and shopping malls. Your personal wake-up service greets you at the door with fresh hot coffee, orange juice and the newspaper.

Rock Eddy Bluff Country Stay and Bed and Breakfast

HCR 62, Box 241
Dixon, Missouri 65459
800-335-5921 • (573) 759-6081
Web Site: www.rockeddy.com

Room Rates:	$65 – $95, including full breakfast.
Pet Charges or Deposits:	Horses welcome. Manager's prior approval required.
Rated: 3 Paws 🐾🐾🐾	2 guest rooms, 1 secluded cottage and a cabin on 150 acres. Refrigerators, microwaves, hot tubs.

T his is where the Gasconade River enters the valley, sweeps between an island and a willowed gravel bar, then relaxes into a pool or "eddy." Viewed from the bluff, meadows appear below and wooded ridges stretch to the horizon.

The Rock Eddy Bluff Country Stay and Bed and Breakfast offers two picturesque bed and breakfast rooms, a secluded cottage and a cozy 1880s cabin on 150 acres of scenic Ozark forest. You'll find unpretentious, old-time furnishings, handmade quilts, fireplaces and a romantic atmosphere.

Hiking, canoeing, fishing, swimming and Amish wagon tours are among the free pleasures you'll find. Relaxation is for the taking — a sense of "nothing must I do but please myself."

Serendipity Bed and Breakfast

116 South Pleasant Street
Independence, Missouri 64050
800-203-4299 • (816) 833-4719

Room Rates:	$65 – $85, including full breakfast.
Pet Charges or Deposits:	$10 per day. One night's refundable deposit. Manager's prior approval required.
Rated: 3 Paws 🐾🐾🐾	5 guest rooms.

This delightful 1887 three-story brick home transports you back to the Victorian era, with antique walnut furniture, rugs and period lighting. The details include Victorian children's books and toys, a myriad of china figurines and vividly colored glassware adorning shelves and tables. The dining room is filled with the luxuries that a middle-class family could obtain from the latest Sears and Wards catalogues of the 1890s. From century-old books to antique medicine bottles and shaving paraphernalia in the bathrooms — this house is overflowing with genuine articles of daily life from the turn-of-the-century era.

Outside, a three-tiered fountain provides a glorious bath for the many birds that flock to the flower-bedecked gardens. A full breakfast of quiche, fruit, muffins, juice and coffee or tea is served on antique china, graced by lace table-cloths and candlelight.

Regal Riverfront Hotel

200 South Fourth Street
St. Louis, Missouri 63102
800-325-7353 • (314) 241-9500

Room Rates:	$139 – $199.
Pet Charges or Deposits:	$50 refundable deposit.
Rated: 4 Paws 🐾🐾🐾🐾	780 guest rooms and 28 suites. Indoor and outdoor swimming pools, exercise room, game room, laundry, 3 restaurants and 2 lounges.

onveniently located downtown, the Regal Riverfront Hotel puts you in touch with all that St. Louis is famous for: the Gateway Arch, Busch Stadium, river-boat gaming and historic Laclede's Landing.

Choose from stylish and spacious guest rooms, executive and hospitality suites or Regal Class accommodations featuring added amenities and services. Many rooms provide exceptional views of the Mississippi River and the Gateway Arch.

On the 28th floor you'll find the Top of the Riverfront, the city's only revolving restaurant. Enjoy spectacular St. Louis vistas along with classic American cuisine and the most popular Sunday brunch in town.

Sharpe House

301 Northwest Second Street
Checotah, Oklahoma 74426
(918) 473-2832

Room Rates: $35 – $50, including full breakfast.
Pet Charges or Deposits: None.
Rated: 3 Paws   3 guest rooms and 1 suite.

The Sharpe House is a reminder of a more gracious, leisurely era. It has been scraped and painted and papered and buffed and shined. It is furnished with heirlooms and lovingly hand-crafted accessories.

The look of the house is antebellum, but the specialty of the kitchen is Mexican cuisine. All the food served is something special — and breakfast is included in your room rate. Try the eggs, bacon, biscuits, waffles and fresh fruit in season or indulge yourself with their breakfast burrito, Mexican omelets, huevos rancheros or menudo. Delicious!

There's even a screened porch with an old-fashioned swing. Have your morning coffee with orioles, cardinals, hummingbirds and an occasional squirrel.

Ramada Plaza Hotel

930 East Second Street
Edmond, Oklahoma 73034
800-322-4686 • (405) 341-3577

Room Rates:	$64 – $79, including full breakfast. AAA, AARP, AKC and ABA discounts.
Pet Charges or Deposits:	$15 per stay.
Rated: 3 Paws 🐾 🐾 🐾	145 guest rooms including 16 suites. Pool, whirlpool and Jacuzzi. Restaurant.

T he Ramada Plaza Hotel, in Edmond, invites you and your pets to discover the elegance of their eight-story, newly renovated, full-service hotel. Located on historic Route 66, the Hotel is a short 15-minute drive from all Oklahoma City attractions, with easy access to all major Interstate Highways.

Relax in the atrium by the waterfall, listening to the chime of the grandfather clock, or kick back by the pool-side in the Jacuzzi. The hotel includes a complimentary full breakfast, free local telephone calls and in-room coffeemakers in all guest rooms and suites.

Carrington's Bluff

1900 David Street
Austin, Texas 78705
800-871-8908 • (512) 479-0638
E-mail: governorsinn@earthlink.net

Room Rates:	$59 – $109, including full breakfast. AARP discount.
Pet Charges or Deposits:	None.
Rated: 4 Paws	8 guest rooms and 1 suite. Pet treats, bedding and walking service.

Carrington's Bluff is Austin's country inn in the city. Enjoy the peacefulness on an acre of tree-covered bluff in the heart of Austin. This 1877 English country house was part of an original homestead of the Republic of Texas.

Inside you'll find rooms filled with English and American antiques, accented with English country fabrics and decor. Outside, the spacious porch invites you to linger under gentle breezes rustling through a 500-year-old native oak. The smell of fresh-brewed coffee beckons you to a full breakfast of fresh fruit, homemade granola, yogurt, bakery items and hot specialty entrées, served on fine china.

A few minutes away you'll discover the University of Texas, the state Capitol, parks, museums, fine shopping, excellent restaurants and Austin's famous Sixth Street.

Governors Inn

611 West 22nd Street
Austin, Texas 78705
800-871-8908 • (512) 477-0711
E-mail: governorsinn@earthlink.net

Room Rates:	$59 – $119, including full breakfast. Call for discounts.
Pet Charges or Deposits:	None.
Rated: 4 Paws 🐾🐾🐾🐾	10 guest rooms. Pet treats, bedding and walking service.

R elive Texas' colorful history at the Governors Inn. Built in 1897, this neoclassical Victorian was restored to its former glory in 1993.

Each guest room, named for a Texas governor, is furnished with beautiful and tasteful antiques. You'll luxuriate in comfort and charm in this well-appointed mansion. Soak in a claw-footed tub in your private bath. Relax in the parlor or on the wraparound porch.

Large trees shade the porches, which are complete with Victorian rockers and porch swings. Every morning, a full breakfast will satisfy your appetite for fine food and good taste.

Cool Water Acres

Route 1, Box 785
Bandera, Texas 78003
(830) 796-4866

Room Rates:	$70 – $85.
Pet Charges or Deposits:	$5 per day. Manager's prior approval required. Sorry, no cats. One night's refundable deposit.
Rated: 3 Paws 🐾🐾🐾	1 two-bedroom cabin on 54 acres.

Cool Water Acres is located about 5 miles from downtown Bandera and it encompasses 54 acres of beautiful hill country. A private, seven-acre, spring-fed lake provides cool, clear water for swimming, snorkeling, fishing and relaxing. Bass, perch and catfish are plentiful and easily caught, when they're in the mood. Two floating docks provide for fishing and sunbathing. The rest of the ranch's topography has varied terrain and elevations, which make for wonderful hiking excursions.

The private cabin is an old homestead, originally built in 1870, with a full kitchen, bedroom and bath. Care was taken to preserve the old beams and the feel of the cabin, including an old rock fireplace. Fresh fruit and eggs are provided when you arrive. The cabin is located about fifty feet from the water and it has its own private floating dock.

Hideaway Country Log Cabins

Route 2, Box 148
Bluffdale, Texas 76433
(254) 823-6606

Room Rates:	$83 – $98, including expanded continental breakfast.
Pet Charges or Deposits:	$10 per stay.
Rated: 3 Paws	5 cabins with kitchens, pool, hot tubs and spa.

T his secluded country retreat offers hideaway cabins among 155 acres of oaks, a short drive from Dallas/Fort Worth. Each of the five cabins is secluded so guests cannot see other cabins from their own.

Each cabin features a private hot tub, a covered porch with a swing, air conditioning, ceiling fans, linens and a color TV/VCR; two have fireplaces. You have your choice of a continental breakfast with homemade breads, muffins, cereals and fruit, or you can have your refrigerator stocked with the makings. All cabins have fully equipped kitchens with microwaves, range/ovens, refrigerators and cooking utensils.

Within 30 minutes you can be in a good restaurant or a cozy nightclub or out shopping for antiques. Most people, however, prefer just to stay at the Hideaway and enjoy the seclusion. Swim and sun at the pool, explore the surrounding countryside, fish in the ponds, hike in the woods or star-gaze from your hot tub or front-porch swing.

Ragtime Ranch Inn

P.O. Box 575
Elgin, Texas 78621
800-800-9743 • (512) 285-9599
E-mail: ragtimeinn@earthlink.net

Room Rates:	$95 – $125, including continental breakfast.
Pet Charges or Deposits:	$20 refundable deposit. Horses welcome.
Rated: 4 Paws	4 guest rooms on 37 acres with refrigerators, microwaves, fireplaces, pool.

E nter the gate to the Ragtime Ranch Inn and immediately feel its country grace. Green pastures on one side, thick woods on the other. The Ragtime Ranch Inn offers you a quiet Texas getaway, with traditional ranch-style porches and a stocked pond, a cool, shaded swimming pool, stabling facilities and 37 acres of nature trails.

Four private 450-square-foot rooms offer individual screened porches or decks with scenic views and wood-burning fireplaces. Guests may use the stabling facilities of 12-foot x 12-foot stalls with 40-foot runs, or two private pastures, if you prefer to turn your horses out.

The fields of wildflowers are brilliant throughout the spring and summer. In fall the leaves turn colors while you cozy up in front of your own fireplace during the mild Texas winter. You will enjoy the solitude here. There's a rocking chair waiting for you.

Hotel Limpia

Main Street on the Square
P.O. Box 1341
Fort Davis, Texas 79734
800-662-5517 • (915) 426-3237
Web Site: www.hotellimpia.com

Room Rates: $79 – $150.
Pet Charges or Deposits: $10 per day.
Rated: 3 Paws 🐾 🐾 🐾   27 guest rooms and 9 suites.

T he Hotel Limpia, named after nearby Limpia Creek, is nestled in the picturesque mile-high town of Fort Davis in the Davis Mountains. For more than 80 years the native limestone structure has provided safe haven and rest for tourists and travelers alike.

Many of the individually decorated rooms and suites are complete with kitchens. This is a good place to relax on one of the many porches, verandahs and gardens in the trademark rocking chairs.

Luckenbach Inn

HC 13, Box 9
Fredericksburg, Texas 78624
800-997-1124 • (830) 997-2205
Web Site: www.luckenbachtx.com
E-mail: theinn@luckenbachtx.com

Room Rates:	$95 – $125, including full breakfast.
Pet Charges or Deposits:	$10 per day. $10 refundable deposit. Manager's prior approval required.
Rated: 3 Paws 🐾🐾🐾	5 guest rooms and 1 suite on 12 acres.

 ocated in the heart of the Texas Hill Country, the Luckenbach Inn is bordered by South Grape Creek, providing an abundance of wildlife and opportunities to enjoy fishing, swimming, hiking, nature walks and fly-fishing.

The 1800s log cabin has 2 bedrooms decorated with antiques, with a rustic but elegant decor. The Grape Creek Suite has a comfortable bedroom with a full kitchen and a porch outside — perfect for relaxing. The Cypress and Coral rooms feature whirlpool tubs and fireplaces.

A full country breakfast of farm-fresh eggs, apple-smoked bacon, assorted juices, seasonal fresh fruit, banana nut pancakes, hash browns and pretty darn good coffee await you each morning.

Lovett Inn

501 Lovett Boulevard
Houston, Texas 77006
800-799-5224 • (713) 522-5224
Web Site: www.lovettinn.com
E-mail: lovettinn@aol.com

Room Rates:	$85 – $150, including continental breakfast.
Pet Charges or Deposits:	Sorry, no cats.
Rated: 4 Paws 🐾🐾🐾🐾	8 guest rooms and 2 guest suites. Pool and Jacuzzi.

Nestled in the heart of the Montrose Museum District, the historic Lovett Inn offers distinctive lodging and catering. The Inn was once the home of Houston Mayor and Federal Court Judge Joseph C. Hutcheson, and it offers all the amenities of a first-class hotel, with the charm and ambiance of a fine historic home.

Each of the eight rooms has been comfortably decorated to evoke the Inn's historic past, while enjoying such modern amenities as in-room phones, remote-controlled color television and private bathrooms. Most rooms overlook the Inn's quarter block of magnificently landscaped grounds, pool and spa.

Whiskey Mountain Inn

HCR 1, Box 555
Leakey, Texas 78873
800-370-6797 • (830) 232-6797
Web Site: www.lcstech.com/whiskey
E-mail: dbjadams@hctc.net

Room Rates:	$40 – $80, including full breakfast in the main house.
Pet Charges or Deposits:	None.
Rated: 3 Paws	3 guest rooms in main house and 6 cabins with cooking facilities.

Spend a night or many nights in this German farmhouse with cypress plank exterior, a tin roof and a 50-foot porch held up by huge cedar tree trunks. Built in 1869, this antique house is a perfect place to relax in wicker rockers, watching the wildlife of deer, rabbits, raccoons and the occasional bobcat.

Located near Garner State Park and Lost Maples State Park, the area offers extensive hiking trails, fishing and cycling.

Gage Hotel

P.O. Box 46
Marathon, Texas 79842
800-884-GAGE • (915) 386-4205
Web Site: www.gagehotel.com
E-mail: welcome@gagehotel.com

Room Rates: $65 – $175.
Pet Charges or Deposits: None.
Rated: 3 Paws 🐾🐾🐾   41 guest rooms and 2 suites. Restaurant and bar.

L ocated in Marathon, Texas, the official gateway to Big Bend National Park, the Gage Hotel offers today's traveler rooms uniquely decorated with artifacts and furnishings that represent the Mexican, Indian and Anglo cultures of the Big Bend.

Guest rooms enjoy cool breezes from the courtyard, where the sound of the trickling fountain offers cool relief from the desert sun. All rooms are near the pool, which is under a shade ramada. Guest rooms with working fireplaces are available for the cooler season.

The high desert of Marathon, at over 4,000 feet, offers warm, dry days, cool, clear nights, and, of course, the scenic drama of Big Bend. Enjoy river-rafting trips on the Rio Grande, tours of Big Bend National Park and horseback riding.

Laguna Reef Hotel

1021 Water Street
Rockport, Texas 78382
800-248-1057 • (512) 729-1742
Web Site: www.lagunareef.com
E-mail: laguna@shelley.dbstech.com

Room Rates:	$50 – $220, including continental breakfast. Corporate and military discounts.
Pet Charges or Deposits:	$5 per day. $40 refundable deposit. Pets under 30 pounds.
Rated: 3 Paws 🐾 🐾 🐾	21 guest rooms and 49 suites. Pool, putting green, 1,000-foot lighted fishing pier.

W hether you stay for a weekend of fishing or a winter of content, Laguna Reef Hotel offers the beauty of the coast and the comforts of home with a flexibility of accommodations. The popular one- and two-bedroom suites offer fully equipped kitchens, dining room and large living room. The master bedroom has a queen-sized bed. The second bedroom has two double beds. The living room has a double sofa bed.

Located on the major migration path traveled by hundreds of species of birds, Rockport is visited by hummingbirds, herons, cardinals and cranes. First-class fishing starts right outside your door with trout, redfish, flounder and deep-sea tournament action. Whooping cranes, native javelina, deer and alligators are viewed north of Rockport at the Aransas Wildlife Refuge.

Brackenridge House

230 Madison Street
San Antonio, Texas 78204
800-221-1412 • (210) 271-3442
Web Site: www.brackenridgehouse.com
E-mail: benniesueb@aol.com

Room Rates:	$99 – $175, including full breakfast. AAA discount.
Pet Charges or Deposits:	Manager's prior approval required.
Rated: 4 Paws 🐾🐾🐾🐾	3 guest rooms and 3 suites.

 he Brackenridge House is a two-story Greek Revival home with first- and second-floor verandahs featuring four white Corinthian columns. Its original pine floors, double-hung windows and high ceilings are enhanced by antique furnishings and family quilts.

The downstairs rooms have communicating doors that can be left unlocked for families or couples traveling together, or they may be locked for privacy. A hot tub, bent-willow swing and wrought-iron table and chairs make the back garden area a favorite place to relax at the end of a busy day.

Put on a Brackenridge House robe. Pour yourself a glass of cream sherry, eat a chocolate and indulge yourself in one of these beautiful rooms with king- and queen-sized beds, claw-footed tubs and mini refrigerators.

Brookhaven Manor

128 West Mistletoe Avenue
San Antonio, Texas 78212
(210) 733-3939

Room Rates:	$75 – $110, including full breakfast.
Pet Charges or Deposits:	Manager's prior approval required.
Rated: 3 Paws	4 guest rooms and 1 suite in the carriage house.

O n your next visit to South Texas, recapture the charm of a bygone era at the elegant, historic, three-story Brookhaven Manor. Built in 1913, the house features 3 fireplaces and hardwood floors and is lovingly decorated with heirloom antiques. You will enjoy a full gourmet breakfast in the formal dining room or in the privacy of your own room.

Located in the historic Monte Vista district, Brookhaven Manor is just minutes from many of San Antonio's most celebrated attractions, including the Riverwalk, the Alamo and the historic King William district.

Katy House Bed and Breakfast

201 Ramona Street
Smithville, Texas 78957
800-843-5289 • (512) 237-4262
Web Site: www.katyhouse.com

Room Rates:	$75 – $95, including full breakfast. Call for mid-week discounts.
Pet Charges or Deposits:	Manager's prior approval required. Sorry, no cats.
Rated: 3 Paws 🐾 🐾 🐾	4 guest rooms and 1 suite.

T his historic landmark 1909 home, furnished with American period antiques and filled with railroad memorabilia, reflects the spirit and heritage of Central Texas. Graceful columns, high ceilings and detailed millwork, along with original longleaf pine floors, pocket doors and leaded and beveled glass, detail the home. The ambiance is one of gracious comfort.

All rooms have private baths with original claw-foot tubs, televisions and telephones. Antique beds have been converted to queen-sized. Separate from the main house, the Carriage House features Western decor, and the Conductor's Quarters feature a railroad theme. A bountiful breakfast feast is served in the dining room.

A city of beautiful old neighborhoods with tree-lined streets, the Smithville area has everything from recreation to relaxation, antiquing, sightseeing and fine dining.

Homestead Bed and Breakfast

P. O. Box 1034
Wimberly, Texas 78676
800-918-8788 • (512) 847-8788
Web Site: www.homestead-tx.com

Room Rates:	$85 – $95, including continental breakfast.
Pet Charges or Deposits:	$10 per day.
Rated: 3 Paws 🐾 🐾 🐾	12 suites with full kitchens.

 or family vacation rentals, romantic getaways or family reunions, check out the Homestead Bed and Breakfast, which offers twelve cottages ranging in size from 500 to 1,000 square feet.

Located on Cypress Creek, which is six miles long and fed directly from an underground limestone aquifer, Homestead has waterfalls with swimming holes and rope swings. People come here to get away and relax, swim, listen to the water and "veg out."

All cottages are equipped with full kitchens with microwaves, wood-burning fireplaces, decks, some with private Jacuzzis, picnic tables, barbecue pits and two hot springs spas for guests. A continental-plus breakfast is provided in all cottages during your stay.

Ritz-Carlton Chicago

160 East Pearson Street at Water Tower Place
Chicago, Illinois 60611
800-621-6906 • (312) 266-1000
Web Site: www.fourseasons.com

Room Rates: $355 – $3,500.
Pet Charges or Deposits: Pets up to 90 lbs.
Rated: 5 Paws 435 guest rooms and 91 suites with pet welcome gift on
                         arrival. Pool, fitness facilities and spa.

S et atop Water Tower Place, high above prestigious North Michigan Avenue, is the Five Diamond Ritz-Carlton Chicago. A winner of the Condé Nast Travel Award, it features guest rooms that unveil a panorama of the city, lake and skyline. Throughout, an aura of warm welcome is accented by classic furnishings, fine art and fresh flowers.

With its pampering treatments and state-of-the-art facilities, including pool, whirlpool, steam rooms, saunas, aerobics, massage and personal training programs, the exclusive Carlton Club is an oasis of renewal. Chilled towels and filtered water await guests at the end of a workout. Outside, a private rooftop sundeck overlooks spectacular city views.

That the Ritz-Carlton is a singular pleasure will be evident from the instant you step into the magnificent lobby.

Victorian Oaks Bed and Breakfast

435 Locust Street
Minonk, Illinois 61760
(309) 432-2771
E-mail: locust@davesword.net

Room Rates:	$60 – $100, including full breakfast. AARP discount.
Pet Charges or Deposits:	Manager's prior approval required.
Rated: 3 Paws	5 guest rooms and 2 suites with refrigerators and microwaves.

V ictorian Oaks, a twelve-room Victorian home built in 1895, offers fine lodging in a romantic setting. Guests gather in the living room and play the Baldwin organ, chat in front of a roaring fire or enjoy movies while munching on popcorn.

Since no rooms share common walls, guest rooms are quiet and private. All rooms have ceiling fans, color cable TV, VCRs, desks and fluffy bathrobes to enjoy during your stay.

A delicious homemade breakfast is served by candlelight on fine china with gold flatware each morning.

Loeb House Inn Bed and Breakfast

708 Cincinnati Street
Lafayette, Indiana 47901
(765) 420-7737

Room Rates:	$70 – $175, including full breakfast. AAA and corporate discounts.
Pet Charges or Deposits:	Small pets only.
Rated: 3 Paws	5 guest rooms and 1 suite.

L ocated in the heart of Lafayette's historic Centennial district, the Loeb House, built in the Grand Italianate style, offers exceptional service and style. Intricate details such as plaster ceiling medallions and crown moldings have been restored, as have the finely detailed fireplaces, chandeliers and parquet floors, as well as the grand staircase with its original newel-post lamp.

At your doorstep are historic sites, museums, theater and fine dining. Parks are within easy access, including Columbian Park, which offers swimming, rides and a petting zoo. The popular Wolf Park is just a few minutes north in nearby Battle Ground. Fort Quiatenon and the Tippecanoe Battlefield also provide interesting historic views into the past.

Hotel Roberts

420 South High Street
Muncie, Indiana 47305
800-333-3333 • (765) 741-7777

Room Rates:	$72 – $225, including breakfast buffet. AAA, AARP, AKC and ABA discounts.
Pet Charges or Deposits:	None.
Rated: 3 Paws	130 guest rooms and 24 suites with refrigerators, microwaves, pool, Jacuzzi, hot tubs, restaurant and lounge.

R eflecting the architecture and ambiance of the Roaring 20s, the Hotel Roberts is listed in the National Register of Historic Places. From its beautiful facade and imposing portico of Indian limestone and brick, to the lobby's sunny glass atrium and ornate architectural details, the Roberts meets the high expectations of today's lodging and dining guests.

Many of the spacious guest rooms feature a sitting area, dressing area and bath accented with a sophisticated mix of brass, wood and wall coverings. An indoor pool, whirlpool, free parking and an exclusive concierge level — the Grand Quarters — are just a few of the amenities available to guests.

Oliver Inn Bed and Breakfast

630 West Washington Street
South Bend, Indiana 46601
888-697-4466 • (219) 232-4545

Room Rates:	$95 – $192, including continental breakfast and snacks.
Pet Charges or Deposit:	$10 per stay. One night's stay as refundable deposit. Manager's prior approval required.
Rated: 3 Paws 🐾 🐾 🐾	9 guest rooms, several with fireplaces, private balcony and Jacuzzi.

F rom the moment you pull into the stately circular drive and up to the grand porte-cochere, the 10,000-square-foot Oliver Inn will gently nudge you back into the grandeur of another time. Shaded by more than thirty tall maple trees, this twenty-five-room estate, with its seven fireplaces, was home to the Oliver families for more than 100 years. This is the largest bed and breakfast in South Bend and the only one on a one-acre estate with a carriage house and playhouse.

Guest rooms are beautifully decorated with several featuring a fireplace, private balcony and Jacuzzi for two. The richly appointed dining room is adorned with a Waterford crystal chandelier, sconces and fireplace. Large front porches and lawn swings are here for the relaxing.

Sandford House Bed and Breakfast

1026 Russell Street
Covington, Kentucky 41011
888-291-9133 • (606) 291-9133
E-mail: DanRRMiles@aol.com

Room Rates:	$55 – $95, including full breakfast. AARP discount.
Pet Charges or Deposits:	$5 per day. Refundable deposit. Manager's prior approval required.
Rated: 3 Paws 🐾 🐾 🐾	1 guest room and 3 suites. Refrigerators, microwaves, whirlpool.

T he Sandford House was built in the early 1820s and has served a variety of purposes over the last 175 years. Today, this elegant bed and breakfast is listed in the National Register. Originally, the house was of Federal design. After an upper-story fire in the 1880s, the appearance was changed to a Victorian style with mansard roof and a wing with a half-octagonal bay front.

Guest rooms include the Craft Room, which is elegant with a queen-sized bed, doll collection and a variety of art. The Garden Suite offers a whirlpool bath and original stone cooking fireplace. The living room overlooks the garden. The Penthouse is a cozy, furnished apartment with great views of the Cincinnati skyline, and the Carriage House is a self-contained building with two bedrooms, two baths, living/dining room and kitchen. A delicious full breakfast is served in the formal dining room or in the gazebo, which is in their award-winning garden.

Morning Glory Manor and Cottage

244 East Lexington Avenue
Danville, Kentucky 40422
(606) 236-1888
E-mail: jazzy@searnet.com

Room Rates:	$65 – $80, including continental breakfast.
Pet Charges or Deposits:	$5 per day. Manager's prior approval required. Sorry, no cats. Horse boarding available in barn, with box stalls at nearby Paradise Farms.
Rated: 3 Paws	2 guest rooms and 1 cottage.

Enjoy the peace and romance of this 1895 Queen Anne Victorian Manor within easy walking distance of historic downtown Danville. Within the Manor is a working studio for stained glass and jewelry.

Morning Glory Manor and Cottage, which is on the National Register of Historic Places, has the original cherry woodwork and staircase. Guest rooms overlook the private gardens and Victorian fountain. The private cottage is surrounded by lawns and gardens, offering one bedroom, living/dining room, kitchen and private bath. A continental breakfast, exercise room, library and use of washer/dryer are included.

Two dogs, Lexie and Sufie, are in residence, as well as a very large, sociable, pot-bellied pig, Guinevere.

Moors Resort and Marina

570 Moors Road
Gilbertsville, Kentucky 42044
800-626-5472 • (502) 362-8361
Web Site: www.moorsresort.com
E-mail: Moors@apex.net

Room Rates:	$45 – $245.
Pet Charges or Deposits:	$50 refundable deposit.
Rated: 3 Paws 🐾 🐾 🐾	24 guest rooms and 27 cottages with kitchens. Houseboat rentals and full-service marina. Pool and hot tubs. Restaurant.

 njoy log-cabin lodging, nestled on Buckhorn Bay at the spacious lodge. The large deck overlooking Kentucky Lake provides a front-row seat for one of the most beautiful sunsets you can imagine.

The Moors also offers lakeside cottages, duplexes and 4-plexes with a wide range of choices.

The fleet of Jamestowner Houseboat rentals includes all the comforts of home. Fuel-efficient motors provide economical power to experience more of Kentucky Lake. Houseboats sleep ten and feature air conditioners, VCRs, cellular phones and complete kitchens with 4-burner ranges, ovens, microwaves and refrigerators.

Farley Place Bed and Breakfast

166 Farley Place
Paducah, Kentucky 42003
(502) 442-2488

Room Rates:	$65 – $85, including full breakfast. AARP, AKC and ABA discounts.
Pet Charges or Deposits:	$10 per day. Refundable deposit.
Rated: 3 Paws	2 guest rooms and 1 suite. Toys and treats provided for your pet.

R ich in Civil War history, Farley Place was built in the early 1800s and survived the Civil War and General Grant's troops, who came looking for the Confederate flag. Surrounded by a traditional white picket fence, the landscaped yard has a quaint goldfish pond and an arbor swing.

This rambling Victorian home has been authentically renovated, with care taken to preserve its original charm. Period antiques and hardwood floors grace the interior rooms. The spacious sitting room, dining room and bedrooms have all been furnished to make you feel that you have truly stepped back in time.

Each morning awake to a breakfast of your liking.

Rose Hill Inn

233 Rose Hill Avenue
Versailles, Kentucky 40383
800-307-0460 • (606) 873-5957
Web Site: www.rosehillinn.com
E-mail: innkeepers@rosehillinn.com

Room Rates:	$75 – $99, including full breakfast.
Pet Charges or Deposits:	Manager's prior approval required. Sorry, no cats.
Rated: 3 Paws 🐾🐾🐾	4 guest rooms and 1 suite.

uilt in the early 1800s as one of the original estates in Versailles, and part of the Rose Hill Historic District, this lovely Inn was rumored to have been a hospital during the Civil War and a campground for both the North and the South.

The Inn has a large formal parlor, a relaxing library and a cozy second-floor sitting room, complete with guest refrigerator and microwave. Guest rooms are finely appointed with cherry furniture, four-poster beds, marble Jacuzzi and private porches, with a swing for cozy talks or casual reading.

Dewey Lake Bed and Breakfast

11811 Laird Road
Brooklyn, Michigan 49230
(517) 467-7122

Room Rates:	$55 – $72, including hearty breakfast.
Pet Charges or Deposits:	Birds welcome. Sorry, no cats or dogs. Manager's prior approval required. Call for deposits.
Rated: 3 Paws 🐾 🐾 🐾	5 guest rooms on 18 acres.

T his century-old home sits atop a knoll overlooking picturesque Dewey Lake, surrounded by eighteen acres of rolling land. Guests are encouraged to use some or all of the many amenities provided, including a paddleboat, canoe, grills, picnic tables, bonfires, horseshoes and croquet by the lakeshore.

The five guest rooms feature comfortable country Victorian decor. A large deck and glass-enclosed porch, with a view of the lake, provide a pleasant place to enjoy breakfast or just relax. Other common rooms include a parlor with a piano and a sitting room with a bay window overlooking the lake.

The Dewey Lake Bed and Breakfast is a relaxing, romantic getaway in the Irish Hills of southern Michigan. It brings back a time of lamplight and lace, love songs and flowers, picnics and sunsets.

Willow Brook Inn Bed and Breakfast

44255 Warren Road
Canton, Michigan 48187
888-454-1919 • (734) 454-0019

Room Rates:	$85 – $115, including full breakfast.
Pet Charges or Deposits:	Manager's prior approval required. Pets are not permitted in sleeping areas, but are kept in dog kennels downstairs.
Rated: 3 Paws 🐾🐾🐾	1 guest room and 2 suites on one acre. Dog run. Refrigerators, microwaves, whirlpool and hot tubs.

T he beautifully restored Willow Brook Inn sits on a wooded acre, through which Willow Brook winds and wanders. Originally built in 1929, this Arts and Crafts-style semi-bungalow has been updated, while maintaining its distinctive appeal.

Graceful country antiques, polished hardwood floors, local handicrafts and downy pastel quilts bestow a feeling of serenity. Childhood keepsakes grace each room to bring back fond, forgotten memories.

Breakfast is served in the "Teddy Bear" dining room or in the four-season sunroom, with tempting treats of home-baked breads and white chocolate raspberry scones, scrumptious egg dishes, squash griddle cakes and stuffed French toast.

Peaches Bed and Breakfast

29 Gay Avenue Southeast
Grand Rapids, Michigan 49503
(616) 454-8000
E-mail: peachesinn@aol.com

Room Rates:	$75, including full breakfast.
Pet Charges or Deposits:	$10 per day. Manager's prior approval required. Sorry, no cats.
Rated: 3 Paws 🐾 🐾 🐾	5 guest rooms.

T his beautiful Georgian Country Manor-style home, built in 1916, is in nearly original condition. Skylights of cathedral glass adorn the second-floor ceiling in the main foyer and open through the third-floor atrium to the roof.

There are five fireplaces and an extensive library, which includes bookcases with leaded glass doors. The former ballroom is now a game and TV area, complete with maple floor and original wall murals depicting the four seasons of sports in Michigan. The five guest bedrooms occupy the second floor.

A full buffet breakfast is served in the dining room each morning. Private dinners by a 4-star chef are available by reservation.

Harbor Springs Cottage Inn

145 Zoll Street
Harbor Springs, Michigan 49740
(616) 526 5431
Web Site: www.harborsprings-mi.com/cottage
E-mail: cottage@freeway.net

Room Rates:	$68 – $175, including continental breakfast. Senior discount.
Pet Charges or Deposits:	$5 per day.
Rated: 3 Paws 🐾🐾🐾	21 guest rooms and 3 suites with kitchens.

T his traditional, one-story inn offers the convenience of separate entrances and private baths with the warm bed and breakfast atmosphere, which includes breakfast treats and the morning newspaper. A variety of guest rooms offer brass beds with antiques, refrigerators and efficiency kitchens or full kitchens at affordable rates.

Unique shops and restaurants of Harbor Springs, the beach, the harbor and shoreline sights, the deer park and duck pond are all within an easy walk of the Inn. The two resident Harlequin Great Danes are always ready for a W-A-L-K and the iced tea is always cold.

White Rabbit Inn Bed and Breakfast

14634 Red Arrow Highway
Lakeside, Michigan 49116
800-967-2224 • (616) 469-4620
Web Site: www.whiterabbitinn.com
E-mail: info@whiterabbitinn.com

Room Rates:	$90 – $200, including continental breakfast.
Pet Charges or Deposits:	50% refundable deposit. Manager's prior approval required.
Rated: 4 Paws 🐾🐾🐾🐾	8 guest rooms and 2 cabins. Cabins include hot tubs, kitchens with microwaves and wood-burning stoves.

The White Rabbit, a small inn in Lakeside, Michigan, is located in the heart of Harbor Country, yet is less than 90 minutes from the hustle and bustle of downtown Chicago. Here you are surrounded by antique stores, art galleries, gourmet restaurants, majestic dunes, wooded trails and of course, Lake Michigan.

Guest rooms feature uniquely decorated rustic furniture of birch or willow, queen-sized beds, whirlpool baths and some rooms offer wood-burning fireplaces. The cabins are large and comfortable with skylights and log beam ceilings, with a private hot tub/spa on the deck outside.

Breakfast is served in the Lodge, an airy building with large picture windows overlooking the woods. Enjoy a hearty continental buffet while watching for deer, colorful wild birds or visiting with Bill, the extremely friendly orange cat.

Stacy Mansion Bed and Breakfast

710 West Chicago Boulevard
Tecumseh, Michigan 49286
800-891-8782 • (517) 423-6979
Web Site: www.lenawee.net/stacybnb

Room Rates:	$85 – $122, including full breakfast.
Pet Charges or Deposits:	$10 per day. Call for deposit.
Rated: 3 Paws 🐾🐾🐾	5 guest rooms with fireplaces.

The hosts and innkeepers of the Stacy Mansion surround you with pampered elegance of the Victorian era. The home is filled with fine antiques and features a library, a music room with a 160-year-old square grand piano and a grand parlor.

Guest rooms are beautifully appointed with fine furnishings, wood-burning fireplaces, fine linens with hand-embroidered pillow cases, large fluffy towels, down pillows and your morning wake-up tray at your door.

Lafayette Hotel

101 Front Street
Marietta, Ohio 45750
800-331-9336 • (740) 373-5522
Web Site: www.historiclafayette.com
E-mail: lafayette@ee.net

Room Rates:	$60 – $170. AAA, AARP, AKC and ABA discounts.
Pet Charges or Deposits:	$100 refundable deposit. Manager's prior approval required.
Rated: 3 Paws 🐾🐾🐾	78 guest rooms and 25 suites. Restaurant and lounge.

T he charm of Victorian elegance and hospitality awaits you when you visit Marietta and the Lafayette Hotel. One of four "historic hotels of America" in Ohio, the Lafayette is the home of the famous restaurant, the Gun Room, and the Riverview Lounge.

The dining room features fresh steaks, seafood and regional fare served in a riverboat theme, appointed with an antique gun collection. After dinner, head to the Riverview Lounge for cordials while overlooking the confluence of the Ohio and Muskingum Rivers.

Pitzer-Cooper House Bed and Breakfast

6019 White Chapel Road Southeast
Newark, Ohio 43056
800-833-9536 • (740) 323-2680
Web Site: www.pitzercooper.com
E-mail: mail@pitzercooper.com

Room Rates:	$45 – $120, including full breakfast.
Pet Charges or Deposits:	One night's rate as refundable deposit. Manager's prior approval required. Dogs kept in kennels, not in the house. Sorry, no cats.
Rated: 3 Paws	2 guest rooms and 1 suite. Bicycles available.

S ituated in the gently rolling farmland of Licking Township, the Pitzer-Cooper House Bed and Breakfast is a step back into a quieter, simpler time. This authentically restored 1858 country home is listed on the National Register of Historic Places.

Six-panel doors, wide moldings and winding cherry staircases are some of the original architectural features, combined with antique furnishings and quilts throughout the large rooms and common areas.

Guests are encouraged to relax on the porch swings, explore the perennial flower and herb garden and enjoy the tranquillity of the rural setting. Delicious healthful breakfasts feature fresh fruits and specialty breads.

Woodfield Suites

3730 West College Avenue
Appleton, Wisconsin 54914
800-338-0008 • (920) 734-7777

Room Rates:	$90 – $150, including continental breakfast and complimentary cocktails. AARP discount.
Pet Charges or Deposits:	$50 refundable deposit. Manager's prior approval required.
Rated: 3 Paws 🐾 🐾 🐾	98 guest suites with refrigerators, microwaves, pool, fitness center, steam room, hot tubs.

T he spacious Woodfield Suites includes microwaves, refrigerators, wet bars, hair dryers and TV/VCRs. Room configurations vary to accommodate families and couples traveling together.

An indoor pool, whirlpool, steam room, sauna, fitness center, playland, video games, Ping Pong tables and pool table are available for all guests. Complimentary continental breakfast and evening cocktails are included in your room rate. Guest laundry and valet dry-cleaning are available.

Mielke-Mauk House

W 977 Highway F
Campbellsport, Wisconsin 53010
(920) 533-8602

Room Rates:	$90 – $130, including continental breakfast.
Pet Charges or Deposits:	Manager's prior approval required. Sorry, no cats.
Rated: 3 Paws 🐾🐾🐾	4 guest rooms. Microwaves, refrigerators.

T his cozy 1860s Norwegian log house has bedrooms with private baths, a living room with wood stove/fireplace and porches overlooking the lake. The polished wooden floors, antiques, country quilts and Scandinavian decor provide a romantic setting.

Located on Kettle Moraine Lake, one hour north of Milwaukee, it's a place where sports enthusiasts can enjoy cross-country and downhill skiing, fishing and water-skiing, golf and horseback riding. The area is a mecca for biking and hiking enthusiasts.

Edgewater Inn and Resort

5054 Highway 70 West
Eagle River, Wisconsin 54521
888-334-3987 • (715) 479-4011
Web Site: www.edgeinn.com
E-mail: edgewater@edgeinn.com

Room Rates:	$39 – $59, including continental breakfast. AAA and AARP discounts.
Pet Charges or Deposits:	Manager's prior approval required.
Rated: 3 Paws 🐾 🐾 🐾	12 guest rooms and 6 cottages on 5 acres. Waterfront views, fully stocked kitchens, enclosed porches.

T he Edgewater Inn is located half a mile west of downtown Eagle River. You are only minutes away from the Nicolet National Forest and thousands of lakes, not to mention fine restaurants, golf courses, tennis, canoeing, riding stables and historical boat rides. The area is noted for hundreds of miles of hiking and biking trails. The fun doesn't end in the summer — winter offers snowshoeing, scenic cross-country skiing and world-famous snowmobile trails.

The Edgewater sits on more than 5 acres, with a professional volleyball court, basketball court, waterfront beach and kids' play area. An expanded continental breakfast is served each morning on the outdoor verandah.

Harbor House Inn

12666 Highway 42
Gills Rock, Wisconsin 54210
(920) 854-8796

Room Rates:	$84 – $125, including continental breakfast.
Pet Charges or Deposits:	$10 per day.
Rated: 3 Paws 🐾🐾🐾	12 guest rooms, 1 suite and 2 cottages. Refrigerators, microwaves, spa.

arbor House is located across from Weborg's Wharf in the quaint fishing village of Gills Rock, on the northern tip of Door County. This is a great place to kick back on the private beach and enjoy the colorful sunsets over the harbor and bluffs of the Green Bay waters.

With more than 90 years of history, the inn is thoughtfully restored, with guest rooms tastefully done in period furniture. All offer private baths and most have refrigerators and microwaves.

Each morning an inviting continental breakfast is served either in the sitting room in front of the fireplace, in the gazebo or on one of the many decks overlooking the fishing harbor.

Ross' Teal Lake Lodge and Teal Wind Golf Club

12425 North Ross Road
Hayward, Wisconsin 54843
(714) 462-3631
Web Site: www.rossteal.com
E-mail: rossteal@win.bright.net

Room Rates:	$84 – $110.
Pet Charges or Deposits:	$5 per pet per day.
Rated: 4 Paws 🐾🐾🐾🐾	Vacation homes from 1-room studios to 3-bedroom houses. Pool. Call for specific information.

 elax, revive and renew yourself in the recreation offered in nature's playground on the water and in the woods. Ross' is primarily a three-season resort (mid-May to late October). On the water you can fish, boat, swim or just relax to the sound of lapping water as the sun sets. On land there's golf, hiking, biking, cross-country skiing and snowshoeing.

The old main lodge, built of huge tamarack logs, is the classic heart and soul of this traditional resort. Casual and comfortable in style, you'll be able to feel the passage of four generations of guests and owners. The accommodations are delightfully designed to assure comfort and relaxation. The roomy screen porches overlook the lake. Many of the cabins feature fireplaces, their own boat docks and marvelous lake views.

Radisson Hotel La Crosse

200 Harborview Plaza
La Crosse, Wisconsin 54601
800-333-3333 • (608) 784-6680

Room Rates:	$89 – $149, some rates include continental breakfast. AAA and AARP discounts.
Pet Charges or Deposits:	None.
Rated: 3 Paws	170 guest rooms. Indoor pool, exercise room, jogging paths, whirlpool, two restaurants.

The Radisson Hotel La Crosse is located downtown, directly across from Riverside Park and the Mississippi River. Convenient to shopping and entertainment, the hotel features an indoor pool, health club and whirlpool.

Each of the spacious guest rooms features spectacular scenic views of the city, bluff and river. A concierge welcomes you each day with a complimentary breakfast, newspaper and even hors d'oeuvres.

Overlooking the river, the Boatworks Restaurant is one of La Crosse's most popular dining spots. The menu is a tribute to seasonal American cuisine. Live entertainment, hearty buffets and a variety of ethnic dishes are found at the Haberdashery Restaurant.

Ty-Bach Bed and Breakfast

3104 Simpson Lane
Lac du Flambeau, Wisconsin 54538
(715) 588-7851

Room Rates:	$65 – $75, including full breakfast. Seventh night free.
Pet Charges or Deposits:	One night's refundable deposit.
Rated: 3 Paws 🐾 🐾 🐾	2 guest rooms. Refrigerator, hot tub.

 ocated on a Chippewa Indian reservation, this modern home is perched on the shores of a tranquil north woods lake. Surrounded by eighty-five acres of woods, the Ty-Bach Bed and Breakfast is a relaxing getaway any time of the year.

The secluded home is tastefully decorated and offers a separate guest area, a large living area and a patio that opens onto a small deck overlooking the lake. A full breakfast is served each morning.

T.C. Smith Inn

865 Main Street
Lake Geneva, Wisconsin 53147
800-423-0233 • (414) 248-1097
Web Site: www.wwte.com/tcinn.htm

Room Rates: $115 – $350, including full breakfast buffet.
Pet Charges or Deposits: $100 refundable deposit. Sorry, no cats.
Rated: 5 Paws 🐾 🐾 🐾 🐾 🐾 6 guest rooms and 2 suites.

The T.C. Smith mansion, built in 1845 as a private home, is today an elegant bed and breakfast inn located in the heart of downtown Lake Geneva. Its proprietors graciously open the massive carved wood doors to all who seek to experience the luxurious warmth and ambiance of the Grand Victorian era.

This award-winning inn offers eight elegant, sunlit rooms and suites. Each comfortable guest room is fully appointed, many with wood-carved fireplaces. All rooms have private baths, and several offer large whirlpools. Is it any wonder that the T.C. Smith Inn has achieved a reputation as the discriminating Chicagoland getaway?

Be sure to explore the courtyard, where you will be treated to brilliant floral Victorian period gardens replete with neoclassic statuettes, a goldfish pond, water garden and quiet benches. The Inn is a genuine oasis in the center of downtown Lake Geneva.

Sunrise Lodge

5894 West Shore
Land O' Lakes, Wisconsin 54540
800-221-9689 • (715) 547-3684

Room Rates: $39 – $98.
Pet Charges or Deposits: Manager's prior approval required.
Rated: 3 Paws   75 guest rooms and 25 cottages.

Easily one of the best places for a family vacation in northern Wisconsin, this four-season recreational resort is located in the Nicolet National Forest in Wisconsin. Sunrise Lodge is perched on 750 feet of lakeshore property, offering a wide assortment of activities for the entire family.

The newly irrigated Land O'Lakes golf fairways make a popular 9-hole course. Horseback riding is a pleasure on the Eagle River and Conover. Bike, jog or walk the Sunrise Nature Fitness Trail and explore the Nicolet Forest. Antique shops, unique gift stores and craft shows are all close by. In the winter there are snowmobiles, skiing and ice fishing.

Gilman Street Rag

125 East Gilman Street
Madison, Wisconsin 53703
(608) 257-6560
Web Site: www.hawkhill.com/gilmanbb.html

Room Rates:	$70 – $90, including continental breakfast.
Pet Charges or Deposits:	None.
Rated: 3 Paws	2 guest rooms with cable TV and refrigerators.

T his classic 1885 Queen Anne Victorian house on Mansion Hill in Madison is furnished with antiques, unusual art work and book collections. Each guest room has an ample writing and reading table, a full closet, a 51-channel color TV and air conditioning for hot summer nights.

Breakfast is served in the sunny solarium, kitchen and dining room overlooking the backyard garden. The Inn is located near a mix of shops, restaurants, coffee houses and the new Frank Lloyd Wright Convention Center, Monona Terrace, overlooking Lake Monona.

52 Stafford

52 Stafford Street
P.O. Box 217
Plymouth, Wisconsin 53073
800-421-4667 • (920) 893-0552
Web Site: www.classicinns.com

Room Rates:	$80 – $130, including continental breakfast on weekdays and full breakfast on weekends.
Pet Charges or Deposits:	None.
Rated: 4 Paws	19 guest rooms.

his Irish guest house is in Plymouth, in the heart of the Kettle Moraine area. The 1892 building was originally a hotel and is now listed on the National Register of Historic Places.

Guest rooms are plushly appointed, with queen-sized four-poster beds, reading chairs, floral wallpaper and custom carpeting. Brass chandeliers, English highboy dressers, writing desks, and green-shaded reading lamps complete the luxurious yet comfortable setting. Whirlpool baths and cable television add modern conveniences to Old World charm.

A relaxing glass of Guinness stout or Irish whiskey can be had in the 52 Stafford Pub. Etched windows, a cherrywood bar, and green-and-white tiled floor create a European ambiance. The restaurant features excellent fresh food.

Just-N-Trails Country Inn

7452 Kathryn Avenue
Sparta, Wisconsin 54656
800-488-4521 • (608) 269-4522
Web Site: www.justintrails.com
E-mail: justintrailsbb@centuryinter.net

Room Rates:	$80 – $300, including full breakfast.
Pet Charges or Deposits:	$10 per day.
Rated: 4 Paws 🐾🐾🐾🐾	1 guest suite and 3 cabins on 200 acres. Refrigerators, microwaves, whirlpool.

 ust-N-Trails is a third-generation dairy farm that has been in the Justin family since 1914. The diversification into the farm vacation business began with the opening of the Nordic Ski Center, set amidst the scenic, wooded hills and valleys of southwestern Wisconsin.

The quaint 1920s farmhouse is supplemented by three private luxury cottages, with all the comforts of a fine bed and breakfast. Guest rooms feature fluffy pillows, Laura Ashley linens, hand-crafted country decor and daily maid service. Private log cabins offer queen-sized, hand-crafted beds, double whirlpool tubs, gas fireplaces and a porch or deck.

Awake each morning to a full breakfast of homemade muffins, granola, yogurt, fresh fruit, a baked entrée, gourmet coffee and tea.

Lark Inn

229 North Superior Avenue
Tomah, Wisconsin 54660
800-447-LARK • (608) 372-5981

Room Rates:	$55 – $80, including continental breakfast. AAA and AARP discounts.
Pet Charges or Deposits:	$5 per day.
Rated: 3 Paws 🐾🐾🐾	19 guest rooms and 6 suites.

I mpressive with its gambrel roofs, dormer windows and country porches, the Lark Inn has sheltered travelers since the turn of the century, when it consisted of several log cabins. Nestled in the heart of Tomah, Wisconsin, the Inn is an easy stroll from antique shops, museums, craft shops and fine dining. Explore the surrounding Amish community, the Mississippi River Valley near La Crosse or the scenic Wisconsin Dells area while based here.

The beds in the private log cabins, luxury suites and comfortable guest rooms snuggle under handmade quilts. A complimentary continental breakfast of homemade cinnamon rolls, assorted Danish pastries, hot coffee and fresh juice is served each morning.

Tutwiler Hotel

2021 Park Place North
Birmingham, Alabama 35203
800-845-1787 • (205) 322-2100
E-mail: grandheritage@wyndham.com

Room Rates: $89 – $172. AAA, AARP, AKC and ABA discounts.
Pet Charges or Deposits: None.
Rated: 4 Paws 🐾🐾🐾🐾 95 guest rooms and 52 spacious suites furnished with antiques, rich fabrics and marble bathrooms; with complimentary morning paper and shoe shine, health club facilities, 2 award-winning restaurants and cocktail lounge.

An Alabama tradition since 1914, the award-winning Tutwiler Hotel offers luxury, history and Southern hospitality amid the glass and steel office towers and tourist attractions of Birmingham's vibrant downtown area. History buffs and leisure travelers visit the eight-story red brick building to experience a bygone era when Warren G. Harding was president, Charles Lindbergh was an international hero and Will Rogers was a premier stage performer.

This historic four-star hotel features 147 guest rooms and suites and is furnished with original antiques, intricate masonry work, carved oak chandeliers and original marble tiles. Enjoy an extra touch of luxury on the Heritage Executive Level, featuring a private executive floor with an exclusive lounge for breakfast and cocktails. Guests are invited to take advantage of the health club facilities, where you can work out on state-of-the-art equipment.

Christian's Restaurant — winner of numerous accolades, including being named among the Top 25 Restaurants in the Country by Best of the Best Dining Awards — features a menu combining the tastes of Europe, the Southeast and Alabama. The restaurant has also been recognized for serving 30 different varieties of domestic and imported red and white wines by the glass.

Marcella's Tea Room and Inn

114 Fairhope Avenue
Fairhope, Alabama 36532
(334) 990-8520

Room Rates:	$85 – $150, including full breakfast, evening wine and snacks.
Pet Charges or Deposits:	$42.50 refundable deposit.
Rated: 4 Paws 🐾 🐾 🐾 🐾	2 guest rooms and a 3-bedroom cottage.

N estled amid giant, moss-laden live oak trees is the charming town of Fairhope. Located only minutes from Mobile and Pensacola, the town sits atop a scenic bluff overlooking a wide stretch of Mobile Bay. This unforgettable, small Southern town is home to Marcella's Tea Room and Inn. Located just one block from the shops of town, this historical home will entice you to sit a spell on its large, welcoming front porch.

Inside the inn, you will be surrounded by a combination of true Southern hospitality and elegance. A warm atmosphere is prevalent throughout this lovingly decorated home with its antique-filled living and dining rooms, inviting sun room and the two cozy bedrooms with brass and iron beds, lace chintz curtains and private baths.

Your complimentary gourmet breakfast of fresh crêpes with berry sauce, crystal dishes of colorful pears, kiwi and grapes topped with cream sauce, served on heirloom china with sterling silver flatware, will give an elegant start to your day. Be sure to stop by Marcella's Tea Room after your day of sightseeing for a cup of tea. In the evening, guests are invited to enjoy a glass of wine.

Mentone Springs Hotel Bed and Breakfast

6114 Alabama Highway 117
Mentone, Alabama 35984
(205) 634-4040

Room Rates:	$54 – $69, including full breakfast.
Pet Charges or Deposits:	None.
Rated: 3 Paws 🐾 🐾 🐾	9 guest rooms, some with fireplaces and private baths, claw-foot tubs, library room, exercise room, large porch and afternoon tea, resident dog.

Mentone means "musical mountain spring." In 1884, Dr. Frank Caldwell of Pennsylvania visited the local mountain while ill and was restored to health after drinking the mineral spring water. He soon took up permanent residence at Mentone, where he established a health spa called The Mentone Springs Hotel. His first guests came for the curative effects of the mineral springs, to enjoy nature walks and to play croquet on the lawn.

This three-story Queen Anne Victorian has passed through many hands since then. It's now being restored to its original grandeur. Today's guest will find an 1,800-square-foot ballroom, nine guest rooms, some with fireplaces and private baths with claw-foot tubs, and a huge porch where guests may partake of afternoon tea and relax.

For recreation, croquet is still played on the lawn, or you and your dog can venture out to one of the nearby parks. The inn's restaurant, Caldwells, named after the original owner of the inn, is open six days a week.

Grace Hall Bed and Breakfast Inn

506 Lauderdale Street
Selma, Alabama 36701
(334) 875-5744

Room Rates:	$69 – $99, including full breakfast.
Pet Charges or Deposits:	$10 per stay. Manager's prior approval required. Small dogs only.
Rated: 5 Paws 🐾 🐾 🐾 🐾 🐾	6 guest rooms with private baths, furnished in period antiques, with large courtyard and double parlors. Treats and food are available for pets.

Grace Hall Bed and Breakfast Inn was built in 1857 by Henry Ware and was occupied by the Evans, Baker and Jones families for 110 years. The home was then given to the local Historical Society, which spent five years restoring it to its original grandeur. This ante-bellum mansion mixes elements of the older neoclassicism with the newer Victorian trends. Now on the National Register, Grace Hall is once again a prominent part of the community.

The elegant rooms with crystal chandeliers, wooden plank floors and large oil paintings welcome you to relax by the fire or join in conversation with other guests. This ante-bellum mansion offers six exquisitely decorated guest rooms with private baths, furnished in period antiques, lush draperies, plush upholstery and elegant bedding. Each guest room opens onto the landscaped courtyard.

Dreamspinner Bed and Breakfast

117 Diedrich Street
Eustis, Florida 32726
888-479-1229 • (352) 589-8082

Room Rates:	$105 – $150, including full breakfast, afternoon English tea and evening wine and cheese.
Pet Charges or Deposits:	$25 per stay. $50 refundable deposit.
Rated: 4 Paws	5 guest rooms with flowers, fresh fruit, bottled water, hot coffee and a newspaper delivered to your room.

A wraparound porch welcomes you to this charming bed and breakfast and its surrounding gardens filled with moss-laden oaks and romantically shaded benches and ponds. Antique roses, camellias and azaleas embellish over an acre of grounds. Elegant English fabrics adorn the well-appointed rooms. Art, antiques and fireplaces provide an eclectic, comfortable setting.

The historical integrity of the Dreamspinner has been maintained along with modern amenities for your comfort. The Victorian house, now called the Dreamspinner, was built in 1881. The kitchen and servants' quarters were originally separated from the main house by a breezeway, which now connects the two dwellings.

Your day will begin with a generous breakfast of homemade breads, jams and freshly brewed coffee. In the afternoon enjoy traditional English tea, followed later by wine and cheese each evening. Relax and enjoy the peace and tranquillity, or venture to nearby attractions such as Disney World, golf, tennis, antique shopping, fishing, horseback riding, or a visit to the Ocala National Forest.

Center Court – Historic Inn and Cottages

916 Center Street
Key West, Florida 33040
800-797-8787 • (305) 296-9292
E-mail: centerct@aol.com

Room Rates:	$78 – $298, including deluxe continental breakfast.
Pet Charges or Deposits:	$10. Manager's prior approval required.
Rated: 5 Paws 🐾🐾🐾🐾🐾	4 cottages and 10 suites with private bathrooms, some efficiency kitchens, televisions, ceiling fans, telephones, hair dryers, air-conditioning, heated pool, Jacuzzi, European-style sun deck, fish pond and exercise pavilion.

True to its name, Center Court is located on Center Street in one of Key West's oldest and most charming neighborhoods. Just half a block from the celebrated sights and sounds of Duval Street — many of the island's finest restaurants, art galleries and shops are neighbors here. Winner of two historical renovation awards for the buildings, the interiors have been decorated with original and unique local art. The same attention to detail and care have been given to landscaping. Lush tropical foliage laden with fruit and blooming with the vibrant colors of the Caribbean provide a year-round welcome.

Each of the accommodations at Center Court is as diverse as the cottages themselves. Every room is air-conditioned, with amenities generally reserved for resorts, such as a heated pool, relaxing Jacuzzi, European-style sun deck and exercise pavilion. All suites and cottages have private yards to accommodate your pet.

Whispers

409 William Street
Key West, Florida 33040
800-856-SHHH • (305) 294-5969
E-mail: whispersbb@aol.com

Room Rates:	$85 – $175, including gourmet breakfast.
Pet Charges or Deposits:	None.
Rated 4 Paws 🐾 🐾 🐾 🐾	8 guest rooms with private bath, air conditioning, television and refrigerator, hot tub. Private beach and pool club included.

The house, listed on the National Register of Historic Places, sits on a sleepy, shaded street within view of the Gulf harbor, and is surrounded by a thirty-block historic district of distinctive 19th century buildings.

Today, ceiling fans whirl above rooms filled with antique furnishings, and congenial guests enjoy the cool porches and lush gardens at one of the island's most unique inns. A full membership at a nearby spa resort is included in your room rate, offering the use of a sauna, steam room, free weights, exercise equipment, pool and private beach.

A full and varied gourmet breakfast, such as lemon dill omelets, honey-maple ham and hot croissants topped with freshly sliced strawberries, is served daily throughout the year, and can be enjoyed either in the dining area or in the tropical gardens.

Chalet Suzanne Country Inn and Restaurant

3800 Chalet Suzanne Drive
Lake Wales, Florida 33853-7060
800-433-6011 • (941) 676-6011
Web Site: www.chaletsuzanne.com

Room Rates:	$139 – $195, including full breakfast. AAA discount.
Pet Charges or Deposits:	$20 per pet. Call for deposit.
Rated: 4 Paws 🐾🐾🐾🐾	30 guest rooms with private baths, private entrances, air conditioning, cable color television, swimming pool, beautifully landscaped grounds with a lake, private airstrip, award-winning restaurant and cocktail lounge.

Surrounded by a 70-acre estate, the family-owned Chalet Suzanne Country Inn and Restaurant has been welcoming guests since 1931. This delightful inn of 30 rooms is a gracious oasis amid the excitement of Central Florida attractions.

Each room greets you with a different decor, through a private entrance by either courtyard or patio. Every corner of the inn glows with the charm of stained glass, antiques and old lamps from faraway places.

Chalet Suzanne has earned a glowing reputation for its cuisine. Gourmet Magazine called it "glorious." Meals are served in the unique setting of five quaint rooms located on several levels, overlooking the lake. The Soup Cannery is where the inn's delicious soups are processed and shipped all over the world. The soups have even been to the moon.

Riviera Beach Resort

5451 Gulf of Mexico Drive
Longboat Key, Florida 34228
(941) 383-2552
E-mail: riviera@longboatkey.net

Room Rates:	$500 – $1,075 per week.
Pet Charges or Deposits:	$10 per day. $50 refundable deposit. Small dogs only. Manager's prior approval required. Sorry, no cats.
Rated: 4 Paws 🐾 🐾 🐾 🐾	9 apartments with fully equipped kitchens, separate living areas, color television, air conditioning and heating, private patio, landscaped tropical gardens, private beach, shuffleboard court, barbecue grill, swimming, fishing and laundry facilities.

L ocated on its own private white sand beach in the Gulf of Mexico is the Riviera Beach Resort — one of the most secluded tropical beach settings on Longboat Key.

Spacious apartments overlook tropical gardens and calm blue waters, offering you a choice of one- or two-bedroom apartments with fully equipped kitchens. Each apartment offers the privacy of your own palm-shaded patio, complete with lounge chairs and barbecue.

Shops and gourmet restaurants beckon only a short walk away from the Riviera's tranquillity. Or stay on the beach and listen to the surf as you barbecue on the beach grill.

Club Hotel by DoubleTree

1101 Northwest 57th Avenue
Miami, Florida 33126
888-444-CLUB • (305) 266-0000

Room Rates:	$59 – $135, including complimentary in-room breakfast. AAA, AARP, AKC and ABA discounts.
Pet Charges or Deposits:	$10 per day.
Rated: 3 Paws	264 guest rooms and 2 spacious suites with in-room movies, cable television, some with microwaves, refrigerators, VCRs, laundry facilities, self-service business center, jogging trails, pet exercise area, pool, restaurant and cocktail lounge.

W hen combining business with pleasure on your next trip to Miami, the Club Hotel by DoubleTree offers accommodations that are both business and pet-friendly. Upon check-in you will receive the traditional DoubleTree greeting of two chocolate chip cookies.

Business travelers will appreciate the new "Club Room," a 7,000-square-foot multi-purpose work space allowing business travelers an office on the road. This 24-hour business center has quiet, private work spaces with a desk, bookshelves, electrical outlets, modem ports and a sliding door for privacy.

The Au Bon Pain Bakery Café is open from early morning to late at night with freshly baked food, made on the premises to serve you quickly. Menu selections include soups, salads, sandwiches, croissants, muffins and a variety of beverages.

Fontainebleau Hilton Resort and Towers

4441 Collins Avenue
Miami Beach, Florida 33140
800-548-8886 • (305) 538-2000

Room Rates:	$149 – $255, including continental breakfast.
Pet Charges or Deposits:	None.
Rated: 4 Paws 🐾 🐾 🐾 🐾	1,206 guest rooms and 60 luxury suites, turndown service, in-room safe, iron and ironing board, beach access, saunas, steam rooms, whirlpools, 2 swimming pools (1 heated and 1 saltwater), health club, 7 lighted tennis courts, restaurants, coffee shops and cocktail lounge.

S et among twenty acres of lush tropical gardens overlooking the Atlantic Ocean on Miami Beach is the Fontainebleau Hilton Resort and Towers.

The hotel offers recreational activities for guests of all ages. There are two magnificent outdoor pools — one is a freeform half-acre rock grotto with a cascading waterfall into a fresh water pool. There are also three whirlpool baths, seven lighted tennis courts, parasailing, paddle boats, hobie cats, boogie boards, hydro sleds, volleyball, basketball and two miles of beach. Spa facilities and state-of-the-art fitness and cardiovascular equipment are available as well.

The Fontainebleau Hilton offers award-winning dining and a wide variety of entertainment.

Ocean Front Hotel

1230-38 Ocean Drive
Miami Beach, Florida 33139
800-783-1725 • (305) 672-2579

Room Rates: $135 – $475, including continental breakfast.
Pet Charges or Deposits: $15 per day. Manager's prior approval required.
Rated: 5 Paws 🐾 🐾 🐾 🐾 🐾 8 guest rooms and 21 luxury suites, many with ocean views
                        and balconies, private in-room safe, color television, VCR,
                        stereo with CD player, wet bar with refrigerator, central air
                        conditioning, beach towels, bathrobes, rooms with private
                        Jacuzzis, concierge service, restaurant and lounge.

L ocated in the heart of Miami Beach's world-renowned art deco district, just steps from the beautiful white sand beaches of the warm Atlantic Ocean is the exquisite Ocean Front Hotel.

The hotel's accommodations are delightfully decorated with a Mediterranean theme, complete with authentic furnishings from the 1930s. Each guest room offers a private in-room safe, color television, VCR, stereo with CD player, wet bar with refrigerator, soundproof windows, beach towels, bathrobes and central air conditioning. Many rooms have balconies with breathtaking ocean or courtyard views. For those choosing one of the penthouse suites, not only will you have wonderful ocean views from your private balcony, but the added bonus of a whirlpool tub and a private elevator.

While staying at the Ocean Front Hotel, be sure to sample some of the fine cuisine at the hotel's brasserie-style Les Deux Fontaines French Restaurant, which has a casual atmosphere and impeccable service.

Chesterfield Hotel

363 Cocoanut Row
Palm Beach, Florida 33480
800-243-7871 • (561) 659-5800
E-mail: ChesterPB@aol.com

Room Rates:	$229 – $1,099. AAA and AARP discounts.
Pet Charges or Deposits:	$150 refundable deposit. Dogs up to 40 lbs. Sorry, no cats.
Rated: 5 Paws	43 guest rooms and 11 luxury suites. Heated swimming pool, private cabaña, whirlpool, health club privileges, restaurant and cocktail lounge. Biscuits upon check-in. Pet beds available.

L ocated in the heart of Palm Beach, just off Worth Avenue, is the historic four-star Chesterfield Hotel. The elegant surroundings are an impressive blend of modern conveniences with the gracious standards of the Third Earl of Chesterfield, offering an uncompromised level of comfort and service.

The beautifully appointed accommodations have distinctive styles, specially chosen fabrics, elegant furnishings, deluxe marble bathrooms. Amenities include plush dressing robes, fine soaps, bottled mineral water and 24-hour room service.

The Chesterfield Hotel is located only three short blocks from the beach. The hotel's heated swimming pool, spa and private cabaña offer you a tropical setting in which to relax from dusk 'til dawn.

Heart of Palm Beach Hotel

160 Royal Palm Way
Palm Beach, Florida 33480
800-523-5377 • (561) 655-5600

Room Rates:	$69 – $219. AAA, AARP, AKC and ABA discounts.
Pet Charges or Deposits:	Credit card as deposit. Manager's prior approval required.
Rated: 4 Paws	88 guest rooms and 2 suites with balcony or terrace, mini refrigerator, concierge service, limousine and bicycle rentals, underground parking, heated pool, restaurant and cocktail lounge.

A warm and friendly atmosphere welcomes you at the Heart of Palm Beach Hotel, a charming European-style hotel. Located in the heart of the island, on the ocean block of picturesque Royal Palm Way, you are only steps away from the beautiful blue Atlantic Ocean.

Your spacious accommodations will include such amenities as a refrigerator, color television and a balcony or terrace to enjoy the view. The pool is set in a delightful tropical setting, next to a garden pavilion.

There are world-famous Worth Avenue shops to keep you entertained, as well as the enchanting "Vias" dotted with boutiques and antique stores. The hotel is located within walking distance of many fine restaurants and area night life, or try the hotel's own Pleasant Peasant Restaurant and the Taps and Tapas Lounge, a popular spot to enjoy your favorite libation.

Banana Bay Club

8254 Midnight Pass Road
Sarasota, Florida 34242
888-6-BANBAY • (941) 346-0113

Room Rates: $90 – $220; weekly and monthly rates available.
Pet Charges or Deposits: $100 refundable deposit.
Rated: 4 Paws 🐾🐾🐾🐾   7 one- or two-bedroom apartments with fully equipped
                         kitchens, all linens provided, remote control color cable televi-
                         sion, air conditioning, ceiling fans, laundry facilities, barbecue
                         grills, swimming pool, bikes and boats available.

I f you are looking for a tropical getaway with swaying palm trees, flowering hibiscus and chirping birds, the Banana Bay Club offers all of that
and more. This private paradise has five ground-floor guest rooms, fully
furnished garden apartments, a studio apartment and a house overlooking the
tranquil Heron Lagoon.

Everything is provided for you. Each unit has its own vibrant, Caribbean
color scheme, is charmingly furnished, has a fully equipped kitchen, supplies
all of your linens, beach chairs and its own private deck. There is also an inviting pool with relaxing spa jets, a canoe for exploring the lagoon, a rowboat for
fishing and bicycles to explore the island.

Located a short distance from the resort is the world-famous white-sugar-
sand beach, where sand sculpturing is an art, as well as the less crowded Turtle
Beach. The aqua-colored waters of the Gulf are great for fishing, swimming and
snorkeling.

Turtle Beach Resort

9049 Midnight Pass Road
Siesta Key, Florida 34242
(941) 349-4554
Web Site: www.sarasota-online.com/turtle
E-mail: grubi@ix.netcom.com

Room Rates:	$120 – $280; weekly rates available. AAA discount.
Pet Charges or Deposits:	10% of room rate as deposit on large dogs only. Manager's prior approval required.
Rated: 4 Paws 🐾🐾🐾🐾	2 guest rooms and 3 suites with fully equipped kitchens with microwaves and coffee makers, honor bars, telephones, color cable television, air conditioning, private hot tubs and patios, laundry facilities, daily maid service available, paddle boats, fishing rods, beach chairs, bicycles, gazebo, room service and docking facilities.

T urtle Beach Resort is a small, Key West-style resort located on the south end of the island, where the large sea turtles nest. There are spectacular views of the Gulf of Mexico and room to dock your boat. You can fish off the pier, go paddle boating, bike along the shoreline, or head into Siesta Village to browse through shops. For those seeking solitude with a good book, a hammock and warm breeze await.

Guest villas are one or two bedrooms. All are equipped with a kitchen area, an enclosed private patio with outdoor spa and a barbecue grill. The larger units have a living and dining room. Lush landscape surrounds you while you enjoy a swim in the outdoor heated pool. Banana trees, giant elephant ear and red hibiscus plants grow unchecked in the warm climate.

Steinhatchee Landing Resort and Inn

Highway 51 North
P.O. Box 789
Steinhatchee, Florida 32359
800-584-1709 • (352) 498-3513
E-mail: sli@dixie.4easy.com

Room Rates:	$120 – $280; weekly and monthly rates available. AAA, AARP, AKC and ABA discounts.
Pet Charges or Deposits:	$250 refundable deposit.
Rated: 4 Paws 🐾 🐾 🐾 🐾	17 spacious suites, many with fully equipped kitchens and separate living areas; 20 Victorian-style cottages with fully equipped kitchens, fireplaces, spas, whirlpool baths, health club, river views and private docks, in a wooded setting on or near the river.

T he Steinhatchee area has been a favorite destination for those who enjoy the beauty of the great outdoors. Some of the best fresh water and saltwater fishing in the nation takes place here. Great care has been taken to preserve the rustic beauty of this wooded river setting. There are gazebos and footbridges scattered throughout, providing guests with peaceful places to relax in tranquil surroundings.

The Steinhatchee Landing Resort and Inn offers the choice of a spacious suite or a private Victorian cottage, set amongst the beautiful Spanish-moss-draped oak trees.

Hundreds of miles of old wooded Indian trails are here for you to hike or bicycle, and there is swimming, horseback riding and bird watching.

Royal Palm House Bed and Breakfast

3215 Spruce Avenue
West Palm Beach, Florida 33407
800-655-3196 • (561) 863-9836
E-mail: royalpalmhouse@compuserve.com

Room Rates:	$75 – $150, including continental breakfast.
Pet Charges or Deposits:	$5 per day. $25 refundable deposit. Small pets only. Manager's prior approval required.
Rated: 3 Paws	3 guest rooms and 3 suites with private baths, air conditioning, spacious grounds with freeform pool.

T he Royal Palm House Bed and Breakfast was built in 1925, during the West Palm Beach land boom. This tropical Dutch Colonial-style home features single guest rooms and suites with private baths.

Each room has its own unique style of furnishing and atmosphere. The spacious grounds are planted with lush tropical vegetation which surrounds the lovely freeform swimming pool. It is a great place to relax and sun bathe.

The West Palm Beach area is located on Florida's "Gold Coast," named for the gold salvaged from shipwrecks off the coast. Besides having some of the most beautiful beaches in the world, there are numerous theaters and playhouses, Worth Avenue for shopping, plus numerous golf courses, tennis courts, croquet clubs and polo fields here.

Pathway Inn Bed and Breakfast

501 South Lee Street
Americus, Georgia 31709
800-889-1466 • (912) 928-2078
E-mail: pathway@sowega.net

Room Rates:	$70 – $137, including full breakfast. AAA, AARP, AKC and ABA discounts.
Pet Charges or Deposits:	$5 per day. Manager's prior approval required. Small dogs only.
Rated: 4 Paws 🐾 🐾 🐾 🐾	5 guest rooms with private baths, some with whirlpools, king- or queen-sized beds with down comforters, fireplaces, ceiling fans, televisions and telephones. Dog-sitting is available if needed.

When looking for an upscale bed and breakfast inn offering personal attention and pampering, visit the Pathway Inn Bed and Breakfast. Here guests will find attractive, individually decorated rooms with king- or queen-sized beds, luxurious down comforters, fireplaces and private bathrooms with whirlpool tubs.

Make sure to tear yourself away from your room long enough to enjoy the sumptuous candlelit breakfast served each morning, and the complimentary refreshments, wine and assorted beverages served in the evening. You will want to experience the true Southern hospitality of this gracious small town, too. There are plenty of historical sights and lots of antique shops to explore in nearby Andersonville, a Civil War town.

Bed and Breakfast Atlanta

1801 Piedmont Avenue Northeast, Suite 208
Atlanta, Georgia 30324
(404) 875-0525

Room Rates: $55 – $150, most rates include breakfast.
Pet Charges or Deposits: Call for charges and deposits.
Rated: 4 Paws 80 bed and breakfast inns, homestays and cottages, with an assortment of amenities ranging from budget to luxury accommodations.

Bed and Breakfast Atlanta is a professional reservation service, providing visitors to the Atlanta area with lodging in carefully inspected and selected inns, homestays and guest cottages. Most accommodations are centrally located in desirable neighborhoods and suburban communities, offering a variety of amenities to please every traveler.

Each accommodation is unique and reflects the style and tastes of Atlanta. You are assured that each accommodation meets the standards of comfort, cleanliness and hospitality you seek. The service will make sure that your pet is welcome, too.

Georgian Terrace

659 Peachtree Street
Atlanta, Georgia 30308
800-651-2316 • (404) 897-1991

Room Rates: $88 – $350.
Pet Charges or Deposits: Limit 2 pets per room.
Rated: 5 Paws 🐾 🐾 🐾 🐾 🐾 320 elegantly appointed suites with coffee makers,
                               microwaves, honor bars, fully equipped kitchens, roof-top
                               swimming pool, fitness center, room service, three restaurants,
                               retail shops, gourmet market, beauty salon and concierge staff.

S ince 1911, the Georgian Terrace — with its Southern-style Parisian architecture — has been one of Atlanta's grand hotels, reflecting the grandeur and opulence of a bygone era. Listed on the National Register of Historic Places, the hotel has recently been lovingly restored to its original magnificence while maintaining modern amenities expected in an upscale hotel.

The elegant accommodations are perfect for the business traveler as well as a family on vacation. To maintain the historical feel of the hotel, a palette of rich, warm, neutral colors and subtle textures, fine mahogany furniture, specially woven draperies and fine art have been incorporated into the decor of the one-, two- or three-bedroom suites. The Georgian Terrace Health Club features a state-of-the-art exercise room to allow guests to maintain their fitness routines, and a fabulous roof-top junior Olympic swimming pool, perfect for an afternoon of sun-bathing while sipping cool drinks or for an aquatic workout. For the four-legged guests, the concierge will give you directions to favorite neighborhood parks and even arrange for doggie day care if needed.

Radisson Suites Inn

3038 Washington Road
Augusta, Georgia 30907
800-333-3333 • (706) 868-1800

Room Rates:	$59 – $99, including full breakfast and evening cocktails. AAA and AARP discounts.
Pet Charges or Deposits:	$25 per stay.
Rated: 3 Paws 🐾🐾🐾	176 luxury suites with separate living area, refrigerator, microwave, coffee maker, 2 televisions, 3 telephones, outdoor pool, landscaped courtyard, health club passes, restaurant and lounge.

L ocated in the heart of the business and entertainment district, the Radisson Suites offers handsomely furnished, comfortable and spacious guest rooms. The Jacuzzi Suites and Ambassador Suites come with a separate living room, a kitchenette with microwave oven, refrigerator, coffee maker and all the amenities of home.

Start your day off with the complimentary breakfast buffet before heading out to explore the area attractions, such as the award-winning revitalized Augusta Riverfront (located along the Savannah River), the National Register of Historic Places, the Morris Museum of Art or the National Golf Club.

Both you and your dog will enjoy a stroll through the attractive landscaped courtyard. In the evening, the inn's restaurant offers casual dining with a varied menu. Don't forget the complimentary evening cocktails.

Misty Mountain Inn and Cottages

4376 Misty Mountain Lane
Blairsville, Georgia 30512
888-MISTY MN • (706) 745-4786

Room Rates:	$50 – $85, including continental breakfast for bed and breakfast guests.
Pet Charges or Deposits:	$25 per stay. $25 refundable deposit. Proof of inoculations and manager's prior approval required.
Rated: 4 Paws 🐾🐾🐾🐾	4 bed and breakfast rooms with private baths, fireplaces, furnished with antiques and queen-sized beds; plus 6 private cottages, each with a full bath, fireplace, private porch and fully equipped kitchen. Personal laundry service available upon request.

W hen looking for a charming mountain retreat for a relaxing vacation or a restful weekend getaway, Misty Mountain Inn and Cottages offers guests their choice of four bed and breakfast accommodations with private baths and whirlpool tubs, comfortable queen-sized beds, charming antique furnishings, private balconies and a complimentary continental breakfast for bed and breakfast guests.

For those traveling with their pets, there are six private cottages, all with fully equipped eat-in kitchens, wood-burning fireplaces and queen-sized beds. The private porches are perfect for grilling your dinner on the supplied hibachi, as you watch the sun go down.

There are three ponds and a picnic area for your enjoyment before you venture out into the neighboring areas for a day at one of the many lakes along the Appalachian Trail.

Blue Ridge Mountain Cabins, Inc.

P.O. Box 1182
Blue Ridge, Georgia 30513
(706) 632-8999

Room Rates:	$75 – $100 per day; weekly rates available.
Pet Charges or Deposits:	$20 per pet per stay. Pets up to 35 lbs.
Rated: 3 Paws 🐾🐾🐾	36 furnished cabins located on the mountainside, near a lake, stream, creek, river, or set in the woods; with fully equipped kitchens, grills, large porches, fireplaces with wood supplied, linens, heat and air conditioning, laundry facilities, dishwasher, microwave, telephone, TV, VCR and some dog runs.

E scape to the beautiful north Georgia mountains and relax on the front porch of one of the Blue Ridge Mountain Cabins. These completely furnished cabins have fully equipped kitchens and supplies you need for a weekend getaway or a relaxing vacation. All you need to bring is your food and your spirit of adventure. The cabins are located either on the mountainside or set in the woods, all with beautiful views, near a lake, stream, creek or river.

There are plenty of places to enjoy tubing or white-water rafting on the Toccoa or Ocoee rivers, or go swimming, boating or fishing on Lake Blue Ridge. You and your pet can commune with nature while enjoying a picnic in the Chattahoochee National Forest. The cabins are all centrally located near shops, grocery stores, restaurants and recreational areas to keep you entertained and well-fed.

Villas by the Sea

1175 North Beachview Drive
Jekyll Island, Georgia 31527
800-841-6262 • (912) 635-2521

Room Rates:	$84 – $239; weekly rates available.
Pet Charges or Deposits:	$50 – $100 per stay.
Rated: 4 Paws 🐾 🐾 🐾 🐾	168 condominium, oceanfront villas offering one to three bedrooms with fully equipped kitchens, separate living and dining areas, full maid service, climate-controlled environment, televisions, balconies, laundry facilities, baby-sitting services, 18-hole golf course, tennis, restaurant and cocktail lounge.

Nestled among 17 acres of windswept oaks and lush natural landscaping, Villas by the Sea offers one-, two- and three-bedroom villas, many of which overlook 2,000 feet of beautiful white sand beach. Each unit comes complete with a fully equipped kitchen, separate living and dining areas with private balconies or decks offering breathtaking views of the island or the sea. Each villa is individually owned and attractively decorated to make you feel right at home, with the added bonus of optional maid service.

Experience the Island's famed amenities, such as 63 holes of championship golf, lighted indoor-outdoor tennis, cable water skiing and the celebrated Historic District. You'll also enjoy a fishing pier, fishing charters, 14 miles of scenic bike paths, a Nautilus-equipped fitness center and a water park. In the summer months, there is professional entertainment in the nearby outdoor amphitheater.

Royal Windsor Cottage

4490 Highway 356
Sautee, Georgia 30571
(706) 878-1322

Room Rates:	$95 – $145, including full breakfast.
Pet Charges or Deposits:	$10 per stay. Small dogs only. Manager's prior approval required.
Rated: 4 Paws 🐾🐾🐾🐾	4 English-style guest rooms with private baths, furnished in antiques, down comforters, central air and heat, large porches, English breakfast and afternoon tea.

S ituated on 22 wooded acres near the Unicoi State Park and Anna Ruby Falls is the lovely Royal Windsor Cottage. Featured in Southern Living magazine, this tasteful English-style cottage brings a touch of Old England to the South by re-establishing the philosophy of being pampered.

Guests will find four distinctive, beautifully decorated rooms to choose from, all with private baths, queen-sized beds, lovely linens and down comforters and a private balcony to enjoy the magnificent mountain views.

Your day will begin with a traditional fireside English breakfast served on fine china with sterling silver cutlery in the dining room, or out on the large porch, where guests are encouraged to "sit a spell" and relax in true Southern tradition.

You and your dog will enjoy exploring the 22 wooded acres of property before heading out for a day of hiking, fishing, swimming or picnicking at Unicoi State Park. Make sure you return to the cottage in time to enjoy English tea and crumpets.

Joan's on Jones Bed and Breakfast

17 West Jones Street
Savannah, Georgia 31401
800-407-3863 • (912) 234-3863

Room Rates: $115 – $140, including continental breakfast.
Pet Charges or Deposits: $50 per stay. Room rate as deposit. Sorry, no cats.
Rated: 3 Paws   2 luxury suites with private sitting rooms, private baths, kitchen or kitchenette, one with fireplace and off-street parking.

J oan's on Jones Bed and Breakfast is a charming 1883 Victorian townhouse set in the heart of Savannah's National Historic Landmark District. Here guests can relax in Victorian splendor surrounded by an array of antiques, offering a glimpse into an elegant past.

The splendid Jones Street Suite, with its private front parlor and sliding pocket doors leading into the charming bedroom with a four-poster, carved rice bed — normally reserved for the head of the plantation — also comes with a kitchenette, fresh fruit and wine to make you feel welcome. The Garden Suite has a secluded, walled garden, heady with the lush scent of Southern plantings, accompanied by the tinkling sounds of the splashing garden fountain, only steps from your sunny, private sitting room, and a sleeping area with a queen-sized iron bed and period furnishings and a large fireplace once used for cooking. If you wish, you may prepare your own breakfast in the suite's full kitchen; all the fixings will be provided.

You and your dog can take advantage of the central location near several city squares and all the interesting sites in the National Historic Landmark District.

Culpepper House Bed and Breakfast

35 Broad Street
Senoia, Georgia 30276
(770) 599-8182
E-mail: culpepperhouse@worldnet.att.net

Room Rates:	$85, including full breakfast. AAA, AARP, AKC and ABA discounts.
Pet Charges or Deposits:	Manager's prior approval required.
Rated: 3 Paws 🐾 🐾 🐾	3 guest rooms furnished in period antiques and reproductions with private baths. Wraparound porch, tandem bikes and golf carts for touring.

S tep back 120 years to the gracious Victorian elegance of the Culpepper House Bed and Breakfast. Set among lovely old oak trees, this charming inn was built in 1871 for Dr. John Addy, a Confederate soldier and a faithful area physician for more than fifty years.

This inn still has its original woodwork, reminiscent of the Steamboat Gothic style. The architectural theme begins with the wraparound porch, and is carried throughout the house in the trimwork and staircases, the stained glass windows in the stairwell, the original light fixtures and massive sliding pocket doors leading into the parlor. This fully restored inn showcases period antiques and wonderful reproductions on heart-pine floors amid a backdrop of massive 12-foot ceilings.

Enjoy a four-poster, canopy bed next to a fireplace, with sounds of the night coming through the window. Wake to a gourmet breakfast, then take a tandem bike ride through the historic town, visiting area shops and the picturesque countryside, or just sit on the porch and rock.

Statesboro Inn and Restaurant

106 South Main Street
Statesboro, Georgia 30453
800-846-9466 • (912) 489-8628

Room Rates:	$75 – $120, including full breakfast. AAA and AARP discounts.
Pet Charges or Deposits:	Manager's prior approval required.
Rated: 4 Paws	18 guest rooms and 1 luxury suite, all with private baths, whirlpool tubs, ceiling fans, remote-control televisions, furnished with antiques, featuring fireplaces, private entrances, screened porches and restaurant.

Built in 1904, the Statesboro Inn and Restaurant integrates the elements of late Victorian bay windows and gables with the Neoclassical features of the Palladian entry and Tuscan columns. The beautifully decorated rooms are furnished with antiques, working fireplaces and private bathrooms with whirlpool tubs.

Guests may relax and enjoy a good book on their private porch or retire to the parlor and visit with other guests. The homey feeling of this country inn has been combined with modern amenities to make your stay an experience to remember. Located on the property is the Hattie Holloway cabin where Georgia Music Hall of Fame member "Blind Willie" is said to have written "Statesboro Blues," made famous by the Allman Brothers Band.

The Inn's "Three Diamond" public dining room is renowned for its atmosphere of casual but elegant dining, offering an ever-evolving Continental and regional menu. The restaurant features many old family recipes and makes its own breads and desserts fresh daily.

Coleman House Inn

323 North Main Street
Swainsboro, Georgia 30401
(912) 237-9100

Room Rates: $55 – $85, including continental breakfast.
Pet Charges or Deposits: None.
Rated: 4 Paws 🐾 🐾 🐾 🐾   7 guest rooms with private baths and showers, antiques, cable
                         television, telephones, individually controlled heat and air con-
                         ditioning.

T he Coleman House Inn is a picturesque, three-story clapboard, turn-of-the-century Victorian bed and breakfast inn, eclectically combining the Queen Anne and Neoclassical Revival styles of decor that are commonly found in Georgia.

Your accommodations are furnished with charming antiques that include a cozy queen, double or twin bed as well as a private bath with footed tub and shower.

This was the first house in Emanuel County to have indoor plumbing and electricity. The front parlor exhibits many Victorian characteristics, such as wooden floors, high ceilings, large pocket doors and bay windows. The grand inn has 11 fireplaces, a central tower projecting from the roof, which includes a balcony and a lovely verandah that surrounds the building's facade, inviting guests to sit down, relax with their dog, sip a glass of iced tea and enjoy the best that Southern hospitality has to offer.

Residence Inn by Marriott

881 East River Place
Jackson, Mississippi 39202
800-331-3131 • (601) 355-3599

Room Rates:	$109 – $149, including continental breakfast. AAA and AARP discounts.
Pet Charges or Deposits:	$75 – $95 cleaning fee.
Rated: 3 Paws 🐾 🐾 🐾	120 luxury suites with separate living room, fully equipped kitchen, fireplace, laundry facilities, barbecue facilities, outdoor pool, two hot tubs, complimentary breakfast buffet, social hour and grocery shopping service.

When you have to be away on business or you are on vacation with your family, the Residence Inn by Marriott gives you that home-away-from-home feeling. The inn's comforts and conveniences, spacious suites with separate sleeping and living areas, fully equipped kitchens, daily maid service, grocery shopping service, laundry facilities, work areas and meeting facilities, as well as the manager-hosted continental breakfast buffet and informal hospitality hour, all add up to make your accommodations more like a home than a hotel. Upon check-in, pets receive complimentary pet dishes for their food and water, plus a special room magnet for the room door to let housekeeping know you have a pet with you.

This restful retreat offers a heated swimming pool, two hot tubs and a barbecue area. The beautifully landscaped grounds and walking path are perfect for morning or evening strolls with pets.

Oliver-Britt House Inn

512 Van Buren Avenue
Oxford, Mississippi 38655
(601) 234-8043

Room Rates:	$45 – $65, including full breakfast on weekends. AAA, AARP, AKC and ABA discounts.
Pet Charges or Deposits:	None.
Rated: 4 Paws 🐾🐾🐾🐾	5 guest rooms furnished with antiques and reproductions, with private baths, cable television, central heat and air.

T he Oliver-Britt House Inn is only a short walk from the University of Mississippi campus and only minutes away from Rowan Oak, the home of William Faulkner, and historical Oxford Square.

The restored manor house offers five spacious guest rooms, uniquely deco-rated with period antiques and reproductions, with queen- or king-sized beds, private baths, cable television and central heating and air conditioning.

On the weekends, guests are treated to a full Southern-style breakfast before they start their day of sightseeing or business meetings. The innkeepers, Glynn Oliver and Mary Ann Britt, are there to assist you with your travel needs. They will help you plan your business trip or vacation to the Oxford area.

La Font Inn – Resort and Conference Center

Highway 90 East
Pascagoula, Mississippi 35968
800-647-6077 • (601) 762-7111

Room Rates: $55 – $69. AAA and AARP discounts.
Pet Charges or Deposits: None.
Rated: 5 Paws 🐾🐾🐾🐾🐾 192 guest rooms with in-room coffee, cable television, clock
radio, some refrigerators stocked with purified water, steam
baths, wet bars, kitchenettes, recliners, sofas, work areas, tennis courts, Olympic-sized swimming pool, heated whirlpool,
playground, shuffleboard, indoor sauna, exercise and weight
room, restaurant and cocktail lounge.

Set amid nine beautifully landscaped acres, the La Font Inn – Resort and
Conference Center offers such amenities as refrigerators stocked with
purified water, wet bars, kitchenettes, steam baths, recliners and sofas,
large dining-work areas, in-room coffee and cable television.

Guests may spend their day relaxing by the Olympic-sized swimming pool,
soaking in the heated whirlpool, working out in the exercise and weight room,
relaxing in the indoor sauna or playing a game or two of shuffleboard or tennis.
For younger guests, there is a playground to enjoy. Four-legged guests will no
doubt love exploring the nine acres of landscaped property.

The La Font Restaurant has a varied menu with a cocktail lounge that offers
nightly entertainment.

Corners Bed and Breakfast Inn

601 Klein Street
Vicksburg, Mississippi 39180
800-444-7421 • (601) 636-7421

Room Rates:	$85 – $120, including full breakfast. AAA discount.
Pet Charges or Deposits:	None.
Rated: 4 Paws	13 guest rooms and 1 luxury suite, all with private baths, whirlpool tubs, furnished with antiques, canopy beds, fireplaces, private terraces, refrigerators and microwaves.

B uilt in 1873, the Corners Bed and Breakfast Inn beckons guests to take a step back in time amid Victorian elegance and country simplicity. The Inn's pierced columns and parterre gardens have earned its registry to the National Register of Historic Places.

Fifteen beautifully appointed guest rooms provide a variety of memorable experiences. Stay in rooms with true Southern elegance or Victorian charm or country simplicity. All are furnished in antiques and have private baths. Choose from canopied beds, fireplaces, whirlpool tubs, private porches and views.

The Inn is perched atop a bluff overlooking the Mississippi Valley, with the Mississippi River off in the distance, so you will want to spend some quiet time taking in the magnificent sunsets from your rocker on your private porch or on the 68-foot front gallery porch.

Duff Green Mansion Inn

1114 First East Street
Vicksburg, Mississippi 39180
800-992-0037 • (601) 636-6968 or 638-6662

Room Rates: $85 – $160, including full breakfast.
Pet Charges or Deposits: Small pets only. Manager's prior approval required.
Rated: 4 Paws 🐾🐾🐾🐾   4 guest rooms and 3 suites, National Register mansion, swim-
                         ming pool.

he Duff Green Mansion Inn in Vicksburg's historical district is consid-
ered one of the finest examples of Palladian architecture in the state of
Mississippi. The property was originally a wedding gift to Mary Lake
Green from her parents, Judge and Mrs. William Lake Green.

Built for his bride in 1856 by the prosperous merchant, Duff Green, the ante-
bellum mansion was the center for many parties and celebrations. When the
Confederate and Union soldiers battled in Vicksburg, the estate was shelled,
but managed to survive and was quickly converted to a hospital, which it
remained until the end of the war.

This 12,000-square-foot mansion has been restored and contains seven
guest rooms offering delightful accommodations, antique furnishings of the
period and hearty Southern breakfasts. There is plenty of room on the grounds
and in several local parks for you and your dog to explore.

Inn at the Bryant House

214 North Poplar Street
Aberdeen, North Carolina 28315
800-453-4019 • (910) 944-3300

Room Rates:	$50 – $85, including continental breakfast.
Pet Charges or Deposits:	None.
Rated: 4 Paws 🐾🐾🐾🐾	9 rooms and 2 luxury suites, twin to king-sized beds, most with private baths, antique furnishings, cable television, non-smoking inn.

 uilt in 1913, the Inn at the Bryant House is a turn-of-the-century home that has been completely restored and converted into a charming bed and breakfast inn. The inn has maintained its Southern splendor of the past, while adding modern conveniences of today.

Welcoming and tranquil pastel colors flow through the entire house. The spacious common rooms offer a friendly, relaxed atmosphere, inviting guests to gather around the fire or relax on the front porch. Guests are invited to enjoy a delicious continental breakfast, served in the dining room or garden room, featuring fresh-baked breads, homemade jams, jellies and preserves, and a wide selection of cereals, homemade granola, seasonal fruits and piping hot coffee or tea. Plus, the resident dog will be glad to show you and your pet some four-legged Southern hospitality.

This non-smoking inn is located in the downtown historic district, set amid the rolling North Carolina hills, close to many regional points of interest such as historical sites, nature preserves, polo and equestrian clubs and more than 30 golf courses.

Dogwood Cottage Inn

40 Canterbury Road North
Asheville, North Carolina 28801-1560
(704) 258-9725

Room Rates:	$95 – $105, including full breakfast.
Pet Charges or Deposits:	Call for deposit.
Rated: 4 Paws 🐾🐾🐾🐾	4 rooms with private baths, large sitting areas, shared balcony, heated pool, large country porch.

Built in the late 1890s, the Dogwood Cottage Inn offers guests 7,000 square feet of Appalachian, rustic, shingle-style architecture. Originally named The Manor, it was built by a visitor to the area, Mr. Raoul, who found it difficult to book hotel rooms for his family of five children and servants. Twenty other similar "cottages" were erected in the area for the same reason. The Manor served as the focal point for most social events for cottage guests.

Now the rustic cottage has been transformed into a quaint bed and breakfast inn. From the 42-foot veranda and the polished hardwood floors to the oak-beamed ceilings and large fireplace in the parlor, the Dogwood Cottage is a charming hideaway and yet is less than 2 miles from downtown Asheville.

Guests may choose from the Colonial Blue Room with French doors looking out onto the pool; the English Country Garden Room, decorated in bounteous flower prints; the Americana Red Room, decorated in Early American, including quilts and rugs; or the Forest Green Room with its rich tones of forest green and gold. All rooms have queen-sized beds, private baths and lots of charm. The spacious grounds and area attractions will beckon you and your dog to explore them.

Banner Elk Inn Bed and Breakfast

407 Main Street East
Banner Elk, North Carolina 28604
800-972-2183 • (704) 898-6223

Room Rates:	$80 – $160, including full breakfast.
Pet Charges or Deposits:	Call for fees and deposits. Manager's prior approval required.
Rated: 4 Paws 🐾🐾🐾🐾	3 guest rooms and 1 large suite, all with down comforters, Victorian or French provincial decor, 3 with private baths.

When looking for a quiet, cozy bed and breakfast inn that welcomes both you and your pet, look no further than the Banner Elk Inn Bed and Breakfast. Once a country church, this 1912 inn is located near Mount Pisgah National Park, great for summer fun or winter skiing. It has been renovated and furnished with antiques collected from around the world.

The lovely rooms offer guests soft, restful hues and Victorian or French provincial decor. Lin's Peach Room has a majestic wooden Victorian queen-sized bed and full private bath. Jeanne's Mauve Room offers a romantic Victorian motif with an antique brass bed and full bath. Jeannie and Linda's Room is colorfully decorated with stripes, bright colors and pewter twin beds. For a French provincial suite that sleeps up to four, Bonnie's Blue Room is a wonderful choice.

No matter which room you choose, you will enjoy the European down comforters, Southern hospitality and a full breakfast of homemade breads, fresh fruit and a variety of special dishes.

Carolina Mornings Inc.

109 Circadian Way
Chapel Hill, North Carolina 27516
888-667-6467 • (919) 929-5553
Web Site: www.carolinamornings.com
E-mail: Carolinamornings@mindspring.com

Room Rates:	$85 and up per night. Weekly rates available.
Pet Charges or Deposits:	Call for fees and deposits. Manager's prior approval required.
Rated: 4 Paws 🐾🐾🐾🐾	6 cabins for 2 to 6 people each with fully equipped kitchens, full baths, telephones, cable television, large porches or decks, some with fireplaces and laundry facilities.

W hen looking for a relaxing, private retreat for your next vacation or weekend getaway, Carolina Mornings Inc.'s reservation service will help you find the perfect place. Choose from The Sugar Creek Studio, Cabin on Eagles Nest, Little House in Hot Springs, Sunny Acres Farm, Dream Wanderer or Dun Romin'.

These cabins are all set in the woods, some near ponds, creeks or mountain streams. Though the accommodations vary by the cabin you choose, most will sleep from two to six people, have fully equipped kitchens, full baths, cable televisions and VCRs, laundry facilities, fireplaces, outdoor grills, covered porches or large decks.

Centrally located near many local attractions and Great Smoky Mountains National Park, there's always plenty to keep you busy. Spend the day with your dog exploring the mountain trails, picnic near a stream, try your hand at fishing or relax with a glass of wine and a good book on your private porch or deck.

River House Inn and Restaurant

1896 Old Field Creek Road
Grassy Creek, North Carolina 28631
(910) 982-2109

Room Rates:	$90 – $170, including full breakfast.
Pet Charges or Deposits:	One night's room rate as deposit.
Rated: 4 Paws 🐾🐾🐾🐾	6 spacious guest rooms with king- or queen-sized beds, private bathrooms, whirlpool hot tubs, decorated with antiques, private porches with river or mountain views, restaurant.

Perched on 125 acres on the banks of the North Fork River is the enchanting River House Inn and Restaurant. This country inn consists of six charming guest rooms decorated with antiques and featuring private baths and inviting private porches with breathtaking views of the river or mountains.

Spend the day relaxing in a rocking chair on the porch, picnic under the giant sycamore trees down by the river or head out for a day of hiking and exploration. If you are feeling truly adventurous, you can rent canoes, go horseback riding or visit the Grayson Highlands State Park, the Creeper Trail or one of the many other local sites. Once you have worked up an appetite, a sumptuous dinner awaits you at the River House Restaurant.

Fire Mountain Inn and Cabins

P.O. Box 2772
Highlands, North Carolina 28741
800-775-4446 • (704) 526-4446

Room Rates:	$85 – $175, including continental breakfast.
Pet Charges or Deposits:	$10 per day. $150 deposit. Dogs under 30 lbs. Sorry, no cats.
Rated: 5 Paws 😺 😺 😺 😺 😺	6 inn rooms, 3 suites and 6 cabins. Amenities include wood-burning stone fireplaces, king- and queen-sized beds, private terraces, private baths, private entrances and parking, separate living rooms, kitchenettes and full kitchens, Jacuzzi tubs, television, VCR, and spectacular views.

F ire Mountain Inn and Cabins are built atop a mountain with uninterrupted, dramatic views. This modern inn is ideal for people who want to bask in the best that Mother Nature has to offer while enjoying the ultimate in sophistication and comfort. Inspired by the beauty of Fire Mountain, this resplendent inn is a private world unto itself. Spectacular views abound from every room and suite. The cabins offer guests full kitchens, native stone fireplaces, vaulted ceilings and plenty of privacy. Each room and cabin opens to a large deck or terrace, perfect for lounging in the mountain splendor, snoozing in the healthy mountain air or taking in the most breathtaking sunrises and sunsets one could imagine.

After you have feasted on the continental breakfast, head out for a day of adventure. There are four hiking trails with ponds, streams and waterfalls, plus the Great Smoky Mountains National Park for you and your dog to explore.

Village at Nags Head — Village Realty

P.O. Box 1807
Nags Head, North Carolina 27959
800-548-9688 • (919) 480-2224

Room Rates: $500 – $5,500 weekly.
Pet Charges or Deposits: $75 per stay. Refundable security deposit. Limit 2 pets.
Rated: 5 Paws 24 condos and houses, luxuriously furnished, many with membership privileges at the private oceanfront Beach Club.

T he tranquil waterfront of the Roanoke Sound is home to The Village at Nags Head — Village Realty. Here you will find more than 200 of the finest accommodations located within the Village community, plus the oceanfront Beach Club and the Nags Head Golf Links. Twenty-four of these allow you to bring your pet.

Choose from a wide variety of well-appointed, spacious, custom-built homes and condos suited for a family vacation or an intimate beach retreat. The houses and condos are luxuriously furnished, have fully equipped kitchens, housekeeping services, including all linens and towels, and are ready for your arrival. Many of the accommodations have private decks with beautiful ocean views, private swimming pools, large hot tubs, outdoor showers, grills, televisions, VCRs and fireplaces. Guest membership privileges are available at the private oceanfront Beach Club — featuring an Olympic-sized pool, children's wading pool, private beach access, snack bar and grill, game room, bath houses, tennis courts and gift shops — as well as at the Nags Head Golf Links.

Barkley House Bed and Breakfast

2522 North Carolina Highway 16 South
Taylorsville, North Carolina 28681
(704) 632-9060

Room Rates:	$55 – $79, including full breakfast; third night free when mentioning Pets Welcome™.
Pet Charges or Deposits:	Manager's prior approval required. Small pets only. Limit one pet.
Rated: 4 Paws	4 guest rooms with private baths, feather mattresses, a common refrigerator for guests and a cozy den with fireplace. Pet beds available upon request.

When looking for old-fashioned Southern charm and comfort, you need look no further than the Barkley House Bed and Breakfast. Life at the inn is homey and relaxed. Guests are encouraged to kick off their shoes, prop up their feet and relax by the cozy fire in the den. Comfort is of the utmost importance. There is a "Pillow Buffet" where you may select the pillow that meets your needs. You may choose from king, full or twin beds, all with feather mattresses and plush comforters. When it comes to the bedding, the sheets are hung on the line to dry in the sunshine, to give them that wonderful scent of the fresh outdoors. Pets will appreciate the added touch of a special bed with clean sheets just for them.

Awake to a large country breakfast of piping hot coffee, tea, hot chocolate or hot apple cider served with a haystack of eggs, breakfast casserole or omelets, biscuits, gravy, grits, juice, fresh fruit, honey or jelly. There is even a breakfast banana split. You may request a pot of hot coffee or tea to be sent to your room in the morning to help you start your day.

Battery Creek Inn

19 Marina Village Lane
Beaufort, South Carolina 29902
(803) 521-1441

Room Rates:	$78; weekly rates available. AAA discount.
Pet Charges or Deposits:	$50 per stay. $50 refundable deposit.
Rated: 3 Paws	20 suites, private entrances, fully equipped kitchens, outstanding views, cable television and private parking.

Located across from the gates of Parris Island is the waterfront Battery Creek Inn, where you will find delightfully furnished guest suites. Located directly on the waterfront, near the Battery marina, the guest rooms offer private entrances, fully equipped kitchens and outstanding views of Battery Creek and the Intracoastal Waterway.

The Battery Creek Inn is convenient to golf courses, the downtown historic district, Hunting Island State Park and the beaches. Here you and your dog have over 5,000 acres on which to picnic, hike, fish or swim.

Carolina Oaks Bed and Breakfast

127 Union Street
Camden, South Carolina 29020
(803) 432-2366

Room Rates:	$90 – $150, including full breakfast.
Pet Charges or Deposits:	$25 per stay. $50 refundable deposit. Manager's prior approval required.
Rated: 4 Paws 🐾 🐾 🐾 🐾	3 guest rooms, 1 cottage, all with fireplaces, featherbeds, antique quilts, down comforters, central air conditioning. Terry robes provided.

Set in the heart of Camden's historic district is the charming, Federal-style Carolina Oaks Bed and Breakfast Inn, built in the early 1900s. This spacious home in a quiet setting provides a convenient and interesting stepping-off point to other fine homes, wonderful restaurants and Camden's festivals.

In the main house, guests will find well designed, comfortable guest rooms decorated with period antiques and soft textures, antique quilts, down comforters and wood-burning fireplaces.

The private cottage is furnished in antiques with a queen-sized brass bed, freshly ironed cotton bed linens, antique quilts and soft down comforters. The cottage has a separate living room and full kitchen.

Breakfasts are served on damask linen with homemade treats such as fresh jams and preserves, with breads still hot from the oven, omelets laced with Canadian bacon, three kinds of cheese and fresh-picked herbs, an assortment of seasonal fresh fruit and piping hot coffee or tea.

Cedar Grove Plantation Bed and Breakfast

1365 Highway 25 North
Edgefield, South Carolina 29824
(803) 637-3056

Room Rates:	$55 – $75, including full breakfast.
Pet Charges or Deposits:	One night's room rate as deposit. Manager's prior approval required.
Rated: 3 Paws 🐾 🐾 🐾	2 guest rooms with private baths, one with separate sitting area, fireplaces, television and VCR, swimming pool, hot tub/spa, herb and flower garden.

L ocated just outside of town, the Cedar Grove Plantation Bed and Breakfast was built in 1790 by John Blocker. Listed on the National Register of Historic Places, it is one of the oldest plantation houses in the Upstate. The house still retains most of the original features, such as the hand-carved mantels and moldings, fireplaces in every room, lovely hand-painted French wallpaper in the parlor, and a unique barrel-vaulted entry ceiling in the hallway. The original kitchen and slave quarters still stand today.

Only two guest rooms are available. The Blocker Suite features a separate sitting room with television and VCR. The downstairs guest room will accommodate two people, but be forewarned: it is already occupied by a ghost! The room is discounted for those brave enough to spend the night. Once you have made it through the night, you can tell everyone about your ghostly experiences at breakfast in the elegant dining room, or, when the weather permits, dine outdoors on the spacious back porch. Special arrangements can also be made for an elegant, romantic dinner or a picnic box lunch.

Be sure to take a stroll through the plantation's herb and flower garden with your dog, a favorite stopping spot for the local deer, fox and wild turkeys.

Mansfield Plantation Bed and Breakfast Country Inn

1776 Mansfield Road
Georgetown, South Carolina 29440
800-355-3223 • (803) 546-6961

Room Rates:	$95 – $115, including full breakfast.
Pet Charges or Deposits:	None.
Rated: 5 Paws 😺 😺 😺 😺 😺	5 main-house guest rooms furnished in antiques with full private baths, fireplaces and private entrances; 3 guest houses with full private baths and working fireplaces, all set on 900 acres with a pond and a river.

Moonlight and Magnolias. The Mansfield Plantation is a historic pre-Civil War plantation situated on 900 private acres. The avenue of noble live oak trees draped in Spanish moss leads you to the traditional antebellum plantation house which is furnished with antiques. This historic rice plantation, located in the heart of South Carolina's Tidelands, was once the exclusive haunt of aristocrats, and is now open to discriminating guests.

Three charming guest houses feature private entrances, handsome furnishings, floral chintz fabrics, fireplaces with beautifully carved mantelpieces and woodwork and full private baths. Guest are invited to relax in the parlors of the plantation house or on the brick terrace, stroll the expansive lawns, or curl up with a good book in the hammock.

Situated on the Black River, the 900 private acres are a naturalist's paradise, offering guests and their pets a private getaway. Walk in the woods, explore the old rice fields, fish from the private dock, go boating on the river, or picnic on the sandy shores. The serene environment and elegant atmosphere blend beautifully to make your visit a lasting memory.

Red Horse Inn

310 North Campbell Road
Landrum, South Carolina 29356
(864) 895-4968

Room Rates:	$85, including continental breakfast. Weekly rate available.
Pet Charges or Deposits:	$25 deposit. Small dogs only. Horses welcome. Manager's prior approval required.
Rated: 5 Paws 🐾 🐾 🐾 🐾 🐾	5 cottages with kitchens, separate bedrooms, private baths, sleeping lofts, separate living rooms with fireplace, decks or patios, some with Jacuzzis, color television, air conditioning.

Set on 190 acres with trails, streams, fields and ponds in the midst of equestrian country is the delightful Red Horse Inn. Sweeping mountain views, pastoral vistas and endless sky offer the perfect backdrop to each season.

The charming, romantic Victorian cottages are exquisitely furnished and decorated offering a kitchen, bedroom, bath, sleeping loft, living room with fireplace, decks or patios, color television and air-conditioning. A breakfast basket is provided each morning for your room.

Local attractions include two championship golf courses, horseback riding, hiking, fishing, antiquing, sporting clay course and the Foothills Equestrian Nature Center. The spring, summer and fall come alive with various events and festivals.

Southwood Manor Bed and Breakfast

100 East Main Street
Ridge Spring, South Carolina 29129
(803) 685-5100

Room Rates: $65 – $85, including full breakfast. AAA and AARP discounts.
Pet Charges or Deposits: Manager's prior approval required. Horses welcome.
Rated: 5 Paws 4 spacious rooms and 1 suite with fine antiques, four-poster
                         beds, air conditioning, color television, fireplaces, full baths,
                         swimming pool and private air strip.

Surrounded by the flavors of the true South, with cotton fields, pecan groves and a working cotton gin, is the Southwood Manor Bed and Breakfast. This magnificent Georgian Colonial plantation is located in the sleepy country town of Ridge Spring, offering a relaxed atmosphere and gracious accommodations.

The large guest rooms are furnished with queen-sized four-poster beds and period antiques. Start your day with a full country breakfast in the formal dining room, or dine in the privacy of your room.

If relaxation is what you have planned, you have come to the right place. Just imagine sipping fresh lemonade as you lounge poolside. For those who crave an active vacation, set up a game of tennis on the inn's court, try your hand at billiards, or practice your putting, all on site, followed by a sherry on the curved and columned portico. Your dog will appreciate the quarter-acre fenced-in yard, and your horse has two box stalls and a pasture.

Magnolia House Bed and Breakfast

230 Church Street
Sumter, South Carolina 29150
888-666-0296 • (803) 775-6694
E-mail: magnoliahouse@sumter.net

Room Rates:	$65 – $125, including full breakfast. AAA discount.
Pet Charges or Deposits:	$65 deposit. Manager's prior approval required.
Rated: 5 Paws 🐾🐾🐾🐾🐾	5 charming rooms and 1 suite, most with fireplaces, stained glass windows, inlaid oak floors, each room decorated in a different era; refreshments in formal garden. Resident pets.

Make yourself at home in the Greek Revival-style Magnolia House Bed and Breakfast Inn with its 5 fireplaces, stained glass windows and inlaid oak floors. Located in the historic district of Sumter, you enter the home expecting to see ladies in flowing gowns and men wearing evening coats. The details of the decorating are tasteful as well as entertaining. There are delightful vignettes at every turn.

Each of the inviting guest rooms is decorated in antiques from a different era with comfortable upholstered chairs and hand-made quilts and the thickest towels you will find. A full breakfast is served in the large dining room, decorated with beautiful French antiques.

This historic home, with its Corinthian columns, wraparound porches with overstuffed chairs and cypress swings, invites you to relax with complimentary afternoon refreshments. The garden blooms year-round with roses, tulips, magnolias and scented gardenias. A collection of birdhouses and feeders encourages a large variety of birds to stop for a visit.

Mt. Carmel Farm Bed and Breakfast

Route 2, Box 580-A
Walterboro, South Carolina 29488
(803) 538-5770

Room Rates:	$75, including full breakfast and light dinner.
Pet Charges or Deposits:	None for cats and dogs. $15 per horse, per day. $20 for each additional horse.
Rated: 4 Paws 🐾🐾🐾🐾	2 guest rooms with two doubles or a queen-sized bed, private baths, ceiling fans, pet blankets and bowls in each room, large den, formal dining room, front and back porches, pool, barn and paddock area. Dogs, horses and pot-bellied pigs in residence.

I f you are looking for a homey country setting for your next getaway, consider the Mt. Carmel Farm Bed and Breakfast. This inn is more like visiting Grandma's house. From the minute you arrive at the front gate, the aroma of fresh-baked goods drifts through the air. The well-decorated guest rooms have private baths and a queen or two double beds with cozy afghans. The larger room overlooks the back field and paddock area. Both rooms have fluffy blankets and bowls for your pet.

Start your day off with a big country breakfast of fresh cinnamon buns, cheese Danish or blueberry cake served in the large country kitchen, where everyone gathers talk to Maureen, the owner/innkeeper, as she prepares the meals.

A comfortable den with a fireplace and two porches entices you to curl up with a good book. Be sure to get a cookie from the jar for yourself, and for Eddie, the resident dog, a pat on the head. Then grab some carrots and head down to the barn to visit the horses and the pot-bellied pigs, Gus and Hammy.

Hachland Hill Inn

1601 Madison Street
Clarksville, Tennessee 37043
(615) 647-4084

Room Rates: $65 – $100.
Pet Charges or Deposits: $10 per day. Manager's prior approval required.
Rated: 3 Paws   8 guest rooms and 3 suites, fireplaces, private entrances, showers and bath tubs. Famous dining.

T he Colonial-style Hachland Hill Inn offers guests more than just charming guest rooms and spacious suites furnished with antiques. There's also plenty of gracious Southern hospitality.

This enchanting inn has unexpected pleasures. While a secluded inn 45 minutes outside of Nashville may seem an unlikely place to find Oysters Rockefeller or Chateaubriand, delectable surprises are a common occurrence at Hachland Hill.

People from around the world have been wooed by the culinary wonders prepared here. The regional flavor of dishes such as fried chicken, country ham and homemade biscuits have been handed down through generations. More cosmopolitan palates will delight in Coquilles Saint Jacques, Moroccan Leg of Lamb and other worldly dishes. The inn's grand ballroom seats up to 300 guests and adjoins a historic 1790 log home.

Guests will no doubt be tempted to take pooches for a stroll around the lovely grounds adorned with fields of wildflowers and even a bird sanctuary. Renowned author, gourmet chef and inn owner Phila Hach prides herself on making the Hachland Hill Inn one of the South's favorite destinations for charming accommodations and fine dining.

Mountain Harbor Inn

1199 Highway 139
Dandridge, Tennessee 37725
(423) 397-3345
Web Site: www.mountainharborinn.com

Room Rates:	$75 – $135, including full breakfast.
Pet Charges or Deposits:	$8 per day. Manager's prior approval required. Call for deposit information.
Rated: 5 Paws 🐾🐾🐾🐾🐾	4 spacious rooms and 9 luxury waterfront suites furnished with antiques and quilts, boat launching and docks, award-winning restaurant; located near Great Smoky Mountain National Park.

T he Mountain Harbor Inn strives for a balance between luxury, comfort and beauty. Ensconced in a scenic mountain setting on Douglas Lake, the inn's charming guest rooms are decorated with antiques and quilts. Pillared porches beckon guests to relax and enjoy the serenity and splendor of the surrounding mountains and lake.

The inn is ideal for a weekend getaway or an extended vacation. There are no time schedules here. Breakfast is served over a two-hour period to allow guests to start their day when they are ready.

No matter what season you choose to visit, each has its own beauty and special events to offer. Spend the day exploring the area with your dog, or head to town and buy one of the locally crafted rockers for your own. Boat launching and docking areas are available for those who wish to spend the day on the lake fishing for bass. There are even charter services available to take anglers to the best fishing spots.

Morning Star Bed and Breakfast

460 Jones Lane
Hendersonville, Tennessee 37075
(615) 264-2614
E-mail: murrays@NC5.infi.net

Room Rates:	$95 – $120, including full breakfast. AAA, AARP, AKC and ABA discounts
Pet Charges or Deposits:	Manager's prior approval required.
Rated: 4 Paws 🐾🐾🐾🐾	3 guest rooms and 1 suite, large wrap-around porches, two Par 3 practice golf tees, large patio and gazebo, high tea and complimentary beverages. Dog runs and exercise areas.

T he Morning Star Bed and Breakfast inn offers guests beautifully decorated rooms with private vanities, claw-foot tubs and showers, with brass fixtures throughout. This custom country Victorian home was featured in the January 1995 special edition of Elite Unique Homes magazine. Common rooms are comfortable and inviting, with four fireplaces.

A large wrap-around front porch with white wicker swings and rockers encourages guests to sit awhile and view the Nashville skyline, the sparkling city lights and colorful sunsets.

Start your day off with the complimentary full breakfast, served in the formal dining room or on the porch, before heading out for a day of adventure. Located minutes away are downtown Nashville; Opryland, home of the Grand Ole' Opry; Opryland USA Themepark; and TBN's Trinity Music City. If relaxation is what you are craving, then stay put and work on your golf game on the inn's practice range or curl up with a good book and relax with your dog in the gazebo.

Union Station Hotel

1001 Broadway
Nashville, Tennessee 37203
800-331-2123 • (615) 726-1001

Room Rates: $137 – $173.
Pet Charges or Deposits: Pets under 25 lbs. Manager's prior approval required.
Rated: 5 Paws 🐾🐾🐾🐾🐾 124 rooms with cable television, some refrigerators, 2 restaurants, cocktails, laundry service, area transportation and valet parking.

 uilt at the height of Nashville's social and economic growth, the Union Station Hotel is a landmark in the heart of Music City and has earned a place on the National Register of Historic Places.

Originally opened in 1900 as a train station, the building now features a modern lobby with a stained-glass skylight, silvered mirrors, bas-relief artwork with gold trim and a black marble fountain. The barrel-vaulted ceiling has original stained-glass panels. A classic example of Romanesque-Revival architecture, the hotel is a limestone building with a massive clock tower and guest rooms with 22-foot-high ceilings.

Over the past 16 years, Arthur's Restaurant has been serving up award-winning meals to Nashvillians, as well as celebrities, journalists, government dignitaries and business leaders from around the nation and the world. The restaurant features an eclectic menu with recipes from North America, Europe, Africa and Asia.

Smokey Ridge Chalet and Cabin Rentals

2225 Parkway, Suite 1
Pigeon Forge, Tennessee 37868
800-634-5814 • (423) 428-5427
E-mail: smokeyridge@smokymtnmall.com

Room Rates:	$85 – $150. Weekly and group rates available.
Pet Charges or Deposits:	Call for fees and deposit requirements. Manager's prior approval required.
Rated: 4 Paws 🐾 🐾 🐾 🐾	60 individual chalets and cabins that sleep up to 12 people, with full kitchens, complete with linens and towels, color televisions, some with VCRs, fireplaces, Jacuzzis, pool.

I f you are looking for a home away from home for your next vacation, Smokey Ridge Chalet and Cabin Rentals has fully furnished chalets and log cabins with complete kitchens and all your linens provided. Choose from accommodations with one to five bedrooms and one to three bathrooms; built over a running stream or nestled on a ridge with beautiful views of the Smoky Mountains. Most rooms offer wood-burning fireplaces, perfect for an intimate evening or a cozy place to snuggle up with a good book.

There are plenty of activities to keep you busy in the area. Pigeon Forge offers the Dollywood theme park featuring homespun fun and traditions of the Smoky Mountains. The Dixie Stampede presents a program of music, comedy rodeo and Wild West-style performances. Then, of course, there's the Great Smoky Mountain National Park with more than 520,000 acres of natural landscape for picnicking, hiking and fishing.

Little Round Top Cabins

3319 Mountain Lakes Way
Sevierville, Tennessee 37862
(423) 428-5984

Room Rates:	$100 – $140; weekly rates available.
Pet Charges or Deposits:	Small pets only. Must bring carrier to confine pet when not in room. Manager's prior approval required.
Rated: 5 Paws 🐾🐾🐾🐾🐾	7 cabins with 2–5 bedrooms, king- and queen-sized beds, whirlpools and hot tubs, satellite TV, wood-burning fireplaces, laundry facilities, full kitchens, central air and heat, gas barbecue grills, porches with rockers, all on 32 acres of private mountain.

S et amid 32 breathtaking acres of the scenic Wears Valley, between Townsend and Pigeon Forge, bordered by the Great Smoky Mountains National Park, are the Little Round Top Cabins. These charming, fully furnished cabins feature two to five bedrooms, with two or three bathrooms, fully equipped kitchens, wood-burning stone fireplaces with firewood supplied, large decks with gas barbecue grills and rocking chairs, laundry facilities in the cabins, whirlpool tubs and satellite television. Everything is furnished for you, including linens and towels. The fully stocked kitchens are complete with microwaves, toasters and a coffee makers.

Start your day off with a brisk hike through the hills, which are covered with mountain laurel, rhododendron, hemlock, numerous types of hardwood trees and large varieties of wildlife. Spectacular mountain views abound.

There are also plenty of attractions and shops to explore in the neighboring towns, as well as fishing, horseback riding, river rafting and golf.

Carnes' Log Cabin Rentals

P.O. Box 153
Townsend, Tennessee 37882
(423) 448-1021
Web Site: www.carneslogcabins.com

Room Rates:	$85 – $115.
Pet Charges or Deposits:	$10 per day. $50 deposit. Small pets only. Manager's prior approval required.
Rated: 5 Paws 🐾🐾🐾🐾🐾	7 furnished log cabins with king-sized beds, fully equipped kitchens, stone fireplaces, large covered porches with rocking chairs and swings, Jacuzzis, private outdoor hot tubs, cable TV with VCR, central air and heat, all linens and towels provided.

L ooking for the perfect Smoky Mountain getaway? Carnes' Log Cabins offers a peaceful alternative to traditional accommodations. Nestled in the secluded wooded setting are completely furnished, private cabins that blend rustic charm with modern conveniences such as fully equipped kitchens, full baths, stone fireplaces, private outdoor hot tubs, central air and heat, with all your linens and towels provided.

The cabins are only one mile from the entrance to the Great Smoky Mountains National Park and mere steps from the Little River, one of the nation's purest watersheds, where you and your dog can roam the five-mile stretch of river, try your luck at some of the fishing holes or go tubing and swimming. Just a short drive over the hill lies Gatlinburg, Pigeon Forge and Dollywood.

The large front porch, with its rocking chairs and swings, is the perfect place to relax after a busy or a not-so-busy day.

Pearl's of the Mountains Cabin Rentals

7717 East Lamar Alexander Parkway
P.O. Box 378
Townsend, Tennessee 37882
800-324-8415 • (423) 448-8801

Room Rates:	$70 – $95.
Pet Charges or Deposits:	$10 per stay. Manager's prior approval required.
Rated: 4 Paws 🐾🐾🐾🐾	3 cabins, each with fully equipped kitchen, microwave, dishwasher, laundry facilities, telephone, cable television, VCR, fireplace, large porches with swings and rockers, heating and air conditioning, charcoal grills, linens, towels, soaps and firewood.

L ocated in the Smoky Mountains near the Great Smoky Mountains National Park are the Pearl's of the Mountains Cabin Rentals. Here you will have the best views of the Smokies from your own private cabin. Choose a four-bedroom, two-level rental that sleeps from two to 10 people. It's perched high on a bluff overlooking the Little River, with lots of mature trees, making it a very private retreat. Stroll down to the river with the dog and wet your fishing line, have a picnic or go for a swim in the river.

Or you may choose a new two-bedroom cabin in the valley with spacious bedrooms which sleeps up to six people, has two private baths, a Jacuzzi and a large porch with rockers for relaxing. All cabins come fully equipped with towels, linens, soaps, firewood for the fireplace, cable television, VCRs, telephones, laundry facilities, heating, air conditioning, as well as kitchens with microwaves and dishwashers, making them an excellent choice for a private getaway.

Twin Valley Ranch Bed and Breakfast Horse Ranch

2848 Old Chihowee Road
Walland, Tennessee 37886-2144
800-872-2235 • (423) 984-0980

Room Rates:	$75 – $95, including full breakfast. Vacation packages available.
Pet Charges or Deposits:	Manager's prior approval required. Horses welcome.
Rated: 4 Paws 🐾🐾🐾🐾	2 guest rooms and 1 cabin on a 260-acre horse ranch with homey accommodations, private cabins with kitchenette, full bath and deck. Horseback riding instructions and guided tours.

Wake up to the mountain's morning mist and breathtaking views at Twin Valley Ranch Bed and Breakfast Horse Ranch. Surrounded by tranquillity and simple country living, guests may choose to share the unique log home with its rustic log interior, two-story mountain stone fireplace and individually decorated rooms featuring special homey touches, or stay in the private log cabin nestled in the hills. The fully equipped cabin sleeps up to six people, offers a kitchenette, full bath and a sunny deck to enjoy the mountain views.

This mountain resort is a perfect place to bring your horse. The ranch has a grassy corral, complete with its own stream and shelter; or use one of the paddocks, with a shelter and running water. There are many trails throughout the scenic hills and valleys of this 260-acre ranch. You may arrange for a guided tour or head out on your own. For those who would rather "rough it" on the trail, there is a one-room primitive shelter, where you can stop and relax in the hammock for two. When the stars come out, build a roaring campfire and breathe in the peace and quiet of nature.

Kings Inn

151 Kings Highway
Lewes, Delaware 19958
(302) 645-6438
E-mail: prockett@juno.com

Room Rates:	$65 – $85, including full breakfast. Call for discounts.
Pet Charges or Deposits:	$5 per day. Credit card imprint required. Manager's prior approval required.
Rated: 3 Paws	5 guest rooms.

L ewes, the "First Town in the First State," is full of small-town charm. Dating from 1631, it has an interesting and varied history, which can be savored on a walking tour of historical houses, churches and parks. The downtown area is replete with shops, boutiques and excellent restaurants, while maintaining a relaxed, tree-lined quietness. Lewes, centrally located for many tourists, is 21/2 hours from Washington D.C., Philadelphia and Baltimore and 4 hours from New York City.

The Kings Inn, built in 1888, features a large period room with high ceilings and stained glass. Guest rooms are reached by an impressive staircase in the foyer or by the convenient back stairs. Quiet, personal entertainment includes a Jacuzzi for two, videos, cable TV, and a stereo with classical, operatic and jazz collections. Bicycles are available for guest use. Swedish coffee and hot cinnamon bread with berries are served each morning in the plant-filled sunroom.

Corner Cupboard Inn

50 Park Avenue
Rehoboth Beach, Delaware 19971
(302) 227-8553
Web Site: www.dmv.com/business/ccinn
E-mail: ccinn@dmv.com

Room Rates:	$80 – $250, including breakfast and dinner.
Pet Charges or Deposits:	$15 per day.
Rated: 3 Paws 🐾🐾🐾	18 guest rooms.

A tradition in some families for generations, the Corner Cupboard Inn is a quiet oasis in this thriving resort town. A short walk will bring you into the hustle and bustle of downtown Rehoboth, with its many shops and boutiques. The ocean is so near, you can often hear the surf above the wind in the pine trees surrounding the Inn.

Air-conditioned guest rooms feature private baths with rooms in the main house, charming annex or cottage rooms with either private or shared patios.

The restaurant is open to the public from Memorial Day weekend through the middle of September. Dine on such local favorites as soft-shell crabs, lobster and prime rib. A selection of homemade desserts is always available.

Hereford House Bed and Breakfast

604 South Carolina Avenue
Washington, District of Columbia 20003
(202) 543-0102
E-mail: herefordhs@aol.com

Room Rates:	$45 – $68, including full breakfast.
Pet Charges or Deposits:	$50 refundable deposit. Manager's prior approval required.
Rated: 3 Paws 🐾 🐾 🐾	4 guest rooms.

 ereford House Bed and Breakfast, now in its 12th year, is an early 1900s brick townhouse that has been converted into a private home, bed and breakfast and guest cottage on an attractive, quiet, residential avenue on Capitol Hill, one block from the underground subway train. This ideal location is a ten-minute walk to the U.S. Capitol, Supreme Court, Library of Congress and tourmobile for guided tours of the city. Easily reached on foot or by public transportation are the Mall, art galleries and Smithsonian museums.

Guest rooms are clean, well furnished and economical. Three blocks away from the Hereford House is the guest house — a two-bedroom, two-bath cottage with living room. A traditional full breakfast or a healthy continental breakfast is included in your room rates.

Hotel Washington

515 15th Street Northwest
Washington, District of Columbia 20004
800-424-9540 • (202) 638-5900
Web Site: www.hotelwashington.com
E-mail: sales@hotelwashington.com

Room Rates:	$174 – $680. Call for discounts.
Pet Charges or Deposits:	Manager's prior approval required. Sorry, no cats.
Rated: 4 Paws 🐾🐾🐾🐾	350 guest rooms and 16 suites. Restaurants and lounge.

R ecognized as Washington's most prestigious address, at the corner of 15th Street and Pennsylvania Avenue. The hotel overlooks the White House and is at the center of Washington's national landmarks and corporate and federal offices. Unquestionably the consummate location is worthy of a hotel that has hosted virtually every president and vice president of the United States since 1918.

Designed by noted New York architects, the Hotel Washington was created in the European style inspired by the Italian Renaissance. Deep-toned woods and exquisite fabrics inspire a gracious flourish of hues that delight your visual senses.

Madison Hotel

15th and M Streets Northwest
Washington, District of Columbia 20005
800-424-8577 • (202) 862-1600

Room Rates:	$225 – $275. AAA discount.
Pet Charges or Deposits:	$30 per day.
Rated: 4 Paws 🐾🐾🐾🐾	318 guest rooms and 35 suites with refrigerators, mini-bars, 24-room service. Health Club. Restaurants and lounge.

 his prestigious landmark hotel provides a high standard of personalized service in an atmosphere of Old World elegance. The public areas are graced by original paintings and antiques from the owner's private collection.

Set in the heart of the business and government district, the Madison Hotel is within walking distance of the White House, Capitol, museums and Georgetown.

Attractive European-style guest rooms and suites offer magnificent city views, some with balconies. A state-of-the-art Health Club includes a gym, massage room, steam shower, exercise equipment and aerobics.

Swiss Inn

1204 Massachusetts Avenue Northwest
Washington, District of Columbia 20005
800-955-7947 • (202) 371-1816
Web Site: www.theswissinn.com
E-mail: Swissinndc@aol.com

Room Rates:	$59 – $99. AAA, AARP, AKC and ABA discounts.
Pet Charges or Deposits:	Manager's prior approval required.
Rated: 3 Paws	7 guest rooms with kitchens.

T he Swiss Inn has the distinction of being the smallest hotel in downtown Washington, D.C. Family-owned and operated for over a decade, the hotel is a renovated turn-of-the-century, four-level brownstone with high ceilings and bay windows.

Each room has individual heating and air conditioning, a television, a fully equipped kitchenette, a telephone and a private bath. The Inn is surrounded by a well-tended flower garden and offers adjacent parking, free on weekends.

Conveniently located on Massachusetts Avenue, in the heart of Washington, you are within walking distance of the White House, the Smithsonian Museums, Embassy Row, the Washington Convention Center, Chinatown, the monuments and across the street from historic St. Agnes Church.

Willard Inter-Continental

1401 Pennsylvania Avenue Northwest
Washington, District of Columbia 20004
800-327-0200 • (202) 628-9100
Web Site: www.interconti.com
E-mail: washington@interconti.com

Room Rates: $350 – $410. Senior citizen's discount.
Pet Charges or Deposits: None.
Rated: 5 Paws 🐾🐾🐾🐾🐾 341 guest rooms and 37 suites. Fitness facility, restaurant and
                        lounge, featuring national jazz musicians.

 eticulously restored to its 1904 grandeur, the Willard is a national landmark that has hosted presidents and others dignitaries. Guest accommodations reflect the charm of the past, while providing all the modern conveniences you expect today. Each lavishly appointed suite features a separate dining room, sitting area and kitchen.

Consistently rated one of the best restaurants in Washington, the elegant Willard Room offers fine contemporary French-American cuisine.

Located two blocks from the White House, the Willard is set amidst Washington's most fashionable shops, restaurants and museums.

Admiral Fell Inn

888 South Broadway
Baltimore, Maryland 21231
800-292-4667 • (410) 522-7377
Web Site: www.admiralfell.com
E-mail: pet@admiralfell.com

Room Rates:	$135 – $195, including continental breakfast. AAA and AARP discounts.
Pet Charges or Deposits:	$75 per day. Sorry, no cats.
Rated: 3 Paws 🐾🐾🐾	75 guest rooms and 5 suites. Three restaurants.

This historic urban inn is located downtown at water's edge in historic Fell's Point, Baltimore's original deep-water port. This lively and colorful community is renowned for its Belgian block streets and brick sidewalks, and its many antique shops, boutiques, art galleries, pubs and gourmet restaurants.

Comprised of eight adjoining buildings, some of which date back more than 200 years, the Admiral Fell Inn is just a water taxi ride away from Baltimore's acclaimed Inner Harbor attractions as well as Little Italy, Oriole Park at Camden Yards, museums, theaters and other cultural activities.

Guest rooms are custom-designed with Federal Period furnishings, each with a modern bathroom, color cable television and air conditioning. The two-story suites feature fireplaces and Jacuzzis.

Biltmore Suites Hotel

205 West Madison Street
Baltimore, Maryland 21201
800-868-5064 • (410) 728-6550
Web Site: www.inn-guide.com/biltmoresuites

Room Rates:	$99 – $139, including deluxe continental breakfast. Call for discounts.
Pet Charges or Deposits:	$20 per stay. Small pets only.
Rated: 3 Paws 🐾 🐾 🐾	26 guest rooms and 17 suites.

T he Biltmore Suites Hotel is a small luxury hotel providing guests with distinctive services and contemporary luxuries. Thoughtful details include mini-bars in every room or suite, the Wall Street Journal and USA Today, complimentary limousine and 24-hour concierge service, in a setting of elegance, with world-class accommodations. Your car is valet-parked, your bags are placed in your room, dinner reservations are made at the most popular restaurants and the staff is dedicated to your service.

A full European breakfast and an evening reception featuring an international wine tasting are compliments of the Biltmore. The hotel is located a few blocks from the central business district within the historic Mount Vernon area, adjacent to Antique Row and within walking distance of the Inner Harbor and Oriole Park at Camden Yards.

River Inn at Rolph's Wharf

1008 Rolph's Wharf Road
Chestertown, Maryland 21620
800-894-6347 • (410) 778-6389
E-mail: rolphs@aol.com

Room Rates:	$75 – $115, including continental breakfast.
Pet Charges or Deposits:	Manager's prior approval required. Credit card number for deposit.
Rated: 3 Paws	6 guest rooms on 6 acres on the Chester River.

This 1830s Victorian home, situated amid 6 acres on the scenic Chester River, is only three miles from historic Chestertown. You have your choice of six charming, air-conditioned guest rooms, all with private baths.

A continental breakfast is included, with home-baked breads, fresh-squeezed orange juice, cereal, hot coffee and tea.

Tidewater Inn and Conference Center

101 East Dover Street
Easton, Maryland 21601
800-237-8775 • (410) 822-1300
Web Site: www.tidewaterinn.com
E-mail: info@tidewaterinn.com

Room Rates:	$95 – $170. AAA and AARP discounts.
Pet Charges or Deposits:	Dogs are not allowed in guest rooms, but are kept in kennels on property. Sorry, no cats. Manager's prior approval required.
Rated: 3 Paws	114 guest rooms and 6 suites. Refrigerators, pool.

From the moment you enter the lobby of the Tidewater Inn, you feel like a guest in a fine home. Warm, rich mahogany doors, fine 18th-century reproduction furniture, the glow of brass lamps and crackling, open fireplaces invite you to relax and enjoy your visit.

Located in Easton, Maryland, where the tree-lined streets invite you to explore a patchwork of charming antique shops and boutiques. Guests can relax at the outdoor pool or take advantage of excellent nearby golfing, fishing and sailing.

Combsberry

4837 Evergreen Road
Oxford, Maryland 21654
(410) 226-5253
Web Site: www.combsberry.com
E-mail: info@combsberry.com

Room Rates:	$250 – $395, including full breakfast and cocktail/tea hour.
Pet Charges or Deposits:	$50 refundable deposit. Manager's prior approval required.
Rated: 4 Paws 🐾🐾🐾🐾	5 guest rooms and 2 suites on 9 acres with formal gardens.

S et among mature magnolias and arching willows on the banks of Island Creek, Combsberry is one of Talbot County's premier historic homes, designed for unsurpassed comfort and privacy.

The unusual stair tower, hidden cellar and eight-arched fireplaces represent unique period design. All guest rooms provide splendid water views and are beautifully appointed with custom furnishings, fireplaces and large baths with Jacuzzis.

At Combsberry you will enjoy the kind of gracious hospitality and casual elegance for which the Eastern Shore of Maryland is well known. After a day of exploring the many sights in nearby Oxford, Easton and St. Michaels, returning home to Combsberry refreshes your spirit with the best of yesterday and today.

Down the Shore Bed and Breakfast

201 Seventh Avenue
Belmar, New Jersey 07719
(732) 681-9023
Web Site: www.belmar.com/downtheshore

Room Rates:	$55 – $90, including full breakfast.
Pet Charges or Deposits:	Manager's prior approval required.
Rated: 3 Paws 🐾🐾🐾	3 guest rooms.

L ocated one block from the boardwalk and beach, Down the Shore Bed and Breakfast offers comfortable, air-conditioned, tastefully decorated guest rooms at reasonable rates. A parlor and a shaded porch are reserved for guests, where they can kick back with a good book, play games or watch TV. Each morning a full breakfast is served, included in your room rate.

The town of Belmar has much to offer — beaches, boat rentals, evening concerts and a variety of restaurant menus that feature everything from fresh seafood to home-style barbecue. Nearby are thoroughbred racing at Monmouth Park, trotters at Freehold Raceway and world-class entertainment at the Garden States Arts Center.

Pillars of Plainfield Bed and Breakfast

922 Central Avenue
Plainfield, New Jersey 07060
888 PILLARS • (908) 753-0922
E-mail: pillars2@juno.com

Room Rates:	$79 – $99, including full breakfast, evening snacks and wine.
Pet Charges or Deposits:	$10 per day. Sorry, no cats. Manager's prior approval required.
Rated: 3 Paws	3 guest rooms and 1 suite. Refrigerators, microwaves, wood-burning fireplaces.

T he moment you drive through the wrought-iron gates, you'll know the Pillars is a special place. Surrounding the house are wildflowers, roses, dogwood, cherry trees and the rhododendrons and azaleas for which Plainfield is famous.

Once inside, in the grand foyer, you're greeted by a handsome circular staircase winding up three stories to a stained-glass skylight. Off the foyer you'll find the music room, with its nautical theme, wood-burning fireplace, organ, stereo and game table. You will enjoy a grand breakfast and your complimentary newspaper each morning in the dining room, with its oversized windows and colored glass.

This restored Victorian-Georgian mansion is nestled on a secluded acre of trees and wildflowers in the Van Wyck Brooks historic district. Golf, tennis and health clubs are nearby.

La Maison Bed and Breakfast and Gallery

404 Jersey Avenue
Spring Lake, New Jersey 07762
(732) 449-0969
Web Site: www.bbianj.com/lamaison

Room Rates: $115 – $285, including full breakfast and happy hour.
Pet Charges or Deposits: 50% refundable deposit or $25 per day for dogs.
Rated: 5 Paws 🐾🐾🐾🐾🐾 5 guest rooms, 2 suites and 1 cottage; beach, pool, tennis, free
                         access to fitness and spa facility.

T he reviews are in: "A top Northeast romantic escape…" states USA Weekend. "Even first-time guests feel as though they've returned to their favorite vacation home," says Country Inns Magazine. And one of 1998's Top 25 B&Bs in the nation, according to America's Favorite Inns, B&Bs & Small Hotels.

In the Victorian seaside village of Spring Lake, New Jersey, you will luxuriate in this quiet, French 1870s inn with an art gallery. Louis Philippe rooms with queen-sized sleigh beds and fluffy comforters combine with discreetly modernized private baths, air conditioning and cable TV. Awake each morning to a full breakfast of specialty omelets, Belgian waffles and French toast, accompanied by freshly squeezed orange juice, mimosas, cappuccino or espresso.

Blue Berry Mountain Inn

HC1, Box 1102
Thomas Road
Blakeslee, Pennsylvania 18610
(717) 646-7144
Web Site: www.blueberrymountaininn.com

Room Rates:	$90 – $115, including full breakfast.
Pet Charges or Deposits:	$50 refundable deposit. Manager's prior approval required.
Rated: 3 Paws 🐾🐾🐾	6 guest rooms and 1 suite on 440 acres with lake. Indoor pool.

 estled among mountains, streams, lakes and ponds on hundreds of acres of glacial wetlands is the Blue Berry Mountain Inn. Six modern, well-appointed guest rooms offer spectacular views of nature from each room.

A game room, a library, an indoor heated pool, an outside spa and an extraordinary Great Room that boasts a massive stone fireplace are available to guests. A full breakfast is served daily in the sun room, as well as tea and sweets in the afternoon. The Inn is friendly to the physically challenged.

Inn at Turkey Hill

991 Central Road
Bloomsburg, Pennsylvania 17815
(717) 387-1500
Web Site: www.enterpe.com/turkeyhill
E-mail: turkyinn@prolog.net

Room Rates:	$95 – $185, including continental breakfast.
Pet Charges or Deposits:	$15 per stay. Credit card refundable deposit. Treat bags provided for your pet.
Rated: 4 Paws	16 guest rooms and 7 suites. Restaurant.

Y ou would probably never suspect that a moment's drive from the Interstate would transport you into a world of peaceful strolls by a duck pond and personal wake-up calls.

This is an oasis along the highway, where continuous attention to detail is evident. It is apparent that the goal here is to make everyone feel pampered, whether you are eating a distinctive gourmet meal, or whether you are spending a night in one of the country cottages surrounding the informal courtyard or in the main house, an 1839 white brick farmhouse.

Fine dining at the Inn at Turkey Hill offers a creative, well-balanced menu in a relaxed, attractive setting.

Merry Inn

Route 390
P.O. Box 757
Canadensis, Pennsylvania 18325
800-858-4182 • (717) 595-2011

Room Rates:	$90 – $95, including full breakfast.
Pet Charges or Deposits:	$25 refundable deposit.
Rated: 3 Paws	6 guest rooms. Outdoor hot tub.

Built Cape Cod-style in the 1940s as a boardinghouse, the Merry Inn was a private home for about twenty years, until 1994.

Owner-innkeepers Chris and Meredyth Huggard have decorated their Inn with comfortable, eclectic furnishings in a country and Victorian style. On the rear, second-level deck, "built over a piece of mountain," is a year-round hot tub that faces the woods. Awake each morning to Western or three-cheese omelets, stuffed French toast or apple or chocolate-chip pancakes served overlooking a brook.

You are within minutes of the Pocono Playhouse, Promised Land State Park, Alpine Mountain and Camelback ski areas. Area shopping, including candle factories and outlets, and white-water rafting, horseback riding and antiquing are nearby.

Lodge at Chalk Hill

Route 40 East, Box 240
Chalk Hill, Pennsylvania 15421
800-833-4283 • (724) 438-8880
E-mail: thelodge@borg.pulsenet.com

Room Rates:	$73 – $104, including continental breakfast. AAA and AARP discounts.
Pet Charges or Deposits:	$10 per day. Manager's prior approval required.
Rated: 3 Paws	61 guest rooms and 6 suites with kitchenettes.

The Lodge at Chalk Hill sits atop 37 lush acres in the heart of the scenic Laurel Highlands. Guest rooms and suites offer private decks, with views of the famous mountain foliage and scenic Lake Lenore.

Here you will enjoy whitewater rafting, premier bike trails, skiing and PGA golf. Shop a variety of unique galleries and boutiques or just relax and observe nature from your own private deck. Downhill and cross-country skiing and sleigh rides are within minutes of the Lodge.

Victorian Loft Bed and Breakfast and Cedarwood Lodge

216 South Front Street
Clearfield, Pennsylvania 16830
800-798-0456 • (814) 765-4805

Room Rates:	$95 – $105, including full breakfast.
Pet Charges or Deposits:	$50 refundable deposit. Manager's prior approval required.
Rated: 4 Paws 🐾🐾🐾🐾	2 guest rooms, 1 suite, 1 mountain cabin. Kitchen, fireplaces, whirlpool.

T he Victorian Loft Bed and Breakfast is an elegant 1894 Victorian home, whose hosts offer warm hospitality and a friendly atmosphere. The house itself is located along the river in historic Clearfield, just minutes from the theater, restaurants and parks.

Featuring double-decker gingerbread porches, cherry and oak woodwork, stained glass and period furnishings, guest rooms are comfortable, air-conditioned and private. A memorable full breakfast is included with your night's stay and features homemade baked goods and freshly squeezed juice.

Cedarwood Lodge, for secluded privacy on 8 forested acres in the Moshannon State Forest, offers a charming post-and-beam, three-bedroom cabin, completely equipped with all the conveniences in a wilderness setting. There is a screened-in porch, deck, picnic table, gas grill and campfire, making this a wonderful base camp from which to explore the natural surroundings.

Golden Pheasant Inn

River Road, Route 32
Erwinna, Pennsylvania 18920
800-830-4GPI • (610) 294-9595
Web Site: www.goldenpheasant.com

Room Rates: $75 – $155, including continental breakfast.
Pet Charges or Deposits: $10 per day. Manager's prior approval required.
Rated: 4 Paws 🐾🐾🐾🐾   6 guest rooms, 1 suite.

T his magical country inn and restaurant is nestled between the Delaware River and the Pennsylvania Canal in Bucks County, Pennsylvania. Perfect for a weekend getaway or an exquisite country meal, the Golden Pheasant Inn is just over an hour from New York City or Philadelphia and only 20 minutes north of New Hope, Pennsylvania. Celebrating its tenth anniversary this year, this Inn remains a Bucks County gem.

Sleep soundly in one of the six romantic guest rooms or the cottage suite, featuring four-poster queen-sized canopy beds, private baths and a generous continental breakfast. All rooms have river and canal views and are furnished in French, English and American antiques. The cottage suite has a peaceful porch overlooking the Delaware Canal and comes equipped with a kitchenette and sitting room.

General Sutter Inn

14 East Main Street
Lititz, Pennsylvania 17543
(717) 626-2115

Room Rates:	$78 – $108.
Pet Charges or Deposits:	One night's refundable deposit.
Rated: 3 Paws 🐾 🐾 🐾	12 guest rooms and 4 suites, 2 restaurants, tavern, outdoor patio.

F ounded in 1764 by the Moravian Church and known then as Zum Anker, or Sign of the Anchor, the Inn from its inception has been considered one of the finest in Pennsylvania. In 1803 and again in 1848 the Inn underwent significant structural changes, evolving into the handsome, three-story brick building of today.

The General Sutter Inn features 16 spacious rooms and suites decorated in antique country and Victorian style, two fine restaurants, a full-service tavern and a seasonal outdoor patio. Regional boutiques, interesting local crafts and a myriad of sights and pastimes are only steps from the front door.

Black Bass Hotel

3774 River Road
Lumberville, Pennsylvania 18933
(215) 297-5770
Web Site: www.blackbasshotel.com
E-mail: info@blackbasshotel.com

Room Rates: $65 – $175, including continental breakfast.
Pet Charges or Deposits: Small dogs only.
Rated: 3 Paws 🐾🐾🐾   7 guest rooms and 2 suites. Restaurants.

 he Black Bass Hotel was built as a fortified haven for river travelers in the turbulent days of the 1740s, when hostile Indian bands roamed the forests. It prospered as an inn for early traders and offered comfort to many travelers.

Though far more civilized today than when boatman and rafters called the inn home, there is the unmistakable sense of history here. Be it in the period-furnished guest rooms and suites, the fine dining rooms, the public room filled with 19th-century antiques and British royal memorabilia, or merely the facade or hallways of the building, there is a rekindling of Colonial spirit that is the very essence of the country inn.

As for provisions, the dining rooms of the Black Bass Hotel have earned a renowned reputation for their culinary reflections of European and American country traditions.

If you are one of those people who, when they imagine a country inn, conjure up the image of antique beds and good food, with a country store across the way, you will feel very much at home at the Black Bass Hotel.

Green Acres Farm Bed and Breakfast

1382 Pinkerton Road
Mount Joy, Pennsylvania 17552
(717) 653-4028
Web Site: www.castyournet.com/greenacres

Room Rates:	$85, including full breakfast.
Pet Charges or Deposits:	$5 per day. Sorry, no cats.
Rated: 3 Paws 🐾🐾🐾	7 guest rooms on 150-acre farm.

This farm is truly family-friendly. From your arrival, your welcoming committee includes your hosts, along with a sociable group of kittens, pygmy goats, sheep, peacocks, chickens and a pony. And the pigs won't mind if you take a peek in the pens as well. Children will enjoy the trampolines, volleyball and basketball courts, bicycles and a ride in the hay wagon.

The main farmhouse is furnished with antiques, offering comfortable air-conditioned guest rooms with private baths. A large balcony and porch set the relaxing tone, as you overlook the beautiful countryside.

Rittenhouse Hotel

210 West Rittenhouse Square
Philadelphia, Pennsylvania 19103
800-635-1042 • (215) 546-9000
Web Site: www.rittenhousehotel.com
E-mail: info@rittenhousehotel.com

Room Rates: $190 – $315.
Pet Charges or Deposits: Call for refundable deposit.
Rated: 5 Paws ❤ ❤ ❤ ❤ ❤ 87 guest rooms and 11 suites with kitchens. Health club and
                          spa, 5 restaurants and lounge.

The Rittenhouse Hotel has received the coveted AAA Five-Diamond Award every year since 1992. Located on the west side of Rittenhouse Square, this upscale residential area is within walking distance of luxurious shops, fine dining, museums and the business district.

Guest accommodations are oversized and exquisite, either overlooking the park or the cityscape to the west. Staterooms are decorated in country French themes, with Queen Anne chairs and writing desks, thick duvet-style bedspreads, beautiful marble baths and original artwork.

The Adolf Biecker Spa and Salon is Center City's premier health club and spa, with an indoor pool lit by an overhead skylight, extensive equipment, free weights and numerous aerobic machines. Take time to enjoy the sauna and steam room or indulge in the spa treatments of a facial, herbal and aromatherapy wraps, massage and manicure.

Pantall Hotel

135 East Mahoning Street
Punxsutawney, Pennsylvania 15767
800-872-6825 • (814) 938-6600

Room Rates: $50 – $85.
Pet Charges or Deposits: Manager's prior approval required.
Rated: 3 Paws 🐾 🐾 🐾   75 guest rooms and 2 suites.

From the first step inside the door, the historic Pantall Hotel welcomes you with its touches of small-town hospitality. All 75 guest rooms have modern conveniences such as cable television, air conditioning and newly renovated baths with showers.

The Coach Room of the Pantall Hotel serves fine food at breakfast, lunch and dinner, in a warm and comfortable setting. The room is filled with antiques, old and new framed prints, paintings and collector plates. An authentic Victorian Bar, made of curly maple-stained cherry with round, ornate columns and arches, has been recently restored here. If the bar could talk, it would fill volumes of history books. Hans Olson, a partner in the Olson & Fisher Drilling Company in the early 1900s, bought diamonds at the bar from dealers who would come from New York to meet him there.

Pegasus Bed and Breakfast

R.R. 2, Box 2066
Shohola, Pennsylvania 18458
(717) 296-4017

Room Rates:	$50 – $100, including full breakfast.
Pet Charges or Deposits:	Manager's prior approval required.
Rated: 3 Paws 🐾 🐾 🐾	8 guest rooms and 2 suites with refrigerators and microwaves.

uilt as a country inn in 1910, Pegasus offers an ideal place for a relaxing getaway. Guests make themselves at home in the cozy living room, parlor game room, library or the big wraparound porch.

   The Pegasus woodland is part of the tri-state forest and nature reserve surrounding Delaware River National Park, in the northeastern corner of the Pocono Mountains. The nearby Delaware River offers swimming and three-season floating in canoes, rafts, and kayaks — for beginners and whitewater experts. River, stream and lake fishing, golf, skiing and horseback riding are here to enjoy.

Benita's Bed and Breakfast

16620 Amelia Avenue
Amelia, Virginia 23002
(804) 561-6321
Web Site: www.bbonline.com/va/benita
E-mail: Davisr79@hotmail.com

Room Rates:	$50 – $70, including full breakfast and evening dessert.
Pet Charges or Deposits:	Manager's prior approval required.
Rated: 3 Paws 🐾🐾🐾	4 guest rooms.

Y ou'll find all the comforts of home at this bed and breakfast. Relax in a rocking chair on the front porch of this ante-bellum home or enjoy sitting by a warm fireplace in the winter. Snack on cookies and milk before you go to bed in one of the four guest rooms furnished with family antiques. In the morning feast on a hearty, Southern-style breakfast served in the dining room, or in bed if you like.

Area attractions include historic sites to explore, a treasure hunt for precious stones at the Morefield Mine, numerous antique stores to investigate and the Amelia wildlife area, which is great for fishing.

Sky Chalet Mountain Lodge

280 Sky Chalet Lane
Route 263
P.O. Box 300
Basye, Virginia 22810
(540) 856-2147
Web Site: www.skychalet.com
E-mail: skychalet@skychalet.com

Room Rates:	$34 – $79, including continental breakfast. AAA, AARP, AKC and ABA discounts.
Pet Charges or Deposits:	Manager's prior approval required.
Rated: 3 Paws 🐾🐾🐾	10 guest cabins and 2 suites, with fireplaces and spectacular views.

 ky Chalet is a warm, friendly place where travelers find good country food, refreshing spirits for the soul and a restful bed in a homey room. The proprietors are there to greet you as their guest, not as a stranger. Each morning a complimentary continental breakfast is delivered to your room.

Sky Chalet is a mountain lodge in its truest sense. First of all, it sits on the very top of a mountain, with views all around. It's rustic, it's old, and it does need work, but the rooms are clean and neat and very reasonably priced.

You are surrounded by hiking trails and woods, the George Washington National Forest and the Shenandoah National Park, in addition to antique and craft shops, skiing, golfing, horseback riding, tennis, swimming, canoeing and numerous lake activities.

Milton Hall Bed and Breakfast Inn

207 Thorny Lane
Covington, Virginia 24426
(540) 965-0196

Room Rates:	$75 – $140, including full breakfast. AARP discount.
Pet Charges or Deposits:	Manager's prior approval required.
Rated: 3 Paws 🐾🐾🐾	5 guest rooms and 1 suite on 17 acres.

Milton Hall, a unique English country manor, was built in 1874 in the Allegheny Mountains of western Virginia. The house presents an exotic contrast to its rustic surroundings, with its many gables, buttressed porch towers and Gothic trimmings. The house is spacious, but more of a large country home than a mansion.

Guest rooms are spacious with private baths, sitting areas and original fireplaces. Room rates include a full English breakfast, with menu highlights of fresh fruits in season, eggs prepared with herbs, Allegheny Mountain trout or local country-style sausage and red potatoes. Home-baked muffins are stuffed with fresh berries or apples in season.

Stratford Inn

2500 Riverside Drive
Danville, Virginia 24540
800-326-8455 • (804) 793-2500

Room Rates:	$50 – $92, including full breakfast. AAA, AARP, AKC and ABA discounts.
Pet Charges or Deposits:	Small pets only.
Rated: 3 Paws	151 guest rooms and 9 suites, with refrigerators, microwaves, pool, whirlpool and Jacuzzi. On-site fitness center. Restaurant.

T he rooms are spacious and comfortable and feature in-room coffee, free newspapers, hair dryers and other amenities, including room service. Suites are equipped with whirlpools, saunas, parlors and two baths.

The fitness facility features the treadmill, stepper and stationary bike. The heated pool, hot tub and sun deck are for guests to enjoy. Nearby is an indoor pool, steam room, Nautilus, racquetball and a fully equipped local health club. Just ask for a free pass at the front desk.

Doe Run Lodge Resort and Conference Center

Milepost 189 Blue Ridge Parkway
P.O. Box 280
Fancy Gap, Virginia 24328
800-325-6189 • (540) 398-2212
Web Site: www.doerunlodge.com
E-mail: doerun@tcia.net

Room Rates:	$109 – $254. AAA and AARP discounts.
Pet Charges or Deposits:	$45 refundable deposit.
Rated: 5 Paws 🐾🐾🐾🐾🐾	Cabins and chalets with refrigerators, microwaves, pool, Jacuzzi, hot tubs, tennis courts.

 t Milepost 189, a spot between Roanoke and Fancy Gap, Virginia, at a place called Groundhog Mountain, you'll find an accommodating alpine lodge and resort where you can stop the world and imbibe the Appalachian experience. Doe Run Lodge offers an inviting retreat with comfortable accommodations nestled in a remote mountain setting along the Blue Ridge Parkway.

You'll find a pre-laid fire ready for your match when you arrive in any of the chalets or villas. All accommodations are spacious and comfortably furnished. Many feature convenient kitchens. The swimming pool and carpeted deck are comfortable throughout the season, and you can get even warmer in the adjacent saunas.

The rustically designed stone-and-timber lodge features top-rated dining, a fabulous wine cellar and a fully stocked bar. Floor-to-ceiling windows and a spacious granite patio add spectacular views at every meal.

Dunning Mills Inn

2305-C Jefferson Davis Highway
Fredericksburg, Virginia 22401
(540) 373-1256

Room Rates:	$67 – $90, including doughnuts and coffee. AAA discount.
Pet Charges or Deposits:	$2.50 per day per pet. $200 refundable deposit for stays of 30 days or longer.
Rated: 3 Paws	44 queen-sized suites. Refrigerators, microwaves, laundry facilities, pool.

T he Dunning Mills Inn features comfortable suites at reasonable rates. Each suite includes a fully equipped kitchen, dining area, living area and a spacious bedroom/bath. There are separate entrances to each suite, with convenient free parking.

While the Inn is centrally located on the Route 1 bypass in Fredericksburg, it is nestled near the woods, away from the noise and congestion of the highway. Most suites offer a wooded view and daily maid service.

Sleepy Hollow Farm Bed and Breakfast

16280 Blue Ridge Turnpike
Gordonsville, Virginia 22738
800-215-4804 • (540) 832-5555

Room Rates:	$65 – $135, including full breakfast.
Pet Charges or Deposits:	$5 – $10 per stay. Manager's prior approval required.
Rated: 4 Paws 🐾 🐾 🐾 🐾	3 guest rooms and 3 suites. Refrigerator, microwave, whirlpool and Jacuzzi.

 njoy country life in a charming old farmhouse or in the chestnut cottage. The warmth and hospitality of Sleepy Hollow reflect Virginia's traditions.

Terraces, porches, a croquet lawn and rooms with views and fireplaces provide opportunities to relax in the family atmosphere. The main house with its antique furnishings and eclectic accessories offers a pleasing and comfortable place to relax.

Each morning a delicious country breakfast is served in the two dining rooms. Sleepy Hollow grows its own herbs, vegetables and flowers for cooking and for decorations.

Hummingbird Inn

30 Wood Lane
P.O. Box 147
Goshen, Virginia 24439
800-397-3214 • (540) 997-9065
Web Site: www.hummingbird.com
E-mail: hmgbird@hummingbird.com

Room Rates:	$105 – $135, including full breakfast. AAA, AARP, AKC and ABA discounts.
Pet Charges or Deposits:	Sorry, no cats. Manager's prior approval required. $20 per stay. One night's refundable deposit.
Rated: 4 Paws	5 guest rooms with whirlpools and fireplaces.

T his unique Victorian villa, born in 1780 and completed in 1853, is just west of the scenic Goshen Pass on the western edge of the Shenandoah Valley. Here you will find country elegance amid perennial gardens and an old livery stable on the edge of a wide trout stream. The atmosphere is relaxed and informal.

Guest rooms are beautifully appointed with period antiques, natural linens, down comforters, ceiling fans, room air conditioners and thick, fluffy towels in modern bathrooms.

A typical gourmet breakfast features fresh fruit, entrées such as oven-baked French toast, cornmeal pancakes or Dutch babies, bacon, sausage or ham, potatoes or baked apples, coffee cake, muffins and scones. Guests have described the cuisine here as "five star" and "fabulous."

Village Inn

Route 1, Box 76
Harrisonburg, Virginia 22801
800-736-7355 • (540) 434-7355

Room Rates:	$42 – $58.
Pet Charges or Deposits:	None.
Rated: 3 Paws	36 guest rooms and suites, many with decks and whirlpool baths.

T he Village Inn of Harrisonburg is conveniently located on Highway 11, just off Interstate 81, in the picturesque Shenandoah Valley of Virginia. Opportunities for fun and recreation abound within easy reach of the Inn. Explore interesting underground caverns or experience the scenic beauty of famous Skyline Drive. The Valley's rich heritage is evident in the many historical monuments and markers along the roads and at the Civil War battlefield and museum in nearby New Market.

Guest rooms are spacious and comfortable, many with whirlpool baths and decks overlooking the scenic Virginia countryside. The Inn offers a pool and a playground as well as parking at your door for easy access.

Tides Inn

480 King Carter Drive
Irvington, Virginia 22480
800-TIDES INN • (804) 438-5000
Web Site: www.tidesinn.com

Room Rates: $130 – $175.
Pet Charges or Deposits: $10 per day.
Rated: 5 Paws 🐾🐾🐾🐾🐾 194 guest rooms and 10 suites, with a restaurant. 175-acre
                         peninsula offering golf, tennis, yacht cruises and a pool.

T he Tides Inn is a charming resort, tucked away from civilization and nestled on the Rappahannock River and Chesapeake Bay. Once a wonderful secret among friends, the Tides Inn has recently been recognized by Condé Nast Traveler readers as one of the premier resorts in the world.

Spoil yourself with a moonlight cruise aboard the exquisite private yacht, the Miss Ann or indulge in 45 holes of championship golf, including the Golden Eagle, rated one of the top ten golf courses in Virginia by Golf Digest. Delight in award-winning cuisine, a saltwater swimming pool, boating, bike-riding, tennis, dancing at the Chesapeake Club, luncheons and cocktails at poolside.

The area abounds in antique and craft shops, seafood markets and traditional boat-building. If nature is your interest, there are two excellent nature trails just minutes away that are a bird-watcher's paradise.

Applewood Inn

Buffalo Bend Road
P.O. Box 1348
Lexington, Virginia 24450
800-463-1902 • (540) 463-1962
Web Site: www.applewoodbb.com
E-mail: applewd@cfw.com

Room Rates:	$80 – $130, including full breakfast, snacks and beverages.
Pet Charges or Deposits:	$20 per stay. Sorry, no cats.
Rated: 3 Paws 🐾 🐾 🐾	4 guest rooms on 35 acres. Llama trekking available.
	Refrigerators, microwaves, pool, whirlpool and hot tubs.

T his special home, perched high above scenic Buffalo Creek in Lexington, combines passive solar technology with historical and natural materials. In addition to four guest bedrooms, all with queen-sized beds and private baths, there is a hot tub with French doors opening out onto the hillside and an in-ground pool with views of the Blue Ridge Mountains. Porches span the entire front of the house on two levels, so that each bedroom opens onto a porch.

The property, consisting of 35 very private acres, has spectacular views of House Mountain and Short Hill, in addition to the Blue Ridge. It abuts more than 900 acres of the Rockbridge Hunt, for hiking and riding, and has access to Buffalo Creek for fishing and tubing. Birds and other wildlife are abundant.

Breakfast is heart-healthy, with whole-grain baked goods, such as hazelnut pancakes, wheat germ and cornmeal waffles, fresh fruit, herbal teas and coffee.

Creek Crossing Farm at Chappelle Hill

P.O. Box 18
Lincoln, Virginia 22078
(540) 338-7550
E-mail: creekcrossingfarm@erols.com

Room Rates:	$95 – $115, including full breakfast.
Pet Charges or Deposits:	Credit card imprint. Horse boarding available.
Rated: 4 Paws	2 guest rooms and 1 suite on 25-acre farm.

Since 1773, Creek Crossing Farm at Chappelle Hill has been providing gracious hospitality to all who stay. The farm is encompasses twenty-five acres, which are located in Virginia's Hunt Country, in a secluded valley just outside the present-day village of Lincoln. Walking trails wind around the creek and a cultivated blueberry field is part of the farm. Horses are boarded here.

Guests can choose from 3 exquisitely appointed rooms, each with a private bath, luxurious thick towels, a fluffy down comforter and all-natural cotton bedding.

Breakfast is served in the large, sunny, 40-foot kitchen or on the deck.

Inn at Meander Plantation

HCR 5, Box 460A
Locust Dale, Virginia 22948
800-385-4936 • (540) 672-4912
Web Site: www.meander.net

Room Rates: $95 – $195, including full breakfast.
Pet Charges or Deposits: Horses welcome. Stables for horses.
Rated: 5 Paws 🐾 🐾 🐾 🐾 🐾 3 guest rooms and 5 suites on 80 acres.

C radled in the heart of Jefferson's Virginia, the Inn at Meander Plantation offers a rare opportunity to experience the charm and elegance of Colonial living at its best. This historic country estate, which dates to 1766, allows guests to return to an earlier, more romantic time, when hospitality was a matter of pride and fine living was an art practiced in restful surroundings. Stroll through formal boxwood gardens or wander woods and fields where wildlife abounds. White rockers line both levels of the expansive back porches, providing peaceful respites for sipping afternoon tea, reading the latest novel or watching breathtaking mountain sunsets.

Guest rooms reflect the elegance and romance of a Virginia country estate, with four-poster queen-sized beds piled high with plump pillows and fluffy down comforters and beautifully appointed with period reproductions and antiques. Join your fellow guests in the formal dining room or under the arched breezeway on sun-warmed mornings for a full country gourmet breakfast.

Widow Kip's Country

355 Orchard Drive
Mount Jackson, Virginia 22842
800-478-8714 • (540) 477-2400
Web Site: www.widow.com

Room Rates:	$65 – $85, including full breakfast. AAA, AARP, AKC and ABA discounts.
Pet Charges or Deposits:	None.
Rated: 4 Paws 🐾 🐾 🐾 🐾	5 guest rooms and 2 cottages; fireplaces; pool, bicycles available.

T his lovingly restored 1830 gem rests on 7 rural acres in the Shenandoah Valley, with views of the Massanutten Mountains. The Widow Kip's is a serene and friendly home offering nostalgia and hospitality in five antique-filled bedrooms of the main house, all with original fireplaces and private baths. Locally crafted quilts grace the four-poster, sleigh and hand-carved Victorian beds. Children and pets are welcome in the two restored cottages that create a charming Williamsburg-style courtyard by the house.

Breakfast is a friendly family-style gathering in the dining room, and the common room welcomes you with backgammon or checkers and old movies on the VCR. A swimming pool is on the property and bikes are provided for rides through the apple orchards.

The Widow Kip's is a perfect jumping-off place for all that the Shenandoah has to offer: caverns, hiking, canoeing, antiquing, battlefields, golf, skiing, horseback riding and fishing on the property — as well as the fine restaurants in the area.

Garden and the Sea Inn

P.O. Box 275
New Church, Virginia 23415
800-842-0672 • (757) 824-0672
Web Site: www.bbonline.com/va/gardensea

Room Rates:	$75 – $165, including continental breakfast. AAA and AARP discounts.
Pet Charges or Deposits:	Manager's prior approval required.
Rated: 5 Paws 🐾 🐾 🐾 🐾 🐾	6 guest rooms with refrigerators, whirlpools, Jacuzzis. Fine dining.

T he romantic Garden and the Sea Inn, circa 1802, is located in New Church, Virginia, an area rich in history, architecture and natural beauty. The Inn offers the best of two worlds. Nestled in a quiet rural setting, it is just minutes from the barrier islands of Chincoteague and Assateague, home of the world-famous wild ponies and one of the most beautiful beaches on the East Coast.

Spacious guest rooms offer queen-sized beds with sitting areas, screened porches and double whirlpool baths. Fine dining at the Inn features a carefully selected menu, with entrées prepared with local produce and seafood from the farms and waters of the Eastern Shore. The menu changes frequently, with an extensive wine list to complement every dish.

Owl and the Pussycat

405 High Street
Petersburg, Virginia 23803
888-733-0505 • (804) 733-0505
Web Site: www.ctg.net/owlcat
E-mail: owlcat@ctg.net

Room Rates:	$75 – $105, including full breakfast.
Pet Charges or Deposits:	$10 per day. $20 refundable deposit.
Rated: 3 Paws	4 guest rooms and 2 guest suites.

T his gracious Queen Anne-style mansion, with a two-story turret and balcony was built around 1895. The Owl and the Pussycat is graced with perennial flower beds and more than twenty herbs, tended to by the English innkeepers John and Juliette Swenson.

The Inn has many unique characteristics such as the original gas-light fixtures, eight fireplaces, all with different tiles and mantels, and polished "heart pine" floors with lovely rugs. Guest rooms are large and comfortable.

Many of Petersburg's attractions are just a brief stroll down High Street. Old Towne is close by, with shops, Civil War museums, antique emporiums and restaurants you can walk to in the evening.

High Meadows Inn

Route 4, Box 6
Scottsville, Virginia 24590
800-232-1832 • (804) 286-2218
Web Site: www.highmeadows.com

Room Rates:	$99 – $185, including full breakfast. Call for discounts.
Pet Charges or Deposits:	$20 per stay. Manager's prior approval required.
Rated: 5 Paws 🐾🐾🐾🐾🐾	7 guest rooms and 7 suites. Refrigerators, microwaves, whirlpool, Jacuzzi and hot tub.

Part of what makes the High Meadows Inn unique is its duality as both a country inn and a vineyard. As Virginia's only Inn that combines its place on the National Register of Historic Homes with a renaissance farm vineyard (it's a leading producer of Pinot Noir grapes), High Meadows offers the discriminating guest a rare opportunity to look at 170 years of architectural history and twelve new, exciting years of viticultural happening.

High Meadows is a grand house, where guests are welcomed with champagne, and stay in individually appointed rooms, furnished with period antiques and art, each with a private bath. The rooms are romantic, each with a story — a fantasy place. The fifty surrounding acres of gardens, footpaths, forests and ponds guarantee privacy and quiet.

There are picnic baskets full of delightful tastes, good wine and poetry books, multicourse dinners and country breakfasts.

Graves' Mountain Lodge

Route 670
Syria, Virginia 22743
(540) 923-4231

Room Rates: $55 – $110, including 3 meals per day.
Pet Charges or Deposits: None.
Rated: 3 Paws   38 guest rooms, kitchens, Olympic-sized outdoor pool.

Graves' Mountain Lodge is nestled deep in the foothills of the Blue Ridge Mountains, near the end of the road in Syria, Virginia. Here you're invited to assume a leisurely pace as you enjoy some of life's simpler pleasures, such as hiking, fishing, tennis, swimming and some good, old-fashioned "porch-sitting." Take a stroll down the lane to observe the activities of the fruit orchard and cattle farm.

Guest accommodations range from the old farmhouse, where you can enjoy comfortable accommodations in an authentically rustic atmosphere, to guest cottages overlooking the river with beautiful mountain views and two or three bedrooms.

In the Lodge itself, you'll find the dining rooms, the gift shop and recreation lounges. At Graves' Mountain, nobody leaves the table hungry. You will enjoy tasty, down-home specialties prepared with foods fresh from the garden.

Inn at 802

802 Jamestown Road
Williamsburg, Virginia 23185
800-672-4086 • (757) 564-0845

Room Rates: $115 – $145, including full breakfast. AAA and AARP discounts.
Pet Charges or Deposits: Manager's prior approval required. Call for refundable deposit.
Rated: 3 Paws 🐾🐾🐾   4 guest rooms.

This new bed and breakfast, decorated in Colonial style, offers four bedrooms, each with its own private bath. Guest rooms are spacious, private, quiet and inviting, with reading chairs and period-style antiques and reproductions.

The common areas of the house include an extensive library with woodburning fireplace, a large living room, a dining room and a delightful sun room that overlooks the garden and patio area.

A candlelight breakfast is served on fine china with crystal and silver. Menu highlights include sumptuous homemade pastries, sizzling hickory-smoked Virginia bacon, ham or sausage and variable mouth-watering entrées.

Cheat River Lodge

Route 1, Box 115
Faulkner Road
Elkins, West Virginia 26241
(304) 636-2301

Room Rates: $58 – $63.
Pet Charges or Deposits: $10 per stay. Sorry, no cats.
Rated: 4 Paws 🐾 🐾 🐾 🐾   6 guest rooms and 6 cabins on 4 miles of riverfront property.
                         Kitchens, fireplaces and hot tubs.

The lodge, made from cedar and fieldstone, is located on a country lane overlooking the river, with large picture windows. Rocking chairs, wicker groupings and picnic tables on the screened porches provide casual areas for lounging.

Six individual log-and-stone homes, each with its own private, 7-foot outdoor hot tub, comprise the rest of the property. Inside, you will delight in the exposed log walls and cathedral ceilings, stone hearths with glass-fronted wood stoves and fully equipped kitchens. The accommodations are well appointed and fully equipped. You will be greeted with freshly made beds and the hot tub warm and ready.

The Cheat River Lodge is located on the Cheat River in the Monongahela National Forest, six miles east of Elkins, West Virginia. Here you will find excellent hiking, biking, birding, rock climbing and cross-country and downhill ski areas. The river provides the ideal place for canoeing, tubing and fishing.

Blennerhassett Hotel

320 Market Street
Parkersburg, West Virginia 26101
800-262-2536 • (304) 422-3131

Room Rates:	$69 – $129, including full breakfast and complimentary newspaper. AAA, AARP, AKC and ABA discounts.
Pet Charges or Deposits:	$25 refundable deposit. Manager's prior approval required. Sorry, no cats.
Rated: 3 Paws 🐾🐾🐾	104 guest rooms and 4 suites. Use of local fitness facility. Restaurants and lounge.

Built before the turn of the century, this hotel exudes the captivating atmosphere of the gaslight era. Registered as a National Historic Landmark, the style of the hotel is seen in its rich crown moldings, authentic English doors, brass and leaded-glass chandeliers and antiques hand-carried from England.

Fine continental and regional American cuisine is enjoyed in the renowned Harman's Restaurant. For the past five consecutive years Harman's has had the distinction of being awarded AAA's 4-Diamond rating.

Pence Springs Hotel

P.O. Box 90
Pence Springs, West Virginia 24962
800-826-1829 • (304) 445-2606
Web Site: www.wvweb.com/www/Pence_Springs_Hotel

Room Rates: $70 – $100, including full breakfast. AAA and AARP discounts.
Pet Charges or Deposits: $15 per stay. Manager's prior approval required.
Rated: 3 Paws 🐾 🐾 🐾   24 guest rooms and 9 suites on a 400-acre plantation.
                         Restaurant.

 nown as The Grand Hotel, this National Registry inn is one of the historic mineral spas of the Virginias. A premier retreat from 1897 until the Great Depression, Pence Springs was the most popular and expensive hotel in West Virginia. Now a fine country inn on a 400-acre plantation, Pence Springs Hotel has attracted national attention.

Guest rooms accommodate every need and are furnished in the style of the 1920s, all with private baths. Room rates include a full breakfast.

You can be as active or inactive as you want to be — relax on the porch with a good book, play croquet and horseshoes on the lawn, ride a bike through the surrounding countryside, ride on horseback on 15,000-year-old buffalo trails, hike along the many trails on the property, take a canoe trip on the Greenbrier River or go smallmouth bass fishing on the hotel's riverfront.

Inn at Chester

318 West Main Street
Chester, Connecticut 06412
800-949-STAY • (860) 526-9541
Web Site: www.innatchester.com

Room Rates:	$105 – $215, including continental breakfast.
Pet Charges or Deposits:	None.
Rated: 4 Paws 🐾 🐾 🐾 🐾	40 guest rooms and 2 guest suites, offering exercise facilities, library, pool table, darts, board games, tennis, hiking trail, touring bicycles, bocci, pub, restaurant and guest laundry services.

he Inn at Chester is the perfect getaway for an escape from the ordinary. Serenity abounds in this country inn located on 12 luscious acres in the Connecticut River Valley. An 18th-century farmhouse was the inspiration for this 42-room full-service inn.

Each room is individually appointed with Eldred Wheeler reproduction antiques to complement the Colonial decor. Rooms are serene, comfortable and unpretentious. Guest amenities include a well-equipped exercise room and the Carriage Parlor, which hosts a library and pool table. Enjoy elegant but comfortable dining in the Post and Beam dining room, which serves award-winning cuisine. Dunk's Landing tavern serves libations and offers lighter but equally delicious fare.

Year-round activities are enjoyed at the inn including tennis, hiking, bocci, croquet, cycling or simply relaxing in the hammock next to a peaceful pond. In winter, you can cross-country ski, downhill ski or ice skate at nearby Powder Ridge or curl up and daydream next to a roaring fire. The surrounding countryside offers many adventures for the traveler, including a visit to a castle by ferryboat, an antique steam train, exploring antique shops, artist boutiques or a show at the Goodspeed Opera House.

Centennial Inn

c/o Nutmeg Bed and Breakfast Agency
P.O. Box 1117
West Hartford, Connecticut 06127-1117
800-727-7592 • (860) 236-6698

Room Rates:	$115 – $150, including continental breakfast.
Pet Charges or Deposits:	None with manager's prior approval.
Rated: 4 Paws	150 guest suites with kitchen, hide-a-beds, fireplace, swimming pool, whirlpool and fitness center.

T he Centennial Inn is located in the aristocratic old town of Farmington, laden with historical treasures and cultural richness. This contemporary inn offers one- and two-bedroom suites featuring comfortable queen-sized beds, with sleeper couches tastefully tucked away, kitchens, full private baths and inviting fireplaces.

Guests can enjoy the outdoor pool and whirlpool during warm weather, as well as the exercise room and jogging trails. In the morning you will awaken to the aroma of freshly brewed coffee and enjoy a deluxe continental breakfast.

The Farmington area offers an unspoiled scenic grandeur, where historic homes and museums are nestled among antique shops and charming restaurants. You may also enjoy a visit to Miss Porter's School, Jackie O's alma mater. Nearby is one of Connecticut's largest and finest shopping malls, West Farms.

Farmington Inn

827 Farmington Avenue
Farmington, Connecticut 06032
800-648-9804 • (860) 677-2821

Room Rates:	$109 – $159, including continental breakfast, afternoon beverages and tea. AAA, AARP, AKC and ABA discounts.
Pet Charges or Deposits:	Manager's prior approval required.
Rated: 4 Paws	59 guest rooms and 13 guest suites with an award-winning restaurant. Off-site health club membership included.

The Farmington Inn is nestled in the heart of one of Connecticut's oldest towns, where stately white homes built by bankers and merchants in post-Revolutionary days still line the main street. Antique buffs will enjoy treasure-hunting through the region's many antique shops. Close by are historic homes, museums and West Farms Mall, one of Connecticut's largest and finest shopping areas. Many recreation activities await the outdoor enthusiast year-round in Farmington.

The Inn welcomes guests in a warm and comfortable lobby decorated with fresh flowers, antiques and original works of art. Awaken to a sumptuous breakfast of steaming flavored coffees, fresh fruit and juices, cereal and freshly baked muffins, croissants and pastries served in the charming Victoria's Café.

Guest rooms are beautifully appointed, featuring white Italian Carrera marble bathrooms, matching Nightengale pattern drapes and bedspreads, cable television and amenities for travelers. The elegant suites offer terry cloth bathrobes and handsome armoires that tastefully house cable televisions. The oversized bathrooms include hair dryers.

Inn at Iron Masters

229 Main Street, Route 44
Lakeville, Connecticut 06039
(860) 435-9844
Web Site: www.innatironmasters.com

Room Rates:	$75 – $135, including deluxe continental breakfast. AAA discount.
Pet Charges or Deposits:	None with signed pet agreement.
Rated: 4 Paws 🐾 🐾 🐾 🐾	28 guest rooms with sitting rooms, swimming pool and restaurant.

K nown as the "Southern Berkshire's best-kept secret," the Inn at Iron Masters offers elegant accommodations in the scenic village of Lakeville, situated in the heart of the Litchfield Hills. The grounds are dotted with authentic Victorian gazebos surrounded by charming English country gardens.

Each guest room is individually decorated, graced with a spacious sitting area and private bath. You can relax by the outdoor swimming pool or warm yourself by the large fieldstone fireplace in the Hearth Room.

Enjoy a generous continental breakfast featuring beverages, cereals, waffles and a selection of muffins, Danish and bagels, served each morning in the café. Lunch and dinner are served at Carriages Restaurant located on the premises.

Discover hundreds of things to do and sights to see, including water sports, mountain climbing, biking, horseback riding, or hiking through numerous nature preserves and gardens. Golf in the splendor of the Berkshires, soar above it all in a hot air balloon, or explore the caves of the Berkshire Mountains with experienced spelunkers. For the winter enthusiast, skating, skiing and snowboarding are enjoyed at nearby Catamount, Mohawk and Butternut Mountains. For the lover of music and the performing arts, Tanglewood, Jacob's Pillow, the Norfolk Chamber Music Festival, Shakespeare & Co., Music Mountain and live theater are within easy reach.

Tollgate Hill Inn

Route 202 and Tollgate Road
P.O. Box 1339
Litchfield, Connecticut 06759
800-445-3903 • (860) 567-4545

Room Rates:	$110 – $175, including continental breakfast.
Pet Charges or Deposits:	$10 per day.
Rated: 4 Paws 🐾 🐾 🐾 🐾	16 guest rooms and 5 suites with wood-burning fireplaces, award-winning restaurant and pub.

T ollgate Hill Inn, situated on ten wooded acres, is designed to live up to its centuries-old heritage of providing memorable hospitality. Listed in the National Register of Historic Places and built in 1745, the main house became a popular way station for travelers during Colonial times. The 18th-century paneling, floorboards and fireplaces have been carefully restored to near-original condition. The guest rooms and suites have been renovated with a meticulous respect for detail, featuring canopied beds and working fireplaces.

The kitchen at Tollgate Hill has won many culinary awards and features a wine list offering more than 100 vintage possibilities. Meals are artfully prepared and served in the gracious quiet of two 18th-century dining rooms.

Litchfield is located in the heart of Connecticut's antique country, where auction-going is a major local sport. Local attractions include the White Memorial Foundation, the state's largest nature center consisting of 4,000 acres with 35 miles of trails for hiking, horseback riding, fishing, cross-country skiing and camping. Visitors also enjoy the White Flower Farm, ten acres of display gardens featuring nationally known English tuberous begonias.

Harbour Inne and Cottage

15 Edgemont Street
Mystic, Connecticut 06355
(860) 572-9253

Room Rates: $75 – $250, including kitchen privileges.
Pet Charges or Deposits: $10 per day, $50 refundable deposit.
Rated: 3 Paws   4 guest rooms and 1 guest suite with hot tub spa on deck,
                         common area with fireplace and antique piano.

L ocated in the heart of historic Mystic, the Harbour Inne invites you to relax and enjoy the beautiful views of the Mystic River from its waterfront gazebo. The Inn is an easy walk from all the shops, restaurants and sights of downtown Mystic, including the Seaport Museum and the Mystic Marinelife Aquarium.

Each of the four bedrooms has a private bath, kitchen privileges and cable TV. The separate cedar cottage features a bedroom with fireplace, a kitchen and private deck with a hot tub.

The Harbour Inne and Cottage is the perfect place to stay while you explore all the attractions of southeastern Connecticut.

High Acres

c/o Nutmeg Bed and Breakfast Agency
P.O. Box 1117
West Hartford, Connecticut 06127-1117
800-727-7592 • (860) 236-6698

Room Rates:	$145, including full breakfast.
Pet Charges or Deposits:	Manager's prior approval required.
Rated: 3 Paws	4 guest rooms on 150-acre horse farm.

T his classic New England farmhouse, circa 1742, is situated on 150 scenic acres. Currently a working equestrian farm, High Acres offers king- and queen-sized beds with private baths in delightfully furnished guest rooms. Guests enjoy relaxing on the spacious glassed-in porch overlooking grassy fields dotted with beautiful horses. A common sitting area is equipped with an inviting fire and color TV. Awake to a delicious full breakfast served in the formal dining room featuring home-baked goods, steaming beverages and fresh juice.

High Acres is said to provide the best views in Connecticut. What better way to enjoy this lovely setting than on horseback during an organized trail ride. If you prefer, get out your hiking boots and explore this beautiful section of southeastern Connecticut.

White Hart

15 Undermountain Road
Salisbury, Connecticut 06068
800-832-0041 • (860) 435-0030

Room Rates: $75 – $195.
Pet Charges or Deposits: $10 per day with manager's prior approval.
Rated: 4 Paws   23 guest rooms and 3 guest suites with tennis, fitness center,
                        baby-sitting services, laundry and dry-cleaning services, 3
                        restaurants, 2 taverns and award-winning wine list.

Nestled in the foothills of the Berkshires in picturesque Salisbury, the White Hart draws its name from its counterpart in England. Enjoying a long and illustrious career as a country inn, the White Hart at one time was owned by Edsel Ford.

The Ford Room is located within the original part of the building and features a canopy bed and view of the Village Green. Each of the 26 guest rooms includes a private bath and furnishings of either Thomasville Mahogany or Lane Country Pine, with Waverly wall coverings and fabrics. Options are many, including rooms with two double beds, queen-sized beds and suites consisting of a bedroom and adjoining sitting area.

There are a number of dining opportunities at the White Hart, with three restaurants to choose from. Breakfast, lunch and dinner are served in the friendly and popular Tap Room and Garden Room. Or enjoy the comfort and dining menu in the American Grill for dinner and Sunday breakfast.

The White Hart's location enables guests to enjoy the recreational activities of both the Litchfield Hills and the Berkshires. Salisbury sports an impressive calendar of year-round events, including live theater, art exhibits, wine and other festivals. Nearby activities include hiking, fishing, boating, biking, antiquing, museums, shopping and dining. Visitors also enjoy auto racing at the Lime Rock Race Track.

Homewood Suites Hotel

65 Ella Grasso Turnpike
Windsor Locks, Connecticut 06096
800-225-5466 • (860) 627-8463

Room Rates:	$125 – $160, including expanded continental breakfast, evening beverages and snacks.
Pet Charges or Deposits:	$100 nonrefundable deposit. Manager's prior approval required.
Rated: 4 Paws 🐾 🐾 🐾 🐾	132 fully equipped suites with on-site convenience store carrying pet food, guest supplies and video rentals; fitness center, sports/activity court, swimming pool and hot tubs.

H omewood Suites is more than a hotel. Here you will enjoy all the comfort, convenience and privacy of home for the price of an ordinary hotel room. Every room is a spacious, apartment-style suite with separate living and sleeping quarters, comfortably furnished with the features and amenities you expect from luxury accommodations. Suites include wood-burning fireplaces, two remote-controlled color TVs, VCRs, ceiling fans, electronic voice-mail system, computer jacks and fully equipped kitchens.

The center of activity at Homewood Suites is the Lodge, where guests can relax and socialize. Start each day with a fresh pantry breakfast and stop by for an evening social and a selection of hot and cold hors d'oeuvres and beverages. The exercise room has aerobic and weight training equipment and the sports court, outdoor pool and whirlpool will complete your workout.

The grounds offer pet exercise areas and Northwest Park is nearby. Twenty-four hour airport transportation is provided, with convenience phones located in the baggage area of the airport.

Senator Inn and Spa

284 Western Avenue at Interstate 95
Augusta, Maine 04330
800-528-1234 • (207) 622-5804

Room Rates:	$59 – $119, including full breakfast. AAA and AARP discounts.
Pet Charges or Deposits:	Dogs only.
Rated: 3 Paws	80 guest rooms and 20 suites with indoor and outdoor swimming pools, whirlpools, Jacuzzi, hot tub, full service health spa, restaurant and oyster bar.

A warm first impression greets you as you enter the Senator Inn, conveniently located in Augusta, the capital of Maine. The guest rooms feature spacious, luxurious accommodations, with a second TV, phone and refrigerator in the bathroom next to the huge, inviting tub.

Enjoy the extensive menu at the award-winning Oyster Bar and Grille. Meals include homemade breads, a huge salad bar, home-grown fresh herbs (even the floral arrangements are made from the garden flora). The spa includes a gym, aerobic classes and services such as facials, manicures and pedicures.

The Senator Inn is consistently voted Greater Augusta's Best Hotel and is conveniently located near the scenic coast, L.L. Bean Retail Outlet and Freeport Outlet Shops. Enjoy year-round outdoor activities with on-site nature trails and the nearby the Augusta Arboretum.

Bar Harbor Inn

Newport Drive, Box 7
Bar Harbor, Maine 04609
800-248-3351 • (207) 288-3351

Room Rates:	$60 – $310, including continental breakfast.
Pet Charges or Deposits:	$15 per day. Manager's prior approval required.
Rated: 4 Paws	153 guest rooms, swimming pool, Jacuzzi.

The Bar Harbor Inn, at the head of picturesque Frenchman Bay, is a full-service oceanfront resort. Noted for exceptional accommodations, service that attends to every need, and elegant dining, the Bar Harbor Inn has long been the destination of choice for discriminating visitors to Bar Harbor, Mount Desert Island and Acadia National Park.

Three separate and distinctively different resort accommodations are available to choose from. The Oceanfront Lodge and Newport Motel are contemporary in design and offer comfortable queen- and king-sized beds and marvelous ocean views. The Newport Building houses 38 comfortable guest rooms, all with private patios or balconies.

Your visit will be complete with an activity for every lifestyle. Stroll or relax on the spacious grounds where flower gardens explode with color. Sail on Frenchman Bay aboard the Natalie Todd, docked at the private pier, or visit the many fine shops, galleries and museums.

Blue Harbor House

67 Elm Street
Camden, Maine 04843-1904
800-248-3196 • (207) 236-3196
Web Site: www.blueharborhouse.com
E-mail: balidog@midcoast.com

Room Rates:	$85 – $145, including full breakfast
Pet Charges or Deposits:	One night's rate refundable deposit. Manager's prior approval required.
Rated: 3 Paws 🐾 🐾 🐾	8 guest rooms, 2 guest suites

R eal hospitality and a refreshingly casual atmosphere await you at Blue Harbor House, a completely restored 1810 New England Cape structure. Nestled by the wayside in Camden, it invites a stay in one of the homey guest rooms inside the Inn or indulgence in the privacy and luxury of the carriage house suites. The suites offer a large sitting area and whirlpool baths. Whichever you choose, the decor is warm and welcoming. Several rooms have canopy beds and all feature period antiques and hand-fashioned quilts.

Begin your day with a full New England breakfast with such specialties as lobster quiche, cheese soufflé and blueberry pancakes with blueberry butter. Dinner is available by reservation and consists of a candlelit presentation of a gourmet, multi-course feast.

Ease into your day with a few quiet hours in a rocker on the porch, or set off to explore all of Camden, where the mountains meet the sea. The irresistible village, with so many delights for visitors, is just beyond the flower gardens.

Inn by the Sea

40 Bowery Beach Road
Cape Elizabeth, Maine 04107
(207) 799-4779
Web Site: www.innbythesea.com
E-mail: innmaine@aol.com

Room Rates: $129 – $449. AAA, AARP, AKC and ABA discounts.
Pet Charges or Deposits: None.
Rated: 5 Paws 😺😺😺😺😺 43 elegant guest suites, tennis, bikes, swimming pool, free
                               movies, refrigerators.

O verlooking the Atlantic from Cape Elizabeth's headlands, the Inn by the
Sea occupies one of the most splendid locations along Maine's coast. In
keeping with this incomparable setting, the Inn is designed to blend
every contemporary amenity with the understated elegance of classic resort
architecture. From the moment you enter the marble-tiled lobby, visit the tea
garden and gazebo or settle into a very private suite, you will be surrounded by
the feeling of an unhurried yesterday.

With just 43 very private one- and two-bedroom suites, the Inn has been
designed with your comfort and convenience in mind. You will find your suite
in the Maine House furnished in Chippendale cherry furniture, complete with a
video cassette player and a fully functional kitchen. The cottage suites, ideally
suited for extended families, feature an additional bedroom in the classic Maine
summer style of wicker and light pine. In the spirit of the Inn's elegance, pets
are welcomed with bones, dishes and turndown treats.

The Inn by the Sea offers boardwalk access to the beach, with hiking, jogging and biking trails nearby.

Craignair Inn

533 Clark Island Road
Clark Island, Maine 04859
800-320-9997 • (207) 594-7644
E-mail: craignair@midcoast.com

Room Rates:	$50 – $110, including full breakfast. AAA discount.
Pet Charges or Deposits:	$8.50 per day. Sorry, no cats. Manager's prior approval required.
Rated: 3 Paws 🐾🐾🐾	24 guest rooms.

The Craignair Inn is situated on four acres of shorefront within the 3,500-odd miles of bay, peninsulas, inlets and headlands that form a coastline unmatched anywhere for its beauty and coastal activity. Set on a granite ledge rising from the sea, and surrounded by flower gardens, Craignair was built in 1928 to house workers from the nearby quarries.

Downstairs is an exceedingly warm and cheery parlor-library, a sunny dining room that looks out on the seas, and an old-fashioned kitchen dominated by an antique cast-iron working stove. Upstairs, the bedrooms are furnished simply but comfortably with antiques, quilt-covered beds, colorful wall coverings and hooked rugs on the floor.

Craignair Inn is attractive to visitors seeking serenity, simplicity, privacy and natural beauty. Some guests wish only to sit in the garden to relax and watch the activities of shorebirds, clammers and lobstermen. Others prefer to explore the coast, along the many miles of paths adjacent to the Inn, or to visit antique shops, art galleries and museums or sail in nearby Camden.

Todd House Bed and Breakfast

1 Capen Avenue
Todd's Head
Eastport, Maine 04631
(207) 853-2328

Room Rates:	$45 – $80, including an expanded continental breakfast.
Pet Charges or Deposits:	None.
Rated: 3 Paws 🐾🐾🐾	6 guest rooms, historic.

Built on Todd's Head during the Revolutionary War, the Todd House is a classic New England Full Cape structure with massive center chimney and unique "good morning" staircase. Guest rooms are furnished with period antiques, enhanced by a collection of local historic artifacts. Owned by a local historian and educator, the Todd House has a library filled with volumes of local history.

Breakfast is served in the common room before a huge fireplace and bake oven, in surroundings reminiscent of the Revolutionary Era. Muffins, especially the wild Maine blueberry variety, are a specialty of the house.

The spacious yard hosts barbecues and affords an ever-changing view of the bay and its islands. Glorious sunrises and sunsets enhance the natural beauty of the area.

Crocker House Country Inn

H.C. 77, Box 171
Hancock, Maine 04640
(207) 422-6806
Web Site: www.maineguide.com/downeast/crocker
E-mail: crocker@acadia.net

Room Rates:	$75 – $130, including full breakfast.
Pet Charges or Deposits:	None.
Rated: 3 Paws 🐾 🐾 🐾	11 guest rooms with hot tub, gourmet restaurant serving select wines, and full bar.

T he Crocker House Country Inn, tucked away on the peninsula of Hancock Point, was built in 1884 and carefully restored in 1986. Its quiet, out-of-the way location, fine cuisine and individually appointed guest rooms, each with a private bath, all combine to make the Crocker House a refreshing and memorable experience. The last sound you hear before retiring is the bell buoy lazily ringing its warning to mariners in Frenchman Bay. Awake to a full gourmet breakfast with fresh, hearty homemade specialties.

Bordered by Frenchman Bay on the south and east, and the Skillings River to the west, Hancock Point is small enough that all roads lead to the water. Moorings are available for guests who arrive by sea, and a few bicycles are on hand for guests' touring. The Inn is conveniently located for visitors to take advantage of sightseeing opportunities in Acadia National Park and Hancock County. Local craftsmen, including potters, weavers and woodworkers, are found throughout the area. Antiquing opportunities, cultural events and the Canadian border are all nearby.

Colony Hotel

Ocean Avenue
P.O. Box 511
Kennebunkport, Maine 04046-0511
800-552-2363 • (207) 967-3331
Web Site: www.thecolonyhotel.com
E-mail: info-me@thecolonyhotel.com
Seasonal: mid-May through mid-October

Room Rates:	$99 – $299, including full breakfast in dining room and afternoon tea.
Pet Charges or Deposits:	$22 per day. $22 refundable deposit.
Rated: 4 Paws 🐾🐾🐾🐾	125 guest rooms with fresh flowers, heated saltwater swimming pool and private sandy beach, designated dog-walking area and restaurant.

T he majestic Colony Hotel, built on a rocky promontory at the mouth of the Kennebunk River in 1914, is a nautical landmark. Its fine Gregorian architecture epitomizes the elegance of the era. Gracious service and friendly pampering complete this unique and rare retreat.

Handmade pet blankets, embroidered with a doggie bone, are provided upon check-in. The heated, filtered saltwater swimming pool delights guests with a warmer version of the same Atlantic waters as the private sandy beach. Enjoy a performance of the Colony water ballet group "The Blue Flames," continuing a performance tradition since 1957. The pool and pool deck offer spectacular views of the breakwater and southern Maine's Mount Agamenticus.

There is plenty of room to roam, both on the property and nearby. Honored as Maine's first environmentally responsible hotel, the Colony Hotel is the only "U.S. backyard wildlife habitat" in the Northeast. A staff naturalist leads guided tours on coastal Maine ecology along the sandy beaches and tidal pools that are free for hotel guests.

Herbert Inn

P.O. Box 67, Main Street
Kingfield, Maine 04947
800-843-4372 • (207) 265-2000
Web Site: www.byme.com/the herbert
E-mail: herbert@somtel.com

Room Rates:	$49 – $165, including continental breakfast.
Pet Charges or Deposits:	None.
Rated: 4 Paws 🐾🐾🐾🐾	40 guest rooms, many with Jacuzzis; hot tub and award-winning restaurant.

Many small historic hotels would lose their distinctiveness — or even be lost to the wrecking ball — it if weren't for entrepreneurs like Bud Dick. The Herbert, a 40-room beaux arts hotel in Kingfield, Maine, is such a place. Following a $1 million-plus restoration, this beautifully restored 1918 jewel is glistening with fumed oak, brass and terrazzo floors.

The rooms are comfy, most with Jacuzzi spas, brass beds and antiques, with cozy comforters and warm apple cider après ski. The dining room is a consistent award-winner, with emphasis on healthy food, accompanied by nearly 100 wines hand-selected and imported by the owner and offered at moderate prices.

The Inn is located 20 minutes from the world renowned Sugarloaf Mountain, home of world-class skiing in winter and one of the finest and most striking mountain golf courses in the country during warmer weather. Visitors also enjoy great hiking, mountain biking and white-water thrills on the Kennebec and Dead rivers.

Enchanted Nights Bed and Breakfast

29 Wentworth Street
Kittery, Maine 03904
(207) 439-1489
Web Site: www.enchanted-nights-bandb.com
E-mail: info@enchanted-nights-bandb.com

Room Rates:	$52 – $180, including full breakfast.
Pet Charges or Deposits:	None.
Rated: 3 Paws 🐾 🐾 🐾	6 guest rooms and 2 guest suites with whirlpools and pet exercise area.

E nchanted Nights is a Victorian fantasy bordering New Hampshire's romantic Portsmouth Harbour area. Each guest room is uniquely decorated with whimsical furnishings, complete with fanciful feather bedding and private bath. Antique claw-footed and whirlpool tubs and elegant French-Victorian decor, including a wrought-iron bed, grace guest quarters. The Turret Room is a tiny but enchanting room for two featuring a 13-foot pointed ceiling, while The Suite features a queen-sized feather bed and whirlpool for two.

Enjoy a full breakfast served on antique china, with freshly ground gourmet coffee, herbal teas and deluxe omelets. Vegetarian selections are always offered.

It is centrally located with easy access to the Kittery Outlet Malls, Boston, Portland and Scenic Route 103's ocean drive. Dine and dance, beach and bike, cliff walk or cruise in a whale-watching craft. Enjoy concerts in the park, quaint shops and outdoor cafes. Water Country, the Children's Museum, the Strawbery Banke Museum of historic homes and Prescott Park Gardens are all nearby.

Sign of the Owl

243 Atlantic Highway
Northport, Maine 04849
(207) 338-4669

Room Rates: $45 – $65, including full breakfast.
Pet Charges or Deposits: Manager's prior approval required.
Rated: 3 Paws   3 guest rooms; pet exercise areas available.

The Sign of the Owl is a 1794 Maine farmhouse, located nine miles north of Camden, that offers three guest rooms. Visitors are invited to explore the private beach just a short walk along a wooded path or to browse the gift and antique shop, filled with an ever-changing selection of fine furniture and accessories.

Nearby Camden Hills State Park offers scenic vistas spanning Acadia National Park to Monhegan Island. Sign of the Owl is centrally located for day trips to Islesboro, Vinalhaven Island, Monhegan, Bar Harbor, Acadia National Park or the Camden-Rockport area.

Waterford Inne

Box 149, Chadbourne Road
Waterford, Maine 04088
(207) 583-4037

Room Rates:	$75 – $105, including full breakfast and dinner.
Pet Charges or Deposits:	$10 per day plus $50 refundable deposit. Manager's prior approval required.
Rated: 3 Paws 🐾 🐾 🐾	8 guest rooms and 1 guest suite in a country setting.

T he Waterford Inne is a 19th-century farmhouse situated on a country lane amidst 25 acres of fields and woods. The interior is finished with hand-hewn beams and wide pine floors, creating a distinctive true country inn. Wander through the gardens, which provide a colorful array of flowers and a bounty of fresh fare for the dining table.

Guest rooms are uniquely decorated with a charming blend of two centuries — the warmth of early pine furnishings, combined with contemporary comforts. An air of quiet, simple elegance pervades the common rooms, rich with antiques, art, barn board, pewter and primitives.

Awake to freshly brewed coffee and a full Maine breakfast featuring home-baked goods and garden-fresh delights. Dinner is a leisurely affair consisting of four courses created to complement one another in taste, color and texture, elegantly presented on fine china.

The Waterford Inne is located in the Oxford Hills and Lakes Region, one of Maine's best-kept secrets — rich in natural beauty offering hiking, biking and skiing. Nearby Waterford is a treasure chest for antique enthusiasts.

Kawanhee Inn Lakeside Lodge and Cabins

Route 142, Box 119
Weld, Maine 04285
(207) 585-2000
E-mail: info@lakeinn.com
Season: May 15 – Oct. 15

Room Rates:	$75 – $165.
Pet Charges or Deposits:	None; with manager's prior approval.
Rated: 4 Paws 🐾🐾🐾🐾	9 guest rooms and 12 guest cabins overlooking Webb Lake offering boat rentals and a restaurant.

 Kawanhee Inn Lakeside Lodge is nestled in the cathedral pines on a knoll overlooking Webb Lake, in the western Maine mountains. On entering the lobby, you are impressed with the rustic and refined decor. A huge fieldstone fireplace, accommodating four-foot logs, crackles a warm welcome. On the second floor of the Lodge are nine comfortable bedrooms – five with private baths, four with shared bath. The cabins face the lake and mountains and vary in size to accommodate parties from two to seven.

Kawanhee Inn is noted for its home cooking, which is served in either the main dining room or on the porch. Picnic lunches are available for guests to take while exploring spots accessible by canoe or while climbing Tumbledown Mountain or gold panning on the Swift River.

The Inn is situated in a region rich in heritage, diversity and recreational pleasures. The Lodge offers an early morning excursion by canoe, when you are likely to see moose feeding by the water's edge with the sun rising over the western Maine mountains. Motorboat or canoe rentals are available for fishing or bird watching. Other daytime activities may include a game of golf 15 minutes away, tennis on clay courts in the charming village of Weld or swimming at nearby waterfalls.

Jenkins Inn and Restaurant

7 West Street
Route 122
Barre, Massachusetts 01005-0779
800-378-7373 • (978) 355-6444

Room Rates:	$95 – $175, including full breakfast.
Pet Charges or Deposits:	$5 per day. One night's refundable deposit. Manager's prior approval required.
Rated: 3 Paws	5 guest rooms, 4-star restaurant on premises, fireplaces, microwaves, landscaped gardens and exercise area for pets.

Whether your visit is a fall foliage retreat, a winter ski vacation, an antiquing weekend or simply a getaway, the Jenkins Inn in historic Barre provides all the comfort and amenities of a home away from home.

Conveniently located in central Massachusetts, the Inn is situated in one of the most pristine areas in central New England. Each guest room is inspired with unique decor, catering to comfort as well as historical significance.

Guests will find shopping and theaters nearby or sightseeing in Old Sturbridge Village. For the outdoor enthusiast, Mount Wachusett, Rutland State Park and the Quabbin Reservoir provide beautiful hiking trails in summer and ski vacations in winter.

Colonnade Hotel

120 Huntington Avenue
Boston, Massachusetts 02116
800-962-3030 • (617) 424-7000
Web Site: www.colonnadehotel.com

Room Rates:	$225 – $425. AAA and AARP discounts.
Pet Charges or Deposits:	None.
Rated: 5 Paws 🐾🐾🐾🐾🐾	285 guest rooms and 15 guest suites (including 3 specialty suites) with swimming pool, umbrellas, rooftop swimming pool with poolside dining, fitness center, 2 restaurants and cocktail lounge.

The Colonnade, located in Boston's Back Bay, is an independent luxury hotel in the European tradition, catering to the discriminating traveler. Lauded for its bold, modern architecture, the building's facade is defined by a series of exterior columns that provide a look of contemporary grace and elegance.

The guest rooms are classically furnished and thoughtfully designed with seating areas and comfortable work desks. The amenities range from plush bathrobes to telephones in the bathrooms. The suites feature Jacuzzi baths, stereo CD systems and wide-screen televisions. The resort-style swimming area commands stunning views of Boston and includes lounge chairs, tables for poolside dining and changing rooms. For indoor recreation, enjoy the fully equipped fitness room. The award-winning cuisine of Café Promenade delights every taste and mood with its innovative seasonal fare.

Colonnade Hotel is located in Back Bay, across from the Hynes Convention Center and the Prudential Center, next to Copley Place, and steps from Newbury Street. Symphony Hall, Fenway Park, the Museum of Fine Arts and Faneuil Hall are minutes away. Special packages, including the special pet package "Cause for Paws," caters to every lifestyle.

Ritz-Carlton, Boston

15 Arlington Street
Boston, Massachusetts 02117
800-241-3333 • (617) 536-5700

Room Rates: $260 – $2,000.
Pet Charges or Deposits: $20 per day.
Rated: 5 Paws 🐾🐾🐾🐾🐾 275 rooms and 42 suites with honor bar, safes, swimming pool, spa, pet exercise area, health and fitness center, 3 restaurants and 2 lounges.

G uest rooms and suites are furnished with French Provincial furnishings, complemented by imported fabrics and distinctive works of art. Windows open to a beautiful view of the Public Garden and Beacon Hill, the Charles River and Commonwealth Avenue or Newbury Street.

Casual or elegant dining is available in one of the three restaurants. Tall, graceful windows provide a magnificent view of the Public Gardens from the Dining Room. An acclaimed seasonal menu offering innovative contemporary French cuisine is complemented by an extensive wine list. The Café is elegantly, simple with soft harp music providing a quaint, romantic setting. The Roof offers fine cuisine with spectacular views and dancing to the Ritz-Carlton Orchestra.

The Ritz-Carlton is central to all sections of the city, with an easy walk to historic monuments and theaters, the Financial District, convention and government centers. Bounded by Commonwealth Avenue, the hotel is at the corner of fashionable Newbury Street, which features exclusive shops, restaurants and art galleries. While offering the convenience of a city location, the Ritz-Carlton, Boston, is unexpectedly quiet and serene.

Bertram Inn

92 Sewall Avenue
Brookline, Massachusetts 02146
800-295-3822 • (617) 566-2234

Room Rates:	$69 – $194, including expanded continental breakfast and afternoon tea.
Pet Charges or Deposits:	$150 refundable deposit. Manager's prior approval required.
Rated: 3 Paws	14 guest rooms and common living room with fireplace.

A stay at the Bertram Inn offers the opportunity to step back into another era. The handsome building was constructed by fine artisans, with oak panels and a sweeping stairway, masterpieces of lead and glass and fireplaces in the tradition of the Old World.

Typical of a large Victorian home, no two rooms are alike. Each of the guest rooms has it own character and size, with accommodations that offer king-sized, queen-sized, double or twin beds. The large living room with fireplace provides a relaxing environment to read or rest and enjoy afternoon tea. In the morning this cozy retreat becomes a cheerful breakfast room, where a hearty continental breakfast of fresh baked muffins and fruits is served.

The elegant Victorian home is located near the Commonwealth Mall, Boston Commons and Charles River Esplanade.

Wainwright Inn

518 South Main Street
Great Barrington, Massachusetts 01230
(413) 528-2062
Web Site: www.wainwrightinn.com

Room Rates:	$65 – $175, including full breakfast.
Pet Charges or Deposits:	One night's rate refundable deposit. Manager's prior approval required. Sorry, no cats.
Rated: 3 Paws	7 guest rooms and 1 suite, handicapped accessible.

O riginally opened as a tavern in 1766, the Inn has been offering New England hospitality for generations. Located in the heart of the southern Berkshire region, the Inn is a four-season destination easily accessible from Boston and New York.

All of the charming guest rooms and suites have private baths and are furnished with comfortable beds and decor. Guests are welcome to take full advantage of the many common areas, including the cozy living room and distinctive wrap-around porches. While enjoying homemade breads at breakfast, guests are free to discuss dinner plans with the chef. The intimate private dining room is reserved for guests, with custom dinners prepared to your request.

Tanglewood is just minutes away, with summer concerts and picnics on the lawn. Enjoy performances by top-name performers at the Berkshire Theater Festival, Shakespeare and Company or the Williamstown Theater Festival. As the seasons change, so do the myriad of colors and activities in the Berkshires.

Brandt House

29 Highland Avenue
Greenfield, Massachusetts 01301
800-235-3329 • (413) 774-3329
Web Site: www.brandt-house.com
E-mail: brandt@crocker.com

Room Rates:	$100 – $175, including lavish continental breakfast and full breakfast on weekends. AAA, AARP AKC and ABA discounts.
Pet Charges or Deposits:	Manager's prior approval required.
Rated: 4 Paws 🐾🐾🐾🐾	8 guest suites on 31/2-acre property that backs up to Highland Park.

T his elegant turn-of-the-century Colonial Revival mansion is located in Western Massachusetts on 31/2 acres of sweeping lawns surrounded by lush vegetation that provides quiet privacy.

Guest rooms include pet treats, featherbeds, complimentary bathrobes and fireplaces. Enjoy relaxing conversation or a good book on the wraparound porch, adjacent patio or in front of a cozy fire.

Guests are invited to walk, hike, bike or cross-country ski in the adjacent woods, play tennis on the clay tennis courts, fish or ice skate on a neighboring pond. The Brandt House is a short drive from historic Deerfield, a championship 18-hole golf course, white-water rafting and major downhill and cross-country ski areas.

Seven Hills Country Inn and Restaurant

40 Plunkett Street
Lenox, Massachusetts 01240
800-869-6518 • (413) 637-0060

Room Rates:	$65 – $250, including seasonal breakfast.
Pet Charges or Deposits:	$20 per day. Manager's prior approval required.
Rated: 4 Paws 🐾🐾🐾🐾	52 guest rooms and 1 guest suite with swimming pool, tennis courts, restaurant and lounge.

O ne of the original Berkshire Cottages, the Seven Hills Country Inn offers you an invitation to enjoy the romantic luxuries of traditional elegance. Furnishings consist of care-worn antiques, hand-carved fireplaces, leaded glass windows and high-ceilinged charm. The Inn's gracious accommodations are comprised of 15 Manor House and 37 Terrace House guest rooms on 27 acres of expansive grounds.

You'll be delighted when you sample the exceptional cuisine. The menu's European influences are complemented by seasonal graciousness, with settings of relaxed fireside dining or meals on the patio surrounded by the Berkshire hills. The lounge features live entertainment for a lively evening after you have enjoyed the many activities the area offers.

The region is a recreation paradise. There are dozens of lakes and rivers perfect for boating, swimming and fishing, with miles of country lanes for biking and walking. During the winter months, the Berkshire hills are home to downhill skiing areas and a number of cross-country touring centers. Other year-round delights include the Berkshire Public Theater, Herman Melville's "Arrowhead," Hancock Shaker Village and the William Cullen Bryant homestead, among other historic homes, sites and cultural institutions worthy of a visit.

Seagull Inn

106 Harbor Avenue
Marblehead, Massachusetts 01945
(781) 631-1893

Room Rates:	$100 – $200, including continental breakfast.
Pet Charges or Deposits:	None.
Rated: 3 Paws 🐾🐾🐾	4 suites with refrigerators and microwaves.

I n Marblehead Neck, with ocean and harbor views from every room, you will enjoy the casual elegance of the Seagull Inn Bed and Breakfast. The suites are all impressive, with many unique features, and furnished with antiques and Shaker-style furniture, cherry floors, private baths and original paintings.

Breakfasts include fresh fruits and juices, homemade granola, oven-warm baked goods, bagels, muffins and breads.

There are many cultural and recreational activities, including golfing at one of the many golf courses, ice skating, museums, yachting and exercising your dog on one of the many beaches.

Salem Inn

7 Summer Street
Salem, Massachusetts 01970
800-446-2995 • (978) 741-0680
Web Page: www.salemweb.com/biz/saleminn
E-mail: saleminn@earthlink.net

Room Rates:	$109 – $190, including continental breakfast. AAA discount.
Pet Charges or Deposits:	None.
Rated: 3 Paws 🐾 🐾 🐾	29 guest rooms, 11 guest suites, Historic Inn on the National Register.

T he Salem Inn, comprised of the West House (circa 1834), the Curwen House (circa 1854) and the Peabody House (circa 1874), testifies to the glory that was 19th-century Salem. These impressive and historic buildings, constructed with the wealth of those seafaring days, are centrally located.

Each of the individually decorated rooms and suites reflects the fine crafts-manship of the Federal period. Guest rooms are spacious and comfortable, many with equipped kitchens and working fireplaces.

A complimentary light breakfast is available in the Breakfast Room each morning. In warmer weather, the private rose garden brick patio is the perfect place to enjoy your breakfast or a quiet moment at the end of the day.

The Inn is a short walk from the National Park Maritime Historical Site, the Essex and Peabody Museum, fine restaurants and the waterfront.

Ivanhoe Country House

254 South Undermountain Road
Route 41
Sheffield, Massachusetts 01257
(413) 229-2143

Room Rates: $65 – $110, including continental breakfast. AAA discount.
Pet Charges or Deposits: $10 per day. Manager's prior approval required. Sorry, no cats.
Rated: 3 Paws 🐾 🐾 🐾   9 guest rooms with swimming pool and kitchenettes.

Built in 1780 at the foot of Mount Race on 25 acres of wooded splendor, Ivanhoe welcomes travelers to the Berkshires. Guest rooms are comfortable country rooms with private baths, some fully equipped with kitchenettes. Enjoy the warmth of a fireplace or the refreshment of the pool. The Chestnut Room, a common area, has a fireplace, library, television, piano and game tables to offer guests a choice of indoor recreation or relaxation. Start your day with a continental breakfast served outside each bedroom, offering a choice of beverage and baked goods. Menus for the excellent nearby restaurants are on hand.

Plan your visit to include the unmatched spectacle of fall foliage. Or challenge the novice-to-expert slopes at nearby Catamount or Butternut Ski Basin. Bike through the rural countryside or hike the Appalachian Trail, Mount Everett, Race Brook Falls or Bartholomew's Cobble. An evening at the Berkshire Playhouse or Jacob's Pillow is a summer's treat for everyone.

Westin Hotel Waltham-Boston

70 Third Avenue
Waltham, Massachusetts 02154
800-WESTIN-1 • (781) 290-5600

Room Rates:	$119 – $255.
Pet Charges or Deposits:	None.
Rated: 3 Paws 🐾🐾🐾	346 guest rooms and 33 guest suites with swimming pool, Jacuzzi, health club, redwood sauna, restaurant, lounge and room service.

T he Westin Hotel is located on Route 128 in Waltham at the heart of the state's "high-tech beltway." Situated on five beautiful acres of land-scaped lawns and gardens overlooking the scenic Cambridge Reservoir, the newly redecorated guest rooms and suites are filled with amenities catering to guests' business and personal comforts.

The Westin features a full-service health club with indoor pool, Jacuzzi, red-wood sauna and cardiovascular equipment. The hotel is less than 10 miles from historic Lexington-Concord Battleground, DeCordova Museum and the Burlington Mall.

Jericho Valley Inn

2541 Hancock Road
P.O. Box 239
Williamstown, Massachusetts 01267
800-JERICHO • (413) 458-9511

Room Rates:	$78 – $238, including continental breakfast.
Pet Charges or Deposits:	None.
Rated: 3 Paws	12 guest rooms and 12 cottages with full kitchens and fireplaces, on 350 acres.

I f you are planning a trip to the Berkshires, Jericho Valley Inn welcomes you and your pet as guests. Located on 350 acres, it is surrounded by the beauty and tranquillity of the New England countryside, yet is minutes away from all the area's major attractions.

Spacious, comfortable guest rooms have been designed for quiet and comfort, offering individually-controlled heat and air-conditioning, full private baths, fine bedding and comfortable furniture. Charming, secluded one-, two- and three-bedroom cottages offer full kitchens and spacious living rooms with fireplaces.

Williamstown is a great place, offering visitors far-ranging cultural and recreational choices — close to the Jiminy Peak Ski Resort, Vermont's Green Mountains and the Berkshire Hills.

Colonial House Inn

Route 6A
Yarmouth Port, Massachusetts 02675
800-999-3416 • (508) 362-4348

Room Rates:	$70 – $95, including breakfast and dinner. AAA, AARP, AKC and ABA discounts.
Pet Charges or Deposits:	$5 per day. Manager's prior approval required.
Rated: 3 Paws 🐾 🐾 🐾	2 guest rooms and 1 suite, restaurant, lounge, fitness area, indoor swimming pool, Jacuzzi, free movies and handicapped accessible.

L ocated on historic Old King's Highway on the north shore of Cape Cod, the Colonial House Inn has been carefully preserved and the tradition of gracious dining and hospitality carried forward. Constructed in the 1730s, with a long list of well-known owners and several renovations, the charm of Cape Cod shines through the Colonial House Inn today.

The large guest rooms are individually decorated and furnished with antiques. Each room has its own private bath and a charming view of the grounds. In addition to the Main House, the renovated Carriage House offers a conference center and additional guest rooms.

The menu at the Inn is continental fare in an elegant yet casual atmosphere. There are three intimate dining rooms, with Cape Cod's fresh seafood forming the basis of the salt-air selections, as well as an extensive wine cellar and a lounge with a full bar.

Yarmouth Port is centrally located on Cape Cod and offers excellent year-round dining, theater, entertainment and dancing, golf courses, tennis courts, churches, antique shops and many historic points of interest. The Inn is convenient to both freshwater and saltwater beaches and 60 acres with nature trails.

Corner House Inn

22 Main Street
Center Sandwich, New Hampshire 03227
800-501-6219 • (603) 284-6219

Room Rates:	$80, including full breakfast.
Pet Charges or Deposits:	None.
Rated: 3 Paws	4 guest rooms, restaurant.

C enter Sandwich, an unspoiled 19th-century village, nestled between the White Mountains and Squam Lake, provides the setting for historic Corner House Inn. The Inn, built in 1849, has been in continuous operation for more than 100 years. The second floor of the Inn still provides lodging for the traveler.

Three of the four guest rooms share bathroom facilities, while one includes a private bath. The rooms reflect a lovely Victorian influence with antiques and handmade quilts. Downstairs, four separate dining rooms serve guests in an intimate, candlelit atmosphere. Guests awaken to the scent of freshly brewed coffee, hand-squeezed orange juice and freshly made omelets. The restaurant serves lunch and dinner, featuring New England seafood and homemade desserts.

An art gallery, weaving designery, numerous antique and craft shops and a historical museum are all within walking distance of the Inn. The more active can swim in Sandwich Bay on Squam Lake, engage in a game of tennis or hike the area's many mountain trails. Winter activities feature cross-country skiing locally and five major down-hill ski areas within an hour's drive.

Payne's Hill Bed and Breakfast

141 Henry Law Avenue
Dover, New Hampshire 03820
(603) 740-9441
Web Site: www.bestinns.net/usa/nh/payneshill.html

Room Rates:	$54 – $65, including continental breakfast and seasonal afternoon beverages and snacks.
Pet Charges or Deposits:	Manager's prior approval required. Sorry, no cats.
Rated: 3 Paws 🐾🐾🐾	4 guest rooms with decks, on 2 acres.

onveniently located near the town of Dover, is Payne's Hill Bed and Breakfast, a recently restored 120-year-old New Englander, situated on two acres. Visitors are encouraged to stroll the grounds, which contain annual, perennial and vegetable gardens.

Each room is individually decorated with comfortable, unique furnishings and cable TV. Guests are invited to enjoy the music room, which has several instruments including a piano, as well as audio equipment. During any season, unwind in the gazebo while enjoying the surrounding natural beauty.

It is within walking distance to downtown, shopping, parks, restaurants, movies and the newly constructed riverwalk. Scenic and historic Portsmouth, the beautiful eastern coastal areas and the new Whittemore Recreational Complex are all conveniently nearby.

Horse and Hound Inn

205 Wells Road
Franconia, New Hampshire 03580
800-450-5501 • (603) 823-5501

Room Rates:	$80 – $92, including full breakfast.
Pet Charges or Deposits:	$8.50 per stay. $50 refundable deposit.
Rated: 3 Paws	8 guest rooms, restaurant.

T he Horse and Hound Inn, which started as a 19th-century farmhouse around 1830, is now one of New England's finest traditional bed and breakfast inns. Rooms are comfortably furnished with king-sized and queen-sized beds, some with adjoining rooms furnished with single or double beds. All rooms offer peaceful views of the surrounding landscape.

Gus and Max, the house cocker spaniels, welcome four-legged guests, and twin cats Boris and Igor may make an appearance.

A complimentary full breakfast is served with a chef's choice of pancakes, eggs and omelets. The dining room also serves continental cuisine each evening at very reasonable prices.

Located "off the beaten path" on the north side of Cannon Mountain, the Inn is adjacent to the White Mountains National Forest and Franconia Notch State Park, with plentiful activities year-round. Enjoy the great outdoors hiking, biking and horseback riding, ride the 80-passenger tram to the top of Cannon Mountain to see the view, or cross-country ski right out the front door – free for guests. The area also offers museums, chamber music, summer theater and antiquing.

Lovett's Inn

1474 Profile Road
Franconia, New Hampshire 03580
800-356-3802 • (603) 823-7761

Room Rates:	$130 – $190, including full breakfast and 4-course dinner.
Pet Charges or Deposits:	None.
Rated: 4 Paws 🐾🐾🐾🐾	22 guest rooms and 3 guest suites, swimming pool, whirlpool, spas, 2 dining rooms and cocktail lounge.

 njoy a peaceful getaway, pampered by true New England hospitality in this beautiful, historic 1794 home. Sample the many seasons of New Hampshire's north country, where relaxation and recreation go hand in hand.

The Inn offers comfortable single, double and suite arrangements, all with private baths. Each room is furnished with antique and period decorations in a comfortable style that proclaims its New England heritage. Comfortable bungalows with fireplaces dot the property, offering woodland privacy or poolside charm. The candlelit dining room provides a soothing atmosphere where guests can enjoy quiet meals chosen from a unique menu.

Situated on ten scenic acres only moments from Franconia Notch State Park, Lovett's offers convenient access to many area attractions. Visit the Old Man of the Mountain, the Basin, the Flume, or Cannon Mountain Aerial Tramway. Enjoy golfing, hiking, bicycling and walking in the summer and fall and downhill and cross-country skiing right from the front door in winter.

Dana Place Inn

Route 16, Pinkham Notch
Jackson, New Hampshire 03846
800-537-9276 • (603) 383-6822
Web Site: www.danaplace.com
E-mail: danaplace@ncia.net

Room Rates:	$85 – $153, including full breakfast and afternoon tea or après ski refreshment. AAA and AARP discounts.
Pet Charges or Deposits:	Manager's prior approval required. Sorry, no cats.
Rated: 4 Paws 🐾 🐾 🐾 🐾	35 guest rooms with indoor swimming pool and Jacuzzi, outdoor swimming hole, clay and asphalt tennis courts, restaurant and lounge.

E xperience more than 100 years of hospitality at historic Dana Place Inn, situated on 300 acres in Pinkham Notch, nestled at the base of the highest mountain in the northeast, Mount Washington. Surrounded by the 750,000-acre White Mountain National Forest, this rural retreat is dotted with apple orchards and mountain pools on the sparkling Ellis River.

Surprisingly sophisticated in decor, facilities and cuisine, the Inn is situated in a charmingly updated Colonial farmhouse. Accommodations include a variety of 35 rooms with king-, double- or queen-sized beds, most with a private bath. The Inn features fine dining, a spirited pub, heated indoor pool and Jacuzzi, a library with a fireplace and complimentary afternoon tea or après ski refreshments. Wake up to a full country breakfast and enjoy classical dining in one of the four dining rooms.

Cross-country ski from the doorsteps in winter or choose from four downhill ski mountains within fifteen miles. Visit Jackson Village for antique shops and galleries or enjoy outlet shopping in North Conway. The Inn is located minutes from the White Mountain attractions that offer year-round recreational fun.

Village House

P.O. Box 359, Route 16A
Jackson, New Hampshire 03846
800-972-8343 • (603) 383-6666

Room Rates:	$65 – $145, including seasonal breakfast and afternoon beverages. Special rates for returning guests.
Pet Charges or Deposits:	$10 per day.
Rated: 3 Paws	14 guest rooms with swimming pool, tennis court, hot tub and Jacuzzi.

J ust behind the famous Jackson Covered Bridge, you'll find the Village House, where guests are welcomed with a tradition that is more than 100 years old. This affordable country inn offers the luxuries of a resort and the atmosphere of a small bed and breakfast.

Put your feet up, read a book on the porch or gazebo or stroll around the six lovely acres of rolling riverfront landscape. Other amenities include a swimming pool, tennis court and a year-round Jacuzzi, which is delightful after a day of hiking or skiing. Breakfast is served on the wrap-around porch on warm mornings.

Jackson is a picturesque village where you can spend your time relaxing in peace and serenity or explore the White Mountain adventure and activity. Enjoy ice skating or sleigh rides under the stars and fine dining and cozy pubs with entertainment and hot chocolate by the fireplace. Jackson also hosts two golf courses, art galleries, antiques and factory outlet shopping.

Peep–Willow Farm

51 Bixby Street
Marlborough, New Hampshire 03455
(603) 876-3807
Web Site: www.top.monad.net/~naderer
E-mail: naderer@top.monad.net

Room Rates:	$35 – $55, including continental breakfast.
Pet Charges or Deposits:	$5 per day. One night's rate refundable deposit.
Rated: 3 Paws	3 guest rooms on an 18-acre working horse farm.

Peep-Willow Farm is an 18-acre working horse farm, where thoroughbreds are born, raised and trained to be top competition horses. Guests are welcome to help with chores, wander around and talk to, feed, or pet the livestock.

Imagine sitting on the terrace and enjoying a view all the way to the Connecticut River Valley, while newborn foals and their moms frolic before you. The ambiance at the farm is casual, comfortable and homey. Flexibility and serendipity are the key ingredients to enjoying your stay here. The twenty-year-old Colonial farmhouse is charming, evoking relaxation and enjoyment of the great outdoors.

Located at the foot of Mount Monadnock, known for great climbing and hiking adventures, this area offers a myriad of activities nearby. Enjoy riding, canoeing, swimming, tennis and nature walks in the state parks or golf at any of several renowned courses. A variety of exceptionally fine dining and cultural offerings abound.

Ram in the Thicket

24 Maple Street
Milford, New Hampshire 03055
(603) 654-6440

Room Rates: $60 – $75, including continental breakfast.
Pet Charges or Deposits: $10 per day. Manager's prior approval required.
Rated: 3 Paws 🐾🐾🐾   9 guest rooms, 2 guest suites, swimming pool, hot tub, restaurant and cocktail lounge.

 ocated in the rolling eastern foothills of the Monadnock Mountain region, Ram in the Thicket is the fruition of a longtime yearning and dream of the owners. The dream began with restoring and completely renovating this grand old Victorian mansion, which now consists of four dining rooms featuring a great crystal chandelier, a hand-carved fireplace and other subdued Victorian touches.

Weather permitting, guests are invited to enjoy the large screened summer garden dining porch. Almost every menu item is made from scratch and cooked to order, using fresh quality seasonal ingredients.

Ram in the Thicket is minutes away from the finest summer theater and year-round outdoor activities. During the spring and summer, enjoy excellent summer hiking trails and swimming beaches in southern New Hampshire. The woods turn into beautiful color foliage trails in autumn and ski areas in winter.

Stonehurst Manor

Route 16
North Conway, New Hampshire 03860-1937
800-525-9100 • (603) 356-3113
Web Site: www.stonehurstmanor.com

Room Rates:	$86 – $176, including full breakfast and dinner.
Pet Charges or Deposits:	$10 per day. $50 refundable deposit.
Rated: 4 Paws 🐾 🐾 🐾 🐾	24 guest suites with pool, Jacuzzi, tennis courts and a restaurant with four intimate dining rooms.

S et on a secluded hillside among 33 acres of tall pines, Stonehurst Manor invites you to enjoy the luxury of this elegant turn-of-the-century mansion. English country manor in style, the architectural highlights feature hand-carved oak woodwork, leaded glass windows, a multitude of stone fireplaces and a screened tile porch. Guest rooms, many with fireplaces, are beautifully and comfortably decorated.

Natural and man-made attractions and activities are abundant in the Mount Washington Valley. In winter, there is cross-country skiing at the doorstep on 65 kilometers of groomed trails, plus six major alpine ski areas are within minutes. You'll also find horse-drawn sleigh rides, ice skating, ice climbing and après ski pubs at locations throughout the valley. In summer, there are several golf courses, miles of hiking, mountain biking and cycling routes, canoeing on the Saco River and lots of great picnic spots.

Woodbound Inn

62 Woodbound Road
Rindge, New Hampshire 03461
800-688-7770 • (603) 532-8341

Room Rates:	$69 – $135, including full breakfast. AAA and AARP discounts.
Pet Charges or Deposits:	None.
Rated: 4 Paws 🐾🐾🐾🐾	44 guest rooms and cabins, with golf, tennis, a gift shop, restaurant and cocktail lounge.

L ocated on the shores of Lake Contoocook, with breathtaking views of Mount Monadnock, the Woodbound Inn offers accommodations to meet every need. Choose from the charm of the historic Main Inn, contemporary rooms in the Edgewood Building or charming lakefront cabins. The cabins are one- and two-bedroom, with either a king-sized bed or two twins, with day beds in the living rooms. Each cabin is equipped with a fireplace and is situated just a few feet from the Inn's private beach. Each day begins with a hearty breakfast.

The property consists of 165 wooded acres, which includes a golf course, clay tennis courts, private beach for swimming or fishing and a network of marked hiking and cross-country ski trails. The Inn also offers picnic grounds, horseshoes, shuffleboard, croquet, badminton, volleyball and a trout pond. The entire Monadnock region is filled with year-round activities, including summer concerts on the Common, regional festivals, a marionette theater and sporting events.

Hilltop Inn

Main Street
Sugar Hill, New Hampshire 03585
800-770-5695 • (603) 823-5695
Web Site: www.hilltopinn.com
E-mail: pw@hilltopinn.com

Room Rates: $70 – $150, including full breakfast and afternoon snacks.
Pet Charges or Deposits: $10 per day. One night's rate for deposit.
Rated: 4 Paws 🐾 🐾 🐾 🐾   3 guest rooms, 3 guest suites and 1 guest cottage.

T he Hilltop Inn is a traditional turn-of-the-century inn nestled in the small and peaceful village of Sugar Hill, in the heart of the White Mountains.

The guest rooms are beautifully furnished with unusual antiques and feature immaculate full private baths with lots of fluffy towels and amenities. Each bed boasts a comfortable extra-firm mattress, hand-painted quilts, European cotton sheets in summer and warm flannel in winter, with lots of plump pillows.

Breakfast specialties include cob-smoked bacon, ham and salmon soufflés, farm fresh eggs and homemade jams, breads and muffins. Fine wines, beers and spirits are always available.

Enjoy year-round recreation at White Mountain National Forest or the many pet-friendly hiking trails right on the property. Stroll along quiet country lanes or relax on the porches and enjoy the show as many species of native birds flock to feeders and hanging flower baskets. Pets are also invited to play in a special fenced-in area off the deck. Golden maremmas "Beemer" and "Bogie" are gracious four-legged hosts.

Tamworth Inn

Main Street
Tamworth, New Hampshire 03886
800-642-7352 • (603) 323-7721
Web Site: www.tamworth.com
E-mail: inn@tamworth.com

Room Rates:	$95 – $140, including full breakfast.
Pet Charges or Deposits:	$5 per day.
Rated: 4 Paws 🐾🐾🐾🐾	9 guest rooms, 7 guest suites, swimming pool, microwaves, restaurant and cocktail lounge.

S urround yourself with the essence of New England hospitality. Each guest room is tastefully accented with a country flavor and the Inn's public areas offer a warm invitation to relax and enjoy the comforts of an authentic New England village inn. Built in 1833, the Tamworth Inn today retains the charm of yesterday — good food with comfortable lodging.

There are picturesque mountains with miles of hiking trails and acres of green lawns. Located within a short drive are the tall peaks of the White Mountain National Forest and the beautiful Lake Winnipesaukee waterfront. Excellent cross-country skiing is at the front door, and the oldest professional theater in the United States is down the lane. Here you can enjoy the river bordering the back lawn with some of the best fishing around, cocktails in the pub or a leisurely dinner.

Spalding Inn

Mountain View Road
Whitefield, New Hampshire 03598
800-368-VIEW • (603) 837-2572
Seasonal: Open June – October

Room Rates:	$150 – $200 including full breakfast and full service dinner. AAA, AARP and AKC discounts.
Pet Charges or Deposits:	None.
Rated: 4 Paws 🐾🐾🐾🐾	36 guest rooms, 6 cottages and a guest house with fireplace on 200 acres, heated swimming pool, clay tennis courts and golf course.

T he Spalding Inn and Country Cottages is located in the heart of the mountains, set amidst 200 acres of manicured orchards and perennial gardens. The broad front porch welcomes you to the inn and on chilly evenings, a fire crackles in the stone fireplace of the main lobby.

Guests will find spacious, romantic rooms with king-sized beds and hand-made quilts, decorated with country cottage antiques. The private cottages have living rooms with fireplaces, service bars and one or more connecting bed-rooms — they are ideal for families. Fresh flowers, silver, crisp linens and candlelight enhance the wonderful food served in elegant yet comfortable surroundings.

Enjoy summer stock theater or a shopping spree at the nearby tax-free outlet. For the sports minded, there is plenty of trout fishing and boating and enticing carriage roads for walking. The Appalachian Trail system is a short walk from the Inn.

Stepping Stones Bed and Breakfast

6 Bennington Battle Trail
Wilton Center, New Hampshire 03086
888-654-9048 • (603) 654-9048

Room Rates: $55 – $60, including full breakfast.
Pet Charges or Deposits: Manager's prior approval required.
Rated: 4 Paws 🐾 🐾 🐾 🐾   3 guest rooms with private baths.

S tepping Stones is a fine bed and breakfast situated at the edge of one of Southern New Hampshire's most charming villages. In friendly European tradition, hostess Ann Carlsmith invites her guests to share an unusually interesting 19th-century house and garden. Furnishings are simple but abundantly comfortable.

Each guest room contains hand-woven throws, pillows and rugs in natural fibers and gentle colors, all created on the looms in the weaving room. Outside, a network of terraces and pathways connects extensive lush gardens, blooming over a long season, ending with brilliant autumn foliage. The country tradition of comfort and quiet hospitality begins with a full breakfast served in the solar breakfast room. During colder months, guests enjoy wood fires, hot cocoa and classical music.

It is located in the Monadnock region of south-central New Hampshire in the peaceful countryside, just beyond the picture-book hamlet of Wilton Center. Visitors enjoy hiking on the Wapack Trail, biking, antiquing and simply enjoying the beautiful setting.

Sedgwick Inn

Route 22
P.O. Box 250
Berlin, New York 12022
800-845-4886 • (518) 658-2334

Room Rates: $68 – $105, including full breakfast.
Pet Charges or Deposits: $5 per day. $50 refundable deposit.
Rated: 3 Paws 10 guest rooms and 1 guest suite.

F requently described as "the quintessential country inn," the Sedgwick Inn sits on twelve wooded acres in the scenic Taconic Valley. Located at the foot of the majestic Berkshire mountains, the Inn is a comfortable yet elegant, two-hundred-year-old Colonial gem.

The main house offers four double rooms and a two-room suite, all with private baths and brimming with collectibles. Each room has its own distinctive period setting, filled with modern amenities. Behind the Carriage House are six more guest rooms, tastefully furnished with Colonial-style maple furniture. A hearty breakfast of cereals, warm muffins and eggs cooked to order is served on the glass-enclosed porch with garden views.

Given its ideal location, the Sedgwick is the perfect springboard for countless area activities including hiking, biking, swimming and skiing. Visitors also enjoy Tanglewood concerts, the Shaker Village, Williamstown and other summer theaters, foliage tours, museums and more. In addition, the history-rich capital of Albany is 30 miles away.

Old Drovers Inn

Old Route 22
Dover Plains, New York 12522
(914) 832-9311

Room Rates: $150 – $395, including full breakfast and full dinner.
Pet Charges or Deposits: $20 each. Small dogs only. Manager's prior approval required.
Rated: 4 Paws 🐾🐾🐾🐾   4 guest rooms located on 12 park-like acres with a restaurant.

O ld Drovers, nestled in the Harlem Valley at the foot of the Berkshires, once served as a haven for New England cowboys known as "drovers," when they were guiding their cattle to market in New York City. Faithfully restored and preserved, the Inn continues to gain worldwide renown for its culinary delights and hospitality. Whether you relax in the Inn's guest rooms, dine in the stone and darkly beamed candlelit taproom or enjoy the seasonal gardens, you will admire this preservation of history.

Gracious guest rooms are furnished with the ambiance of a grand past, with decorative touches throughout and private baths. You can expect outstanding meals starting with a full American breakfast and ending with a dining experience that has won Old Drovers Inn the "Gourmet Retreat of the Year" reward. American country specialties are served, like cheddar cheese soup, seasonal game, browned turkey with mustard sauce and grilled double-cut lamb chops garnished with homemade tomato chutney.

Old Drovers is ideally situated for day trips to nearby cultural and educational sites, vineyards and antiquing. Visitors also enjoy year-round outdoor activities. Discover the hospitality, history and friendliness that have been the tradition for hundreds of years.

Inn at Lake Joseph

400 Saint Joseph Road
Forestburgh, New York 12777
(914) 791-9506

Room Rates:	$158 – $258, including full breakfast.
Pet Charges or Deposits:	None.
Rated: 4 Paws 🐾 🐾 🐾 🐾	10 guest rooms, 2 guest suites and carriage house with fireplaces, whirlpools, pool and lake swimming, health and fitness club, tennis, ski rentals and ski lessons.

 romantic Victorian country estate, tucked high in the Catskill Mountains on an unspoiled 250-acre lake, is the setting for the Inn at Lake Joseph. Surrounded by acres of hardwood forest and a wildlife preserve, the Inn has ten cozy guest rooms, including two suites. Some rooms have working fireplaces, whirlpool baths and private sun decks overlooking the forest. All are tastefully decorated with Victorian furnishings that invite you to step back in time.

You can relax in the comfortable living room or private library in front of a warm fire or enjoy some of the many board games. There is even a Victorian billiard room if you care for friendly competition. The formal dining room features damask wall coverings, Persian rugs, lattice windows and an overhead Venetian glass chandelier. Dining on the verandah overlooks the grounds and pool.

The Lake offers year-round recreational opportunities including fishing, swimming and boating during warm weather and ice skating during winter. There is also white-water rafting, river canoeing, horseback riding, sleigh rides, downhill skiing and water skiing nearby. Visitors may wish to enjoy the summer theater, outlet shopping or hot air ballooning in the neighboring areas.

Schaible's Serendipity Bed and Breakfast

1201 Bruynswick Road
Gardiner, New York 12525
(914) 255-5667

Room Rates:	$65 – $85, including full breakfast.
Pet Charges or Deposits:	$10 per stay. Manager's prior approval required.
Rated: 3 Paws	3 guest rooms and 1 guest suite on 26 acre farm with swimming pool and barn for stabling horses.

T his charming 1850s farmhouse is situated on 26 acres surrounded by meadows with panoramic views of the Shawangunk mountain range. In the quiet of this country setting, stroll acres of wildflowers to the rivers edge or explore the picturesque mountain fed pond. Guest accommodations feature large comfortable rooms with queen-sized beds and inviting decor. Awaken when you like and enjoy a leisurely breakfast consisting of homemade baked goods, fresh fruit and gourmet coffee and tea. Breakfast can be enjoyed in the country dining room or greet the morning with pleasant views outside on the spacious deck.

Outdoor enthusiasts will enjoy the Mohonk Preserve featuring climbing, biking, hiking and horseback riding. Minnewaska State Park offers hiking, biking, picnicking, swimming and cross country skiing. Several historical sites, vineyards and wineries are conveniently located within 15 minutes of the homestay.

Log Country Inn

P.O. Box 581
Ithaca, New York 14851
800-274-4771 • (607) 589-4771
Web Site: www.logtv.com/inn
E-mail: wanda@logtv.com

Room Rates:	$45 – $75, including full breakfast. AAA, AARP, AKC and ABA discounts.
Pet Charges or Deposits:	None.
Rated: 3 Paws	5 guest rooms and 1 guest suite with whirlpool and sauna.

The Log Country Inn resides on 15 wooded acres at the edge of the vast Danby State Forest. This rustic inn, constructed of fine Vermont logs, is a design inspired by the American pioneer cabins of the 18th century. Inside, you will find modern accommodations provided in the spirit of international hospitality. A cathedral ceiling soars over the living room, accented by exposed log ceiling beams.

Each morning, a full European breakfast is served with freshly squeezed juices, selected fruits, local bees' honey, homemade jams, breads and pastries. There is always a jar of homemade cookies for snacking.

The Inn is located at the southern gateway to the Finger Lakes. Tour the Cayuga Wine Trail's unique family vineyards or enjoy the breathtaking gorges and waterfalls of seven nearby state parks. Fish, sail, swim and water ski or watch world-class auto racing in Watkins Glen. The area is a bird watcher's paradise with thousands of migratory birds in the Montezuma Wildlife Reserve or the Sapsucker Woods Bird Sanctuary.

Lake Placid Hilton Resort

One Mirror Lake Drive
Lake Placid, New York 12946
800-755-5598 • (518) 523-4411

Room Rates:	$69 – $159. AAA and AARP discounts.
Pet Charges or Deposits:	$50 refundable deposit. Manager's prior approval required.
Rated: 3 Paws 🐾🐾🐾	177 guest rooms and 2 guest suites with indoor and outdoor swimming pools, private waterfront area, fitness facilities, whirlpool, restaurant and lounge.

O n the shores of Mirror Lake, overlooking the Adirondack's High Peaks, the Lake Placid Hilton Resort offers accommodations with delightful views of the lake and surrounding mountains. Dining in the Terrace Room promises both exceptional cuisine and spectacular views through wrap-around windows. If you are looking for night life, the Dancing Bears Lounge features live entertainment.

Located in the heart of Adirondack State Park, the largest wilderness area in the East, Lake Placid is truly a year-round "getaway" spot. There are venues from the 1932 and 1980 Olympic Winter Games, combined with the U.S. Olympic Training Center, which brings international training and world class competitions. Visitors can attend major shows with top entertainers or professional athletic events. If you prefer the great outdoors, the Adirondack Mountains, with their rivers and lakes, offer year-round recreational opportunities.

Guest House

223 Debruce Road
Livingston Manor, New York 12758
(914) 439-4000

Room Rates:	$100 – $200, including full breakfast, afternoon English tea and cocktails.
Pet Charges or Deposits:	One night's rate refundable deposit. Manager's prior approval required.
Rated: 4 Paws	7 guest rooms with fitness room, whirlpools, Jacuzzi and enclosed large dog run with igloo kennel.

S heltered among mature trees and graceful shrubs, the Guest House overlooks its own private stretch of the Willowemoc River. Forty unspoiled and secluded acres surround the modern house, built to the design of a traditional barn.

Each of the luxurious bedrooms has a private bath and is furnished with king-sized or queen-sized beds, Jacuzzi and a private patio, with impressive views of the river, garden or pond. The common area known as the Great Room has a cathedral ceiling, fireplace and baby grand piano. Windows and French doors open on three sides to enchanting views of the garden and another welcoming patio encircled by multicolored flower baskets. Morning begins with home-baked bread, croissants or muffins piping hot from the oven, followed by a full country breakfast. A fitness area is ready and waiting for a vigorous aerobic workout.

Enjoy the serenity of the woods or test your skills at fly-fishing, horseback riding or cross-country skiing. The Guest House is situated less than two miles from the main shopping street of Livingston Manor, with nine golf courses and indoor and outdoor tennis courts nearby.

Crowne Plaza Manhattan

1605 Broadway
New York City, New York 10019
800-243-6969 • (212) 977-4000
Web Site: www.crowneplaza.com

Room Rates:	$210 – $410. AAA and AARP discounts.
Pet Charges or Deposits:	Small pets only. Pets up to 30 lbs. $500 refundable credit card deposit.
Rated: 4 Paws 🐾🐾🐾🐾	755 guest rooms and 15 suites.

In the heart of New York City's historic theater district and the "new" Times Square sits the 46-story Crowne Plaza Manhattan. With only 26 rooms per floor, it has built its reputation on offering the privacy of a small hotel with the facilities and services of a large one. All the guest rooms feature spectacular cityscape or river views, in-room refreshment center, coffee maker with coffee and tea, personal in-room safe, individual heating controls in winter and air conditioning in summer and cable TV.

The Crowne Plaza Manhattan is conveniently located near LaGuardia, Newark and JFK International airports. Only blocks away are famous New York City must-sees such as Radio City Music Hall, the Rockefeller Center, St. Patrick's Cathedral, Saks Fifth Avenue, the Museum of Modern Art, Carnegie Hall, Central Park, Cartier and Tiffany and Company.

Four Seasons Hotel New York

57 East 57th Street
New York City, New York 10022
800-332-3442 • (212) 758-5700

Room Rates: $475 and up.
Pet Charges or Deposits: Small pets only.
Rated: 5 Paws 367 luxury rooms including 58 suites.

From the columned grand foyer to sunset over the park from your private terrace, the Four Seasons Hotel is an excellent choice for travelers and their pets in the heart of New York City. The 367 guest rooms, including 58 suites, are New York's largest.

Your pet will receive a five-star welcome at check-in, with complimentary dog bowl, snacks and a sleeping pillow. Central Park is only steps away, and you and your pet can enjoy a brisk walk.

The Four Seasons' own Fitness Center and Spa offers an aerobics studio and full strength-training or cardiovascular workouts with personal trainers. Men and women enjoy separate saunas, whirlpools and steam rooms. Spa pampering ranges from facials to massage to reflexology.

The hotel is minutes away from such New York landmarks as Carnegie Hall, Rockefeller Center, Radio City Music Hall, the Trump Tower, the Museum of Modern Art, St. Patrick's Cathedral and the NBC studios.

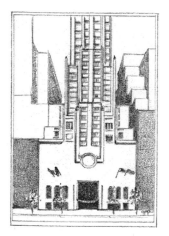

Le Parker Meridien Hotel

118 West 57th Street
New York City, New York 10019
800-543-4300 • (212) 245-5000

Room Rates: $325 – $2,500.
Pet Charges or Deposits: Small pets only.
Rated: 5 Paws 🐾 🐾 🐾 🐾 🐾 500 guest rooms and 200 guest suites with rooftop swimming
                        pool, health spa, award-winning restaurants, room service,
                        cocktail lounge, concierge and valet service.

S eek refuge from the mundane at Le Parker Meridien, where the glamour and charisma of New York meet the sophistication and elegance of Europe in an unforgettable experience. Graceful columns, shimmering marble and abundant greenery greet you in the three-story atrium lobby. An escape to the luxurious guest rooms, outstanding restaurants, newly renovated Club La Raquette and magnificent rooftop pool guarantees your cure for the commonplace. Pamper yourself in the manner you deserve.

Guest rooms offer all the amenities you expect to find in a world-class hotel, as well as magnificent views of the Manhattan skyline and Central Park. Indulge yourself with 24-hour room service, concierge assistance and valet service. Discover Bar Montparnasse, an exquisite lounge evocative of 1930s Europe.

The hotel's fashionable 57th Street address puts you close to Carnegie Hall, Lincoln Center, Broadway theaters, pet-friendly Central Park and Fifth Avenue shopping.

Holiday Inn Express

341 South Road
Poughkeepsie, New York 12601
800-HOLIDAY • (914) 473-1151

Room Rates:	$89 – $109, including continental breakfast. Local restaurant discounts. AAA and AARP discounts.
Pet Charges or Deposits:	None.
Rated: 3 Paws 🐾 🐾 🐾	119 guest rooms and 2 guest suites with swimming pool and fitness center.

T he guest rooms, designed for comfort, feature contemporary decor with extra space for spreading out. Guests receive a local area guide at check-in with a listing of local attractions, entertainment spots, restaurants and maps. A breakfast bar is offered in the Great Room each morning.

Located on Route 9, south of the Mid-Hudson Bridge, the Inn is situated in the heart of the wine country, and the surrounding area is easily accessible. The Metro North Train Station and the Dutchess County and Stewart Airports are all within 20 minutes. Near the Culinary Institute of America, Vassar and Marist colleges, other attractions include the Franklin Roosevelt home, the Vanderbilt Mansion and West Point Military Academy.

Audrey's Farmhouse

2188 Brunswick Road
Wallkill, New York 12589
(914) 895-3440

Room Rates:	$90 – $120, including full gourmet breakfast.
Pet Charges or Deposits:	$50 refundable deposit. Manager's prior approval required.
Rated: 3 Paws 🐾🐾🐾	5 guest rooms, with swimming pool, stabling for horses, Jacuzzi and hot tub.

L ocated at the foot of the Shawangunk Mountains, surrounded by 125 acres of meadows, sits Audrey's Farmhouse. This beautifully restored 1740s farmhouse is handsomely decorated and features period antiques. Guest quarters are furnished with comfy feather beds and fluffy down comforters. This property rates 4 stars in Bikofsky's "Best Places to Kiss," and guests are invited to enjoy star-filled romantic evenings and leisurely strolls along the many paths gracing the spacious acreage.

Enjoy the luxury of country living, relax by the pool or take advantage of the stables, if you're traveling with your horse. There are wonderful opportunities for trail riding and exploring the surrounding areas. Also nearby are world-class mountain climbing, biking, hiking and cross-country skiing through snow-covered mountains. The artists' colony of Woodstock is only a short drive away or you may choose to visit the many local wineries.

Willkommen Hof Bed and Breakfast

Route 86
P.O. Box 240
Wilmington, New York 12997
800-541-9119 • (518) 946-7669

Room Rates:	$50 – $96, including full breakfast, afternoon beverage and snacks. Military discounts.
Pet Charges or Deposits:	$10 per day. $25 refundable deposit.
Rated: 3 Paws 🐾🐾🐾	5 guest rooms and 1 three-room suite with whirlpools, spas and sauna.

A turn-of-the-century farmhouse, the Willkommen Hof Bed and Breakfast is the perfect place to enjoy and explore the Adirondacks. Accommodations range from deluxe rooms featuring king-sized beds with private baths to their standard room with a shared bath.

The common areas include a reading room with a cozy fireplace, providing the perfect place to curl up with a good book. A separate TV room hosts a large-screen TV and VCR with a selection of current movies and games and books for your enjoyment. Guests are also invited to relax in the large cedar sauna. Besides serving a hearty breakfast, your hosts serve afternoon tea where you can sample freshly made cakes and baked goods.

The Adirondack Mountains offer many opportunities to enjoy the outdoors. There are hundreds of miles of hiking trails for both the novice and the expert hiker or backpacker. Some of the best trout fishing in the state of New York is within walking distance. Nearby Lake Placid offers swimming, sailing, wind surfing or water skiing. For the winter enthusiast, skiing, ice skating, luge and bobsled runs are available at Whiteface Mountain, which is the home of several Winter Olympics.

Danske Hus

361 South Street
Windham, New York 12496
(518) 734-6335

Room Rates:	$50 – $85, including full breakfast.
Pet Charges or Deposits:	$5 per day. $50 refundable deposit. Manager's prior approval required. Sorry, no cats.
Rated: 3 Paws	4 guest rooms with sauna.

A circa 1865 farmhouse, Danske Hus has been fully restored as a charming bed and breakfast. The four cozy bedrooms, all with private baths, promise a comfortable rest, with the relaxing sounds of the babbling brook. A large living room, with mountain views and a wood-burning fireplace, is available for reading, socializing or playing the piano. A full breakfast is served in the heirloom-filled dining room.

Each season provides many reasons for a visit. In winter, while others are waiting to park their cars, Danske Hus guests are on the slopes — just across the street. Upon return, homemade soup and bread, gourmet coffees, teas, hot chocolate and cookies are served. The hills on the property lend themselves to great sledding, with a warm fireplace and roasted marshmallows awaiting. Warm weather invites golf, swimming, hiking, biking, horseback riding and antiquing, all nearby.

Sanford-Covell Villa Marina

72 Washington Street
Newport, Rhode Island 02840
(401) 847-0206

Room Rates: $65 – $295, including continental breakfast.
Pet Charges or Deposits: Sorry, no cats.
Rated: 4 Paws 🐾 🐾 🐾 🐾   7 guest rooms and 2 guest suites with swimming pool, Jacuzzi,
                         hot tubs and guest laundry facilities.

 esigned and built as a summer cottage, the Sanford-Covell Villa Marina today stands as an architectural landmark dating back to 1869. Among the extraordinary features are the grand staircase and entrance hall, which rises 35 feet from floor to ceiling, accented by projecting balconies at various levels. The woods used in the house include oak, ash, cherry, hard pine, maple, black walnut, butternut and ebony.

Located on a historic street in Newport, the setting invites guests to relax on the comfortable porch and enjoy spectacular sunsets over the bay, watching the boats sailing by in front of the house.

A delightful continental breakfast is served in the formal dining room featuring a dining set once owned by the founder of the Naval Academy at Annapolis.

Historic Newport offers many attractions and activities, including the Newport Mansion tours, the Newport Music Festival and the International Boat Show. Shopping areas include the Brick Marketplace, America's Cup Avenue and Thames Street which features a large collection of specialty shops.

Westin Hotel

One West Exchange Street
Providence, Rhode Island 02903
800-WESTIN-1 • (401) 598-8000

Room Rates:	$140 – $205, including breakfast allowance. AAA, AARP and American Express Senior Discounts.
Pet Charges or Deposits:	$50 per stay. $25 refundable deposit. Manager's prior approval required. Small pets only.
Rated: 4 Paws 🐾🐾🐾🐾	363 guest rooms and 22 guest suites, with rooftop health spa and indoor swimming pool, video games, 2 restaurants and 3 lounges.

T he Westin Providence, New England's landmark of luxury and neoclassical beauty, is well connected to the heart of Rhode Island's capital city. From the moment you enter the Rotunda Lobby with its dramatic backdrop of the Capitol Building, you can feel the old-world craftsmanship that distinguishes this oasis of new-world comfort.

Furnished with European style and graced with spectacular views of the city, each of the 363 guest rooms and suites is elegantly appointed with a spacious writing desk, an easy chair with ottoman and a private refreshment center. Remote-controlled color cable TV is tastefully tucked away in an armoire.

You'll feel on top of the world in the glass-domed rooftop health spa. Swim under the sun or stars in the indoor heated pool. Schedule a massage or an exercise session with a personal trainer, enjoy a quiet interlude in the elegant Library Lounge or enjoy live music in the Piano Bar. Morning, noon and night, delight in fresh American cuisine or a sumptuous Sunday brunch in the garden-style setting of The Café. You will discover inventive seafood and regional favorites at Agora, the award-winning specialty restaurant.

Filled with historic charm and all the natural wonders of coastal New England, Providence offers the pleasures of one-of-a-kind shops, Tony Award-winning theater, year-round sporting events and a restaurant scene inspired by the largest culinary school in the world.

Larchwood Inn

521 Main Street
Wakefield, Rhode Island 02879
800-275-5450 • (401) 783-5454

Room Rates:	$35 – $120. AAA, AARP, AKC and ABA discounts.
Pet Charges or Deposits:	$5 per day.
Rated: 3 Paws 🐾 🐾 🐾	18 guest rooms, 3 dining rooms, cocktail lounge.

 ocated in the quiet village of Wakefield, Larchwood Inn has survived the necessities of modernization while preserving the charm of its past. Century-old trees dot the grounds of this 160-year-old country inn.

This three-story manor is surrounded by a wide expanse of landscaped grounds and by South County beaches. Each comfortable guest room has been individually decorated and all are furnished with carefully selected period pieces. Most of the rooms have private baths.

Guests may enjoy fine dining throughout the day in one of the three dining rooms, which serve traditional fare along with many interesting daily specials and light suppers.

Local attractions include beautiful surf and sheltered beaches, making Larchwood a perfect base for swimming, fishing, sailing, biking or bird watching.

The Villa

190 Shore Road
Westerly, Rhode Island 02891
800-722-9240 • (401) 596-1054

Room Rates:	$75 – $225, including continental breakfast.
Pet Charges or Deposits:	$25 per stay. Manager's prior approval required.
Rated: 4 Paws	6 guest suites with swimming pool, Jacuzzi, hot tubs, fireplaces and private terrace.

An oasis of privacy and luxury, The Villa is a large, gracious home situated on 11/2 landscaped acres, surrounded by beautiful gardens and spacious lawns. Gracing this delightful setting is a Mediterranean, designer pool and a delightful outdoor Jacuzzi spa.

This deluxe bed and breakfast features six luxury suites, individually inspired and uniquely highlighted with romantic and inviting details. A pleasing breakfast, featuring home-baked goods, is served in the dining area at poolside or in the privacy of your suite.

Located at the crossroads of historic Westerly and Watch Hill, The Villa is minutes from Rhode Island's pristine shoreline. The many nearby attractions include Misquamicut Beach, Foxwoods Resort and Casino and the Mystic Aquarium. Guests can also enjoy shopping at Old Mystic Village, oceanview golf courses and saltwater fishing.

Hill Farm Inn

R.R. 2, Box 2015
Arlington, Vermont 05250
800-882-2545 • (802) 375-2269
Web Site: www.hillfarminn.com
E-mail: hillfarm@vermontel.com

Room Rates:	$75 – $125, including full breakfast and a jar of homemade strawberry-rhubarb jam.
Pet Charges or Deposits:	$5 per day. One night's rate refundable deposit.
Rated: 3 Paws 🐾🐾🐾	11 guest rooms and 2 guest suites with refrigerators and wood stoves.

H ill Farm Inn, one of Vermont's first country inns, still specializes in the warm country hospitality that began 90 years ago. The Inn is surrounded by 50 acres of farmland with a mile of frontage on the famed Battenkill River, offering spectacular mountain views in every direction.

Seven guest rooms are located on the second floor of the 1830s main house, with an additional six rooms in the 1790s guest house next door. New England farmhouse decor is found throughout the guest accommodations, with each room individually and uniquely decorated. The suites have private porches and incomparable views of the Taconic and Green Mountains. Guests enjoy a full country breakfast each morning and for a minimal fee can feast on a four-course dinner served nightly. The Hill Farm Inn specializes in soups, breads and desserts — all from scratch — and vegetables fresh from the garden. The chef offers a choice of vegetarian, light or hearty entrées.

Whatever the season, you will find relaxation or plenty of activities to match every mood. Fish or canoe in the Battenkill, search for and find the elusive fiddlehead fern, hunt for antiques or browse the flea markets. Hike the mountain and forest trails or bike country roads, swim in streams, lakes or the old quarry. Ski downhill or cross-country, ice skate or jog the back roads.

Greenhurst Inn

R.R. 2, Box 60
River Street
Bethel, Vermont 05032-9404
800-510 2553 • (802) 234-9474

Room Rates:	$50 – $100, including continental breakfast. AAA and AARP discounts.
Pet Charges or Deposits:	$50 refundable deposit. Manager's prior approval required.
Rated: 3 Paws 🐾🐾🐾	13 guest rooms with outdoor exercise area.

L ocated midway between Boston and Montreal, in the center of Vermont, this charming country inn offers gracious hospitality and elegant comfort. The Greenhurst Inn is a lovely 1890s Victorian mansion overlooking the White River.

This grand inn, with its turrets, porches and gazebo, houses magnificent woodwork, carved staircases, high ceilings and lovely intricate light fixtures. Guest rooms are comfortably decorated with antiques and original artwork, and many offer fireplaces.

Breakfast is served in the period dining room, offering home-baked goods with an array of jams and preserves. A crackling fire and strains of classical music accompany the sumptuous fare.

Seasonal activities are abundantly available and include Nordic and Alpine skiing, golfing, boating, canoeing and fishing. The historic countryside awaits exploration and the Appalachian Trail is minutes away.

Inn on the Common

North Main Street
Craftsbury Common, Vermont 05827
800-521-2233 • (802) 586-9619
Web Site: www.innonthecommon.com

Room Rates:	$220 – $280, including full breakfast and dinner.
Pet Charges or Deposits:	$15 per stay. Manager's prior approval required.
Rated: 4 Paws	14 guest rooms and 2 guest suites, tennis courts, swimming pool, award-winning chef.

T he Inn is situated on a panoramic hilltop surrounded by 15 beautifully landscaped acres of land. It is located in Craftsbury Common, a village of white clapboard homes in Vermont's pristine Northeast Kingdom, where the roads run along ridges and brilliantly green farmland falls away to the distant mountains.

Sixteen guest rooms with private baths are spread out between three houses. All have sitting areas made for relaxing and are stylishly furnished with fine wallpaper, distinctive artwork and antiques. The meals rival Boston's finest in service and excellence, complimented by an award-winning wine list.

Guests are invited to enjoy the pool or clay tennis courts or simply to explore the back roads throughout this scenic area. During winter, the Craftsbury Nordic Center trails crisscross the kind of red-barn-spotted farmscape that speaks Vermont. After a day on the trails, enjoy The Wellness Barn, a state-of-the-art fitness center featuring spas and saunas that is located 10 minutes away.

Barrows House

P.O. Box 98, Route 30
Dorset, Vermont 05251
800-639-1620 • (802) 867-4455
Web Site: www.barrowshouse.com
E-mail: barhouse@vermontel.com

Room Rates:	$120 – $240, including full breakfast and gourmet dinner.
Pet Charges or Deposits:	$15 per day. Manager's prior approval required. Sorry, no cats.
Rated: 4 Paws 🐾🐾🐾🐾	18 guest rooms and 10 guest suites, with swimming pool, sauna, badminton, croquet green, tennis courts, touring bikes and pub.

 he Barrows House is a historic inn of eight buildings nestled on twelve park-like acres situated in Dorset. The white clapboard buildings, colorful gardens, manicured lawns and stately trees evoke a history dating back to the 1700s.

The unique facilities and extensive grounds feature modern conveniences, with each guest room or cottage uniquely furnished in its own restful style with antiques, old family pieces and modern bedding. Each house has its own sitting room, porch or terrace. The main inn features a living room with a glowing hearth and a cozy tavern, which provide an opportunity for either companionship or privacy.

During warm weather, the inn offers swimming, tennis, lawn games and touring bikes for leisurely rides around Dorset and down the Mettowee River Valley. Nearby Manchester offers an array of shopping adventures and an 18-hole golf course. Horseback riding and trout fishing on the famed Battenkill are found close by and hiking trails abound throughout the area. In winter, the downhill runs of Bromley, Magic and Stratton are within a short drive.

Cortina Inn and Resort

U.S. Route 4
Killington, Vermont 05751-7604
800-451-6108 • (802) 773-3333
Web Site: www.cortinainn.com
E-mail: cortina1@aol.com

Room Rates:	$99 – $179, including full breakfast, afternoon tea and tasty Vermont treats. AAA, AARP, AKC and ABA discounts.
Pet Charges or Deposits:	$5 per day. $50 refundable deposit. Manager's prior approval required.
Rated: 4 Paws 🐾🐾🐾🐾	91 guest rooms and 6 guest suites with pet treats upon arrival; gourmet restaurant, indoor swimming pool, health club, tennis, Jacuzzi, spas, sleigh rides and skating.

T he Cortina Inn, located amidst Vermont's scenic beauty, blends hospitality and cozy charm with the luxury of a fine resort. Each room is decorated individually, offering fresh, fragrant flowers, brass beds and handmade quilts. In some of the deluxe rooms, you can warm yourself by the fireplace or enjoy the scenic beauty surrounding the inn from your balcony or terrace.

Center Court, where a fire blazes, is one of the common areas where guests may enjoy a game of backgammon. The restaurant serves a sumptuous array of foods rich in flavor, artfully prepared and served in the elegant dining room. Take a stroll through the Mountain Art Gallery to view the works of acclaimed regional artists, representing a broad range of styles and media.

Choose from several challenging golf courses nearby or play tennis on one of Cortina's eight courts. Seasonal activities include snowmobiling, sleigh rides, ice skating and snowshoeing in winter. Summer offers fabulous mountain biking, hiking and fly-fishing.

Combes Family Inn

953 East Lake Road
Ludlow, Vermont 05149
800-822-8799 • (802) 228-8799
Web Site: www.combesfamilyinn.com

Room Rates:	$55 – $124, including full breakfast.
Pet Charges or Deposits:	$75 refundable deposit.
Rated: 3 Paws 🐾 🐾 🐾	11 guest rooms with lounge.

As the name indicates, this is a true family inn situated on a quiet country back road in the heart of Vermont's mountain and lake region. There are 50 acres of rolling meadows and woods to explore.

Built in 1891, the dairy farm supplied Ludlow and surrounding towns, and the sugar bushes yielded untold gallons of maple syrup. The Inn now offers a quiet respite with homey ambiance, good food, friendly hosts and spectacular scenery.

The cozy, country-inspired guest rooms, all with private baths, are scattered between the farm house and adjoining units. Meals at the Inn are hearty, Vermont-style, with fresh, home-baked goods and jams. The dining room has exposed beams and a large bay window overlooking the pastures and Okemo Mountain.

There is swimming, boating and fishing on Lake Rescue and Echo Lake, bicycling on country roads, hiking, picnicking, golf, tennis and horseback riding nearby. There are numerous small towns for shopping, live theater, museums and cheese and maple syrup factories. Located minutes from several great ski resorts to challenge every level.

Red Clover Inn

7 Woodward Road
Mendon, Vermont 05701
800-752-0571 • (802) 775-2290
Web Site: www.redcloverinn.com
E-mail: redclovr@vermontel.com

Room Rates:	$100 – $350, including full breakfast and gourmet dinner.
Pet Charges or Deposits:	$5 per day. 50% refundable deposit. Manager's prior approval required.
Rated: 4 Paws 🐾🐾🐾🐾	14 guest rooms with swimming pool, whirlpools, an award-winning restaurant and pub on 13 picturesque acres.

T he Red Clover Inn was built as a private retreat in 1840 by General John Woodward. Once inside, the Inn feels like a large, cozy home with comfortable furniture, exposed wood beams and a roaring fire in the fieldstone fireplace. Guest rooms are beautifully appointed, with private baths. Many rooms boast fireplaces, whirlpools and picturesque mountain views.

You will awake to a country breakfast menu of fresh fruits and home-cooked delights such as Cinnamon Swirl French Toast, served in the sunlit breakfast room. Dinner offerings feature innovative and traditional American cuisine by candlelight, complemented by an award-winning wine list.

The Red Clover Inn is convenient to Killington and the Pico Mountains, minutes away. Cross-country ski on well-groomed trails during winter. During the warmer months, swim in the knoll-top pool, hike, bike or horseback ride the Appalachian or Long Trail. Enjoy Music on the Mountain concerts or summer stock theater. The Inn is a perfect place to view the changing seasons during autumn, pick apples or browse for antiques.

Commodores Inn

Route 100 South
P.O. Box 970
Stowe, Vermont 05672
800-44-STOWE • (802) 253-7131
Web Page: www.stoweinfo.com/saa/commodores
E-mail: commodores@mt-mansfield.com

Room Rates: $62 – $124.
Pet Charges or Deposits: $10 per stay.
Rated: 3 Paws 🐾🐾🐾   50 guest rooms with indoor and outdoor swimming pools,
                         Jacuzzi, hot tubs, spas, restaurant and sports lounge, around a
                         3-acre lake.

C ommodores Inn is located in Stowe, the essence of Vermont, where family-owned farms rub boundaries with world-class ski areas. Enjoy comfortable accommodations, fine food, a host of activities and friendly, courteous service in a tranquil and picturesque 30-acre setting.

Guest rooms feature comfortable king- and queen-sized beds, cable TV and heat lamps in your private bath. Relax in the comfortable living room and enjoy the warmth of a crackling fire in the majestic fieldstone fireplace, the wide-screen TV, quiet reading or board games. Bask in the tropical warmth of the new indoor swimming pool, where state-of-the-art technology creates a relaxing environment complemented by red cedar paneling.

Visit New England icons such as a white-spired community church or the ghost on Emily's Bridge or witness the transformation of sap to syrup at maple sugaring time. Cheer for your favorite Olympic skier at the annual ski challenge. Enjoy model yacht racing and experience the beauty of the 1812 Overture performed by the Vermont Symphony Orchestra in an open meadow at sunset.

Mountain Road Resort

1007 Mountain Road
P.O. Box 8
Stowe, Vermont 05672
800-367-6873 • (802) 253-4566
Web Site: www.stowevtusa.com
E-mail: stowevt@aol.com

Room Rates:	$95 – $195.
Pet Charges or Deposits:	$15 – $25 per stay. Guests must sign pet responsibility/liability form.
Rated: 4 Paws 🐾 🐾 🐾 🐾	24 guest rooms and 6 suites with pool, hot tubs, spa and tennis.

O n seven beautifully landscaped acres, the Mountain Road Resort offers 30 guest rooms and condo-suites, with amenities such as fireplaces, dining areas, lofts, kitchens and tiled baths with whirlpools. Concierge and room service are also provided.

Feast on a French country breakfast outdoors on the Alpine Terrace, and enjoy daily afternoon refreshments beside the massive stone fireplace in the den.

Jog, bicycle or rollerblade the scenic five-mile Stowe recreation path, then plunge into the Mountain Road Resort's large, heated outdoor swimming pool. Or take a break from tennis to relax in the outdoor "MoonSpa," then barbecue or play lawn games. If golf is more your style, the nearby Stowe Country Club offers guests preferred rates.

Millbrook Inn and Restaurant

R.D. Box 62
Waitsfield, Vermont 05673
800-477-2809 • (802) 496-2405
Web Site: www.bbonline.com/vt/millbrook
E-mail: millbrkinn@aol.com

Room Rates:	$50 – $70, including full breakfast and full dinner.
Pet Charges or Deposits:	Sorry, no cats.
Rated: 3 Paws	7 guest rooms on 4 acres, with a restaurant.

Millbrook is a classic Cape-style farmhouse built in the 1850s by Jack Dana. He located the farmhouse close to his lumber and brick mills on nearby Mill Brook. Today the mills are long gone, but the picturesque setting remains, with the Inn situated midway between the ski slopes and the village of Waitsfield.

In the tradition of Vermont innkeeping, guests are treated to personalized service in a friendly, unhurried atmosphere. You enter the Inn through the Warming Room, where the antique parlor stove blazes a warm winter welcome. The seven guest rooms all have private baths and are decorated with hand stenciling, antique bedsteads and handmade quilts.

Fine country gourmet cuisine is served in the comfortably decorated dining room, featuring homemade items using the freshest natural ingredients for soups, breads, pasta, ice cream and desserts. To complement your dinner, a fine selection of wine and Vermont beer is available.

Millbrook is conveniently located five minutes from the finest skiing in the East. Neighboring Mad River Valley offers excellent hiking, road and mountain biking, canoeing, golfing, soaring, tennis, horseback riding and swimming. Back-country roads await your exploration, along with the local antique and crafts shops.

Powderhound Inn

Route 100
P.O. Box 369
Warren, Vermont 05674
800-548-4022 • (802) 496-5100
Web Site: www.powderhoundinn.com

Room Rates:	$68 – $164, including seasonal breakfast.
Pet Charges or Deposits:	$5 per day. One night's rate deposit, partially refundable.
Rated: 3 Paws 🐾🐾🐾	4 guest rooms and 44 guest suites with swimming pool, hot tubs, volleyball, croquet, tennis courts, refrigerators, full bar in winter, restaurant and doggie biscuits at check-in.

T he Powderhound is located in the heart of central Vermont, in the scenic Mad River Valley. The century-old converted farmhouse overlooks a peaceful, rustic setting at the entrance to the Sugarbush resort area.

Each of the 44 suites features a living room area with cable TV, kitchenette, separate bedroom and private bath, offering comfort and privacy for up to four guests. There is a cozy common area for reading or relaxing and spacious grounds for long walks and lawn games. An old-fashioned front porch is a great place to sit a spell and watch the world go by. A hearty breakfast is served in the dining room, with windows offering ample opportunities for bird watching.

The Mad River Valley offers an assortment of year-round activities, from hiking to biking, horseback riding, canoeing and fishing, as well as lots of sightseeing. Sugarbush and Mad River Glen offer some of the best skiing in the East and provide a challenge for every level. The valley also offers a wide variety of winter adventures with cross-country skiing, snowshoeing, sleigh rides and winter fun.

Kedron Valley Inn

Route 106
Woodstock, Vermont 05071
800-836-1193 • (802) 457-1473
E-mail: KedronInn@aol.com

Room Rates: $120 – $195, including full country breakfast.
Pet Charges or Deposits: Manager's prior approval required.
Rated: 4 Paws 🐾🐾🐾🐾   23 guest rooms, 3 suites and a restaurant.

One of Vermont's oldest inns, operating for 168 years, the Kedron Valley Inn's rural pace and scenic surroundings offer a relaxing hideaway. Most rooms have canopy beds and fireplaces or wood-burning stoves. Hooked rugs, antique rockers, heirloom quilts and needlepoint fill the rooms with quality comfort.

Breakfast consists of hearty fare: homemade muffins or scones, fragrant and hot from the oven, rival the sumptuous omelets. The restaurant serves contemporary American cuisine centered around the finest local products.

The Inn has lush bulb and perennial gardens, and several nearby gardens are open for viewing or strolling. Art galleries, antique stores and shopping are close at hand in Woodstock, and the discount Outlet Center is a short drive away in Manchester. Three golf courses are within 15 minutes, and a fitness center and indoor and outdoor tennis courts are available to guests.

Index

About the Author...
From a Dog's Point of View

Dreamer Dawg, office manager and "cover girl" for Bon Vivant Press, is an eleven-year-young Labrador Retriever. When not exploring the food and lodging for each regional book, you can find Dreamer relaxing onboard her boat in the Monterey harbor or running with the horses in Pebble Beach.

Owners Kathleen & Robert Fish, authors of the popular "Secrets" series, have researched and written twenty-seven award-winning cookbooks and travel books, and are always on the lookout for lodgings with style and character.

Other titles in the Pets Welcome™ series are *Pets Welcome™ California, Pets Welcome™ America's South, Pets Welcome™ New England and New York, Pets Welcome™ Southwest, Pets Welcome™ Pacific Northwest* and *Pets Welcome™ Mid-Atlantic and Chesapeake*.